Irish environmental politics after the communicative turn

MANCHESTER
1824
Manchester University Press

Irish environmental politics after the communicative turn

Edited by Patrick O'Mahony and
Kieran Keohane

Manchester University Press
Manchester and New York

*distributed in the United States exclusively
by Palgrave Macmillan*

Published by Manchester University Press
Oxford Road, Manchester M13 9NR, UK
and Room 400, 175 Fifth Avenue, New York, NY 10010, USA
www.manchesteruniversitypress.co.uk

Distributed in the United States exclusively by
Palgrave Macmillan, 175 Fifth Avenue, New York,
NY 10010, USA

Distributed in Canada exclusively by
UBC Press, University of British Columbia, 2029 West Mall,
Vancouver, BC, Canada V6T 1Z2

British Library Cataloguing-in-Publication Data
A catalogue record for this book is available from the British Library

Library of Congress Cataloging-in-Publication Data applied for

ISBN   978 07190 7915 3   hardback
ISBN   978 07190 7916 0   paperback

First published 2011

Typeset
by Toppan Best-set Premedia Limited
Printed in Great Britain
by CPI Antony Rowe Ltd, Chippenham, Wiltshire

Contents

List of figures   *page* vii

List of tables   viii

Contributors   ix

Preface   xi

Introduction   Patrick O'Mahony   1

1   The communicative turn and cosmopolitan ecological
    consciousness in the global risk society: an assessment of
    the discourse   Piet Strydom   12

2   Discourses of transition to sustainability in Ireland:
    outlines of a green republican strategy   John Barry   31

3   Communications practices and Irish environmental politics:
    oral hearings, tribunals, planning and sustainable
    development   Kieran Keohane   54

4   Social positions and dynamics within the cognitive order of
    Irish environmental discourse   Patrick O'Mahony   75

5   Nurturing dissent in the Irish political imagination: the
    contribution of environmental law to a new civic
    cosmopolitanism   Tracey Skillington   97

6   Conventions of quality and governance of artisan food:
    revealing the tyranny of 'sound science' in the regulation of
    Irish raw milk cheese   Colin Sage   117

7   Wasting Ireland and consuming sustainability: the 'Celtic
    Tiger' years and beyond   G. Honor Fagan   140

8   Promoting participatory planning: a West of Ireland
    case study   Catherine Corcoran and Ciaran Lynch   *page* 160

9   Irish environmental discourse: towards
    an ecological ethic?   Patrick O'Mahony   183

Index   209

List of figures

7.1 National profile of waste generated in 2004   *page* 143
9.1 A process model of rational political will formation
     (Habermas, 1996)   188

List of tables

6.1 Comparing constructions of quality as represented in
the court case involving DAF and the West Cork
cheese maker   *page* 132
7.1 Irish total waste generated (2004)   144
7.2 Irish waste indicators (2001–3)   145
9.1 A legal-political typology of norms   189

Contributors

Dr. John Barry is Reader in Politics at Queens University, Belfast. His main interest is in the relationship between moral/political theory and the environment, with particular focus on ecofeminism, the implications of green theory for thinking about justice, and theories of political economy in relation to the environment. He is author of *Environment and Social Theory* (London: Routledge, 2007), which is now in its second edition.

Catherine Corcoran is a Rural Development Specialist in Social & Community Studies at Tipperary Institute. She has worked in community and rural development programmes in Ireland and overseas. Her interest in participatory processes became particularly strong while working in Africa with communities that had to develop their own governance systems in the virtual absence of the State. **Ciaran Lynch** is Director of Rural Development at Tipperary Institute and a Civic & Social Organisation Consultant. He has also worked as a Senior Planning Officer. Catherine and Ciaran have been a facilitators on a number of Integrated Area Plans and their publications include Lynch, C., Corcoran, C., Horgan, C., Keating, P., Kirwan, B., Mccormack, M., Mcgrane, E. and Ryan, M. *Integrated Area planning: A Collaborative Approach to Decision-making* (Cork: Oak Tree Press, 2008).

Dr Honor Fagan is Senior Lecturer in Sociology and Dean of Graduate Studies at National University of Ireland Maynooth. Her research work specifically directs itself towards creating a synergy between sociological knowledge, radical democracy and citizenship. She is the author of *Cultural Politics and Irish Early School Leavers; Constructing Political Identities*, Critical Studies in Education and Culture Series, edited by H. Giroux and P. Freire (Westport, CT: Bergin and Garvey, 1995) and co-editor, with Ronaldo Munck, of *Globalization and Security: An Encyclopaedia* (Santa Barbara, CA: Praeger Security International, 2009) as well as numerous essays on governance, environment and globalisation.

Kieran Keohane B.Soc.Sc, M.A., Ph.D (York, Can. 1994) is Senior Lecturer in Sociology at the School of Sociology and Philosophy, UCC. He is the author of *Cosmopolitan Ireland: Globalization and Quality of Life* (London: Pluto Press, 2007); *Collision Culture: Transformations in Everyday Life in Ireland* (Dublin: The Liffey Press, 2004) and *Symptoms of Canada: An Essay on the Canadian Identity* (Toronto: University of Toronto Press, 1997). His essays have appeared in *Philosophy & Social Criticism*, *Theory Culture & Society*, *Cultural Politics* and *International Political Anthropology*.

Patrick O'Mahony is a Senior Lecturer in Sociology at University College, Cork in the School of Sociology and Philosophy. His interest in sociology of the environment is long-standing and extends to many research projects, reports and publications. He edited the collections of essays on *Nature, Risk and Responsibilty: Discourses of Biotechnology* (Basingstoke: Palgrave/Macmillan, 1999). He is currently writing a book on The Contemporary Theory of the Public Sphere.

Colin Sage is Senior Lecturer in Geography in the School of the Human Environment, University College Cork. His interests in food stretch from the governance of artisan production and alternative networks of food provisioning, through its relationship with the environment and community health and wellbeing. He is the author of *Environment and Food* (Forthcoming).

Tracey Skillington is a Lecturer in Sociology in the School of Sociology and Philosophy at University College Cork. She is a co-editor of the *Irish Journal of Sociology* (Manchester: Manchester University Press) and Senior Research Officer to the College of Arts, Celtic Studies and Social Sciences. She has published in a variety of edited book collections and international journals on issues of environmental sociology, democracy, rights consciousness and social change.

Piet Strydom, an Apartheid émigré, is Senior Lecturer in Sociology, School of Sociology and Philosophy, at University College Cork, Ireland. The thrust of his work is the development of the cognitive core of critical social theory and research. His publications include *Discourse and Knowledge* (Liverpool: Liverpool University Press, 2000); *Risk, Environment and Society* (Open University Press, 2002); *New Horizons of Critical Theory: Collective Learning and Triple Contingency* (Delhi: Shipra Publications, 2009); *Contemporary Critical Theory and Methodology* (Forthcoming) and *Philosophies of Social Science* (Open University Press, 2003, edited and introduced with Gerard Delanty), besides a wide range of articles in anthologies, encyclopaedias and leading journals.

Preface

This book represents scholarship on environmental issues in Ireland that foundationally draws from social and political theory as an orientation and guide to empirical investigations. In this way, the book is intended as both a general illustration of the application of theory in the field of environmental scholarship and as a contribution to understanding the societal implications of environmental politics in Ireland.

The intellectual biography of the book has many strands, variously reflected in the contributions, but one source that deserves special mention is the former Centre for European Social Research. For a number of the contributors, including the lead editor, Piet Strydom, and Tracey Skillington, the experience of working in this centre focalised their theoretical and methodological orientation to the environmental field. From without, the inspiring and creative presence of Klaus Eder, who collaborated with the Centre in the 1990s, contributed greatly to the establishment of an intellectual culture in environmental sociology that was enthusiastically taken up and elaborated within. The remaining editors would also like at this point to draw attention to the immense contribution of Gerard Mullally, one of the original editors, to both the environmental research of the Centre and also to the development of this volume, before ill health forced his withdrawal.

The contributors would also like to acknowledge various funding bodies whose research grants have contributed to the knowledge base of this research, notably the European Union's Environment and Climate and Socio-Economic Sciences and Humanities research programmes, the social science research programmes of the Irish Environmental Protection Agency and Galway County Council. Finally, the editors would like to acknowledge the outstandingly thorough and expeditious copy-editing and layout support offered by Nicholas McMurry and Siobhan O'Sullivan in the finalisation of this volume.

Introduction

Patrick O'Mahony

The central idea of this edited collection can be stated in one sentence. Communicative practices are essential to the coherence of modern societies and cultural models that vary across space and time guide such practices. The essays in the book, more and less explicitly, identify the cultural models and communication practices present in Irish environmental politics, examining how they relate to one another and how they shape societal coordination mechanisms and outcomes.

Further clarification of what this implies can be derived from examining the idea of a 'communicative turn' in the title of the book. The term refers to the increasing recognition in the social and human sciences that communication is essential to the organisation of modern societies. Without advanced communication systems that provide the means to describe common worlds, as well as to evaluate and prescribe collective practices and states of affairs, a differentiated and yet minimally integrated modern society could not be sustained. Such an insight is becoming increasingly intrinsic to modern social thought (see Strydom, Chapter 1 and O'Mahony, chapter 9).

Cultural ideas of what is true, right and good – in other words, cultural models – are essential to the operation of complex communication systems. Such models give form to communication, establishing what is relevant and justifiable according to specific cultural standards. They can be relatively stable over time and space, but even the most stable are subject to contestation, a process that sometimes leads to transformation of what had been previously accepted.

In the environmental sphere, there has been a vast expansion in communication in recent decades. Communication increases as a social sphere achieves the status of a vital collective interest, currently the case in the environmental sphere. By means of this communication, ideas of what is true about the human relation to nature, what are right and appropriate norms and values to guide our relations with nature and with one another through nature, and what is an emotionally sustaining relation to nature are undergoing profound change. The cultural model that guides our relation to nature is being transformed and yet some version of this model is always pivotal to the self-understanding of society (Moscovici, 1984).

These new ideas about nature are not simply political ideas but they are politically mediated – that is to say, shaped by political discourse. Modern politics is pre-eminently a communicative politics. Political discourse takes place in an environment conditioned by the principle of publicity through which the rights and responsibilities of the opinion carried by a public are constitutionally protected. Moreover, political discourse is intrinsic to the coordination of society, as without effective and legitimate political discourse it could not form a meaningful collective will to organise its disparate spheres of action. Major contemporary social and political theorists such as Rawls, Habermas, Sandel, Luhmann and Foucault recognise this state of affairs by stressing the centrality of communication to politics, albeit with differing emphasis.

The potential for cognitive re-orientation in respect of the human relation to nature, in both diagnosing its problems and in articulating its possibilities, varies significantly across different contemporary societies. Moreover, what has come to be regarded as human progress in the spheres of economy and science may be subjected to intense scrutiny or even found inappropriate in future ecologically oriented cultural models. It is an open question whether a benign outcome in the form of a new cultural model that reconciles the needs of nature and modern civilisation will emerge. If it is to emerge, and modern societies more and more grapple with its necessity as well as its difficulty, the extent to which different societies and civilisations will make a positive contribution to it crucially depends on the nature of communication in and across these various societies.

Cognitive re-orientation is therefore carried by communication – above all, public communication. It follows that the resources available for public communication in various societies and the will and capacity of individuals and groups to use these resources will determine whether cognitive re-orientation adequate to the ecological challenges of the times will in fact take place. Such cognitive re-orientation will result in the production of a new cultural model specifying what can and needs to be done and provides an orienting framework for establishing a kind of practical rationality secured in behaviour, law and social technologies.

The collection of essays in this book are concerned in one way or another with these questions on a number of levels. First of all, they are cognisant of the contingency of achieving socially and ecologically good outcomes through the social process of communication and cultural change. Such good outcomes will not only depend on fragile resources of collective will formation on different temporal and spatial scales but also on the performance of various social systems and the biosphere.

Secondly, the essays grapple with normative questions of what should be done set in the sobering, empirically revealed context of what is being done. And, thirdly, they address the issue of the adequacy of communication practices both within Ireland and in its transnational setting.

In relation to the first level – the contingency of achieving benign outcomes arising from interaction between social forces, culture and communication – the essays in the book, far from any sense of the inevitability of ecological progress, concentrate on what they perceive as the lack of ecological sustainability of the Irish model of development. Lack of sustainability is expressed, on the one hand, in immediate environmental dysfunctions in the local setting – water pollution, waste hazards, agricultural contamination through genetic innovations – or, on the other, in the country failing to respond to issues of transnational concern, increasing rather than decreasing its carbon consumption, and contributing to the over-hasty worldwide diffusion of a scientifically transformed agriculture. In general, a number of social systems, notably the economy and science, are considered to have too much autonomy and to drive on an Irish growth and innovation model that pays scant attention to ecological needs.

There is a distinct flavour of epistemological realism in this general laying out of critical perspectives. In this respect, while the essays by no means deny that both culturally variable preferences and the mode of amplification of issues in the communication system 'construct' environmental issues, they respect the scientifically and experientially borne evidence of the exhaustion of natural tolerances and the general proliferation of hazards. They converge, therefore, on the realist perspective that the Irish development path is not sustainable and is contributing to the exhaustion of planetary resources and the diminution of quality of life in both Ireland and elsewhere. Hence, the essays can be said to operate with realist ecological assumptions in this sense. This position gives an edge to the critique of the hegemony of economy and science and generally draws from the realist foundations of the paradigm of ecological sustainability.

However, realism in this sense by no means precludes what is sometimes presented as an opposing constructivist or idealist paradigm. Generally, for the essays in this collection, good outcomes involve the establishment of a sustaining relationship between realist horizons of resource utilisation and hazard management on one side, and the epistemic, normative and evaluative processes of communicative 'construction' on the other. From a constructivist perspective, the essays do not suppose some knowable 'real' point of ecological equilibrium that should direct appropriate communication, a view that communication should merely reflect what is already knowable and hence imperative. Rather, the complex relation between natural balances and complex human social systems requires ongoing communicative elaboration and cultural adjustment.

The status accorded to an appropriate human relation to nature, including the status of nature as a good unto itself that calls for human non-interference on principled grounds, relates closely to the physical capacities of the biosphere but also reaches beyond it. Many questions to do with nature today preoccupy human civilisation that do not bear upon the sustainability of the human species itself but on issues of cultural preference and moral grounding. These issues include how humans want to live within nature, with one another through re-worked and interrelated conceptions of human self-nature and external nature and with other life forms by conferring them autonomy and rights of non-interference. Even if the question of ecological sustainability of human life forms is somehow resolved, these questions will still remain.

The brief remarks in the last paragraph begin to show the complexity of the cultural understanding of nature, which takes on an urgent normative force with respect to the question of what we should do faced with the weakening of the dominant nature code of modernity. This code emphasises efficient nature exploitation, unlimited growth in an economy without limits, nature as a free and unlimited resource, that the purpose of external nature and of other species is merely to serve human needs and maintains the strict separation of culture and communication as human accomplishments from the inert speechlessness of nature, other species and even 'inferior' humans.

The essays in the collective cast a critical eye on the continuing domination of this code in Ireland from the standpoint of an alternative nature code that would be based on both a sustainable and non-dominating relation to nature and that requires democratic innovation to be realised. The essays in various ways, then, engage in exploration and critique of the Irish cultural model of nature as it is politically articulated. This exercise involves critical assessments of negative assumptions among policy makers about the assumed low rationality of the public, the absence of an ecological ethic, the prioritisation of the economy over other social needs, the over-extension of the risk model of sound science, and the pessimistic cognitive construction of participation among policy makers.

The collection does not, however, follow the path of much critical social science of engaging in critique with a merely implicit corrective standard. To the contrary, at various points it asserts strong counter-factual normative standards that could contribute to a better kind of practical rationality than currently obtaining. The examples in this volume, range from Strydom's idea of a responsible, ecocentric cosmopolitanism (Chapter 1), Skillington's similar but case-based idea of cosmopolitan imaginary emerging in legal argument (Chapter 5), Sage's idea, following Thévenot, of an equilibrium between a wide range of orders of worth rather than the domination of industrial and market-based logics (Chapter 6), Keohane's Habermas-inspired idea of the ideal speech situation (Chapter 3), O'Mahony's Apel-inspired idea of an ecological ethic achieved within a real communication community (Chapter 4), Corcoran and Lynch's use of Arnstein's ladder of participation (Chapter 8), Fagan's discussion following Sager of communicative planning (Chapter 7) and Barry's ecological version of a republican political philosophy (Chapter 2).

Across these various normative reference orientations may be found certain recurring and reinforcing normative themes. The first is the engagement in moral and ethical critique, in some cases implicitly and in other cases explicitly. Skillington, for example, explicitly draws attention in Chapter 5 to the dogmatism, authoritarianism and closure of the older Catholic moral code and to the tentative emergence of a new cosmopolitan moral imaginary. O'Mahony in the concluding Chapter 9 similarly draws attention to needed moral learning processes in the context of notably deficient progress towards the realisation of an ecological ethic. Barry's essay in Chapter 2 calls for a different kind of ethos that would combine the common good tenets of republican political philosophy, albeit one that accords space to rights-based pluralism, with a green political philosophy. Sage, in Chapter 6, similar to O'Mahony's critique of the narrow rationality underpinning normative innovation, shows the ethical and ultimately legal deficiencies of too narrow reliance on a few orders of worth that exclude the projects of civil society.

In general, the moral and ethical critique is closely linked to the idea of an ethic of responsibility. Strydom, for example, speaks in Chapter 1 of unresolved questions in the allocation of moral responsibility for ecological hazards and altered practices today. He draws attention to a new kind of perception of risk and responsibility that generates a discourse that is as yet inadequately institutionalised anywhere. Through public discourse, ecological responsibility has come on the agenda and has made practices based on unawareness of ecological problems no longer acceptable. But the precise attribution of responsibility between major actors, individual members of the public, civilisations, societies and social systems has not been worked out. We therefore live in an uncomfortable space between the acceptance of ecological reason, that something should be done, but without a corresponding ecological morality that would galvanise the necessary practical *commitments*. Put differently, we operate with enlightened perception but also with normative agnosticism as to what should practically issue from this perception. In this respect, ideas that link governance, communication and responsibility are prominent in the essays as, for example, in Sage's idea in Chapter 6 of governance as relational co-responsibility.

The critical thrust of the essays suggests that responsibility in this sense is extremely weakly present in the Irish context. Barry in Chapter 2 talks of the individualisation of responsibility that prevents reflections on institutions. Sage, Fagan and Corcoran and Lynch in Chapters 5, 7 and 8 draw attention either to the preference for command and control governance over relational forms or to the poor design of communicative forums that make co-responsibility between public authorities and society difficult.

In general, the absence of an ecological ethos among the public strongly limits the range of discourse and the possibility of generating binding moral norms of ecological responsibility. This kind of moral responsibility would be instantiated in both the moral foundations of everyday and professional practices as well in relevant legal codes. It would necessitate wide-ranging cultural and social change, including relevant norm formation and the institutionalisation of new forms of discourse.

Quite a few of the essays, O'Mahony's in Chapter 4 the most explicitly, document the consequences of the exclusion of moral and ethical consideration from both discourse and the formation of action-guiding norms. It cannot be sufficiently stressed that the point generally raised is not to compare Ireland with accomplished innovation on these lines in other jurisdictions, given that these other jurisdictions are also deficient. Rather, the point is to draw attention to comparatively poor overall advances in Ireland, especially in moral and ethical will-forming discourses that would indicate the prospect of radical practical change down the line. To the contrary, the cases generally exhibit the presence of a political rationality that seeks to exclude moral and ethical considerations altogether and a public that is generally quiescent or apathetic.

However, nearly all of the essays in one way or another do contrast sections of the public that at least carry the fight, even if the moral and ethical principles that guide their alternative semantics – for example, notions of environmental or technological citizenship – are not well established.[1] Moreover, Barry in Chapter 2 proposes a comprehensive normative vision of an alternative green republican political philosophy, whose conditions of possibility are enhanced by recent developments in self-organising and active communities, notably the Transition Town movement dedicated to end dependency on carbon fuels.

The last point articulates a clear practical rationale for a collection of this nature, to draw attention to a deficient aspect of public discourse and hence contribute to a more comprehensive kind of public will formation. In particular, a collection of essays that focuses on communication will draw attention to the role of communication and discourse in generating innovation or in the making real of abstract concepts. Hence, communication is not simply about the introduction of concepts of responsibility and sustainability that can then operate independently of that communication. Rather, communication helps establish ecological cultural models that in turn contribute to norm formation, but it never disappears from the scene. Norms are communicatively instantiated, problematised, modified and ultimately replaced. Cultural models mediate between norms and communication practices, specifying both the kind of communicative procedures and the relevant range of considerations that enter into the reproduction, repair and replacement of action-guiding norms (see Strydom in Chapter 1 and O'Mahony in Chapter 4 for an account of the cognitive basis of communication).

These remarks on the centrality of communication introduce the third central theme of the collection specified above – the significance of resources and capacities of communication. By the standards of long-established and prosperous democracies the Irish public sphere is notably lacking in adequate communication practices with respect to such factors as possibilities for public participation, thematic range, sincerity and resonance on both publics and political office-holders (O'Mahony and Delanty, 2001; Keohane, Chapter 3). The Irish public sphere is colonised both by administrative power and narrow policy networks dominated by economic actors.

While formal democratic rights are in some cases restricted, notably by the censorious effect of libel laws, it is not the constitutional–legal framework *per se* that offers the principal impediment. The problems of publicity in Ireland rather lie on the fault-line of this volume, the culture and practices of communication. Cultures and communicative practices restrict the participation of civil society, exclude certain relevant pragmatic, moral–political and legal considerations due to extremely narrow agenda-setting mechanisms in the mass media, show poor capacity for relevant 'moral memory' and do not hold office-holders adequately accountable. In general, Irish mass-mediated communication in the techno-environmental sphere was found by O'Mahony and Schaefer (2005) to be journalistically dominated, restricted in the extent of its coverage and exhibiting low participation by civil society, including non-science academics.

A number of the essays in this volume address head on the question of resources and capacities of communication in the public sphere. Keohane in Chapter 3, for example, documents the unbalanced nature of a planning hearing and finds the communicative arena dominated by political power-holders. He shows how the communication that results both from imbalances of power and a particular kind of ethos is normatively deeply problematic. Corcoran and Lynch in Chapter 8 do acknowledge the limited success of their study of a communicative planning experiment in the West of Ireland but still document problems with design and procedures.

In contrast to Corcoran and Lynch, Fagan in Chapter 7 has a more marked political sociological approach that is generally critical of the import of communicative planning insofar as it legitimates existing power. Skillington in Chapter 5 endeavours to show more optimistically how the dogmatic, anti-communicative ethos of the form of democracy that historically obtained in Ireland, and that preserves much power, is nonetheless under assault by perceptions of moral injury and dereliction of ecological responsibility that derives animus from a strengthened cosmopolitan context. Finally, O'Mahony in Chapter 4, using a cognitive sociological framework, documents how contrasting cognitive models within a given organisation of the public sphere lead to a kind of indirect, embattled communication due to the breakdown of respectful and sincere communicative relationships.

It should not be supposed, however, that the above remarks suggest that consensual communication is always either necessary or appropriate as a model of communication. Often, communication has to be strident, unruly and raucous to solve problems or to include previously subjugated voices (Fraser, 1989; Young, 2002; Keohane, Chapter 3). Often, too, communication is strategic and conflictual with no direct encounters between contending parties. Furthermore, recognition must be granted to the post-structuralist and system-theoretical insight that non-human actants or systems – for example, technological components or the carrying capacity of the biosphere – interpose themselves into the relational circuits of human communication. Communication makes assumptions about the performance of natural and social systems but these systems frequently undermine the assumptions, forcing revision.

All of these observations reflect the studies of this book in that the latter reveal the variety and complexity of environmental communication in a modern society, its conflictual and unresolved tensions as much as its emerging harmonies.

The complex relation between political communication and the coordination of society is currently entering a new phase, especially marked in the environmental sphere. The channels of mass-mediated political communication appear inadequate in the light of the depth of societal controversy. The 'outputs' of the political system in the form of decisions and policies no longer enjoy widespread legitimacy. In the environmental sphere, conflict and dissatisfaction have become endemic. In these circumstances, new forums of political communication have been advanced as a solution. Hence, in the case studies there is a treatment of a public hearing (Keohane, Chapter 3) and examples of communicative planning (Corcoran and Lynch, Chapter 8 and Fagan, Chapter 7). It is also an aspect of the work of Skillington (Chapter 5) and Sage (Chapter 6), in the sense that the law, always a central deliberative forum of modern societies, is now forced to address new substantive concerns. In the case of Skillington, the idea of judicial review of policy decisions is itself a relatively recent legal–political innovation.

In general, the collection is pessimistic on how these new forums of communication, which depend on extending citizen participation, work in the Irish case. As suggested above, the confidence of the existing legal–political order, linked to traditions of authoritative control, tends to make political power-holders unresponsive to the case for extending public participation (see O'Mahony, 2009). There is some disagreement in the collection in relation to these forums, in that some authors hold out a more optimistic assessment of them, both in Ireland and more generally (Corcoran and Lynch, Chapter 8), whereas Fagan (Chapter 7) holds that the idea of communicative rationality linked to consensus is problematic in itself. What is shared, however, is the sense that power-holders in Ireland do not take participation seriously in the environmental sphere, that it is always restricted to the least ambitious possible form, that it merely follows EU insistence, that the agenda is restricted from the outset and that the mechanisms have little influence on the outcomes.

Overall, this volume examines environmental communication in Ireland as a pivotal dimension of a democratic environmental politics, and finds it seriously lacking. Communication is thematically restricted, deeply and unfairly distorted by power, narrowly instrumental in its range and poor at building collective will. There is, however, some evidence that the context is changing due to the growing accountability of power-holders from within and growing transnational and cosmopolitan influence from without. The global, transnational and EU dimensions pervade many of these cases and exhibit emerging transnational civil societal networks (Sage, Chapter 6), cosmopolitan discourse (Skillington, Strydom, Chapters 1 and 5), and indications of a green political philosophy (Barry, Chapter 2). These and other developments are perhaps beginning to change the balance of forces. O'Mahony's case study of plant genetically modified organisms (GMOs) in Chapter 4 exhibited the pattern of a stalemate rather than the normal repressive hegemony of the public authorities for various internal and external reasons. And Sage's case study of artisanal cheese makers in Chapter 6 showed how the courts found in favour of the cheese makers and against the dominant public narrative.

From the standpoint of this volume it appears clear that only a significant re-balancing of communicative forces will assist in the production of the kinds of discourses and cultural models that could point the way to an ecological ethic. On the practical–political level, the collection can therefore be regarded as itself a critical reflective act of intellectual communication that springs from and feeds back into situated communicative practices. The intervention may help to point a way beyond the current unsatisfactory situation, by clarifying latent structures, mechanisms and themes in Irish environmental communication.

Note

1 Frankenfeld, in a well-known essay from 1992, speaks of 'technological citizenship' as a set of rights, obligations and status that bridges the autonomy of laypersons and that of experts. The concept of technological citizenship involves four kinds of rights – respectively, to knowledge or information, to participation, to informed consent and to reduction of endangerment.

References

Frankenfeld, P. J. (1992) 'Technological Citizenship: A Normative Framework for Risk Studies', *Science, Technology & Human Values*, 17(4), 459–84.
Fraser, N. (1989) *Unruly Practices: Power, Gender and Discourse in Contemporary Social Theory* (Cambridge: Polity).
Fraser, N. (1991) 'Rethinking the Public Sphere: A Contribution to the Critique of Actually Existing Democracy', in C. Calhoun (ed.), *Habermas and the Public Sphere* (Cambridge, MA: MIT Press).

Hausendorf, H. and A. Bora (eds.) (2008) *Analysing Citizenship Talk: Social Positioning in Political and Legal Decision-Making Processes* (Amsterdam: John Benjamins).

Moscovici, S. (1984) *Versuch über die menschliche Geschichte der Natur* (Frankfurt: Suhrkamp).

O'Mahony, P. (2009) 'Sociological Theory, Discourse and the Cognitive Construction of Participation', *Comparative Sociology*, 8, 490–516.

O'Mahony, P. and G. Delanty (2001) *Rethinking Irish History: Nationalism, Identity and Ideology* (New York: St. Martin's Press).

O'Mahony, P. and M. Schaefer (2005) 'The Book of Life in the Press: Comparing German and Irish Media Coverage on Human Genome Research', *Social Studies of Science*, 35, 99–130.

Young, I. M. (2002) *Inclusion and Democracy* (Oxford: Oxford University Press), 265–81.

1

The communicative turn and cosmopolitan ecological consciousness in the global risk society: an assessment of the discourse

Piet Strydom

We knew the world would not be the same. (J. Robert Oppenheimer, 1945)

Now it is the totality that has become the problem and the task. It ushers in a complete transformation of history. The decisive thing is that there is no more 'outside'. The world closes. It is the earth's unity. New threats and opportunities appear. (Karl Jaspers, 1955)

Introduction

A fundamental transformation has taken place in the cognitive organisation of society in the twentieth century. The implicated cognitive structures, both the cultural cosmological world model and its corresponding schema of interpretation, have undergone something like a Gestalt switch. Whereas the modern mechanistic cosmology and industrial world model had framed society since the late eighteenth century, its place was taken by an ontology supporting a new planetary sense of earthiness and worldhood which is interpreted according to a wholly different structure of perception.

A variety of factors conditioned this transformation, yet if one is to understand both the global and planetary reach as well as the particular configuration of the contemporary cognitive order, then one extraordinarily significant event must be singled out – the atom bomb. In the wake of this epoch-making world disclosure, stimulated by other events and developments, a new perspective arose that informs a set of society-wide discourses in which the themes of risk, ecology, globalisation and cosmopolitanism, all refracted through the interpretative prism of the equally novel corresponding cognitive schema, progressively became closely intertwined.

Since modern society's emergence as a self-constituting and self-organising complex of relations, public discourse has been playing a central role in the collective identification and definition of vital problems and challenges, as well as in concurrent collective mobilisation, decision making, regulation and action. Due to a number of developments, including the expressive revolution of the 1960s, recent changes in communications technology, and the intensification of the communicative form of society up to the point where we can justifiably speak of the contemporary communication society, the current discourses have gained an unprecedented potency, both extensively and intensively. Not only have they expanded on an unprecedented scale, but the self-understanding they reflexively generate has been taking hold of increasing numbers of people since the late 1960s, and particularly since the watershed years of 1986 and 1989. The vanishing point is global cosmopolitan being in a cared-for planetary biosocial ecosphere.

The question is how to disentangle the different strands of this the most characteristic discursive complex of our time so as to enable us to assess its significance in terms of impact, direction and prospects.

A new perspective

Under the title of 'nihilism', Martin Heidegger, following Friedrich Nietzsche, regarded technology and science as having undermined the moral basis of life in Europe and the West. On the other hand, he pinned his hope on this very process of the devaluation of all values harbouring and eventually delivering a new redeeming world disclosure. Such an event in fact did occur with the bombing of Hiroshima and Nagasaki. But what Nietzsche could not have foreseen, Heidegger actually lived through, yet, unlike contemporaries of his such as J. Robert Oppenheimer and Karl Jaspers, failed to appreciate fully, despite a reference to 'atomic energy' (1977: 15) in his technology lecture of 1954. Compared to Copernicus' planetary cosmology, human understanding of the earth here became reflexive a second time. Rather than just a round planet circling the sun in its own orbit, we gained the insight that we ourselves now possess the unprecedented and frightening ability to destroy the planet, the very organic foundations of our earthly lives and socio-cultural world. The gaping abyss, the limits of this small and vulnerable planet, emphatically highlighted the real significance of the earth. This insight inaugurated a completely new perspective with implications for both the earth and the world, which contradict, while allowing critical intervention, the continuation of the backward looking nihilism metanarrative of conservative culture criticism.[1]

Initially, the new perspective made itself felt at two levels. First, the destructive potential of nuclear technology induced awareness of the planet, the globe, the totality. Second, the dark underbelly of techno-logical–scientific progress called forth awareness of risk. Considering public discourse, the risk angle is the first to have become articulated – that is, in the 1950s in the context of the emerging nuclear energy industry. The ecological angle followed suit in the 1960s. Stimulated by the detection of low-level radiation emitted by the first generation of nuclear power plants, but also reinforced by the first photograph of the so-called 'Blue Planet'[2] from outer space, the new planetary sense was cast in an ecological semantics.

While the momentous world disclosure of the 1940s occasioned the relatively early assertion of the risk and ecological angles, the funda-mental change in perspective allowed two further significant amplifica-tions – the first encapsulated by the expression 'globalisation', the second by 'cosmopolitanism'. The former term was first introduced in the early 1980s, but the underlying train of thought piggybacked on earlier developments in the ecological field. On all accounts, environ-mental problems and challenges provided the first and most compelling examples of the global shift in human awareness, activities and organi-sation and thus cleared the way for the articulation at a variety of levels of the characteristic global consciousness of our time. It is against this background, but punctuated by the European Revolution of 1989 and reinforced by the coinciding anniversaries in 1995 of Immanuel Kant's proposal for perpetual peace, the end of the Second World War and the establishment of the Charter of the United Nations, that cosmopolitan-ism obtained contemporary significance and became the burning issue it is today in the conflict of different cosmopolitan cultures.

A change in perspective, particularly one of this magnitude, involves a reconfiguration of the cognitive order of society. Such a transforma-tion takes place in accordance with the conditions called for by the new problems and challenges which need to be met in the process of the constitution and organisation of society. On the macro-cultural level, the cosmological world model provides a representational framework that becomes an action-guiding horizon through a corresponding schema of interpretation. As a dynamic processor, the latter makes possible creative interpretations on the meso-level where different socio-cultural groups, collective agents and movements compete with one another and, at the micro-level, such cognitive dynamics find a foothold in the minds of the participating and observing individuals.

The mid-twentieth-century paradigm change at issue here switched the modern Copernican–Newtonian heliocentric–mechanistic cosmology and industrial world model to the background in favour of foregrounding the ecological planetary cosmology and cosmopolitan world model of our own time. By the same token, the interpretative schema of wealth and poverty through which the former was articulated was replaced by the currently dominant schema of safety and danger (Strydom, 2002). It is undoubtedly the case that this schema admits competing cautious, confident and neutral cognitive frames (Simpson, 1996). For a growing number of people, however, a sense of ontological security could derive no longer from the avoidance of pauperisation and participation in the wealth of the nation, but rather had to be sought in risk aversion and enjoyment of living conditions which were technologically, ecologically and cosmopolitically safeguarded on a global scale.

Diagnosis of the times

The contemporary discourse remains impenetrable without recourse to the epoch-making world disclosure and consequent reconfiguration of the cognitive order of society. Within this framework, the dominant pre-understanding of contemporary society, particularly the perception of the problems both threatening and challenging the social situation at a particular point in time, provides the horizon within which the discourse follows its undulant course.

Risk discourse

Initially, this horizon was approached by way of restrictions and possibilities as they became apparent through the prism of risk. The risk discourse originally arose in the 1950s from a restricted and exclusive expert debate in the newly founded civil nuclear energy industry. Celebrating expert accuracy to the exclusion of the public and its potential concerns, it started from the classical safety question to focus on the probability of objectively calculable risks and risk comparison. The ultimate aim was to establish a socially acceptable level of risk which would allow the nuclear industry to forge ahead without interruption. Had the spirit of this positivism and authoritarian paternalism prevailed, then society would have remained an object, totally controlled by scientific, planning and political forces. Instead, however, not only did opposition to the experts, paternalistic institutions and risk start to appear, become mobilised and grow in the course of the 1960s and 1970s, but the attentive public audience also expanded. An organised

opposition played its role at the US Atomic Energy Commission hearings about routine radioactive emissions from power plants in 1971 and
two or three years later, at the time of the international oil crisis, the
anti-nuclear movement had been fully consolidated.

Due to the resultant risk communication and concurrent increase in
public concern, by the late 1970s the closed technical expert debate had
broadened into a virtually full-fledged international public discourse
concerning the societal constitution, including both the production and
social construction, of risk. Through the ensuing competition and conflict, the discourse simultaneously took in increasingly wider dimensions
of potential damage and penetrated deeper into the probability of such
damage – on the one hand, moving from personal, social and political
to environmental damage and, on the other, contemplating not just
known and suspected risks but even – indeed, especially – hypothetical
ones. The latter in time gave rise to both the cognitive question of non-
knowledge or unawareness (Beck, 1999), including the best way of
dealing with it, and its moral or ethical counterpart, the question of
collective or co-responsibility (Jonas, 1973; Apel, 1987; Strydom, 1999a).

Ecology discourse

The inclusion of the natural environment entailed a re-specification of
problems threatening and challenging contemporary society and thus a
shift in the discursive horizon. Not only did the risk discourse prepare
the way for the ecology discourse, but the two discourses started to
overlap. The year 1965 marks the turning point. Concern over nuclear
power was generalised into distrust in high technology and its support-
ive institutional order, and a link was then made to the natural environment. Significantly, this augmentation of perspective, marked by the
UNESCO Biosphere Conference of 1968, brought global environmental
problems, such as acid rain, water and air pollution and the global
commons, as well as the ecology as such into view. Through the discursive intensification, this cognitive shift stimulated a collective learning spurt which eventuated in a dramatic change in collective identity
to include what came to be called 'environmental consciousness' – a
development behind the 'Green Seventies'.

The inescapable diagnostic conclusion that a threatening ecological
imbalance was a major crisis tendency blighting contemporary society
(Habermas, 1976) signalled the moment of the implosion of modernity.
The taken-for-granted boundary between society and nature evapo-
rated, making room for the realisation that there was continuity between
nature and society and, therefore, that the two were coextensive. Besides

the individual psyche and the socio-cultural form of life, a new life support system possessing its own objective teleology emerged with which humans had to identify if they were to maintain themselves (Apel, 1979) – the planetary ecosphere in the sense of the comprehensive biosocial system embracing all the earth's inhabitants as their unitary self-maintenance system. It was clear that a planetary health care programme was urgently required.

The mode of realisation of this most basic interest in identification and self-maintenance, however, became a divisive issue. Despite the by no means insignificant agreement created by the Brundtland Report, UN conferences from Rio de Janeiro to Johannesburg and an unprecedented increase in transnational environmental accords, it has retained this character, especially in view of the potential ecological imbalance with which global warming and climate change are confronting contemporary society. The competition and conflict manifest themselves in particular in relation to the transformation of the function and scope of the political form of society. With the contemporary multilevel security state focusing on prevention tasks at the centre of attention, major participants propound diverging interpretations.

If the appearance of environmental problems in the 1960s indicated the unavoidability of taking into account the global dimension, these arguments over ecological politics already partook of the globalisation discourse.

Globalisation discourse

Having been inaugurated by the world-disclosing bomb, the global perspective was first articulated in terms of environmental problems and the ecology which, in effect, also elevated the preceding risk perspective to the global level. In the course of its consolidation, the global perspective was reinforced by a series of more or less significant events – including the emergence of the 'global village' on the back of the communications media in the 1960s; the impact of the abandonment of the Bretton Woods international exchange rate system in the early 1970s; the closely related emergence of neo-liberal economic and political measures calculated to free capitalism from its perceived regulatory fetters; the European Revolution of 1989 and the end of the Cold War; and, perhaps, having the greatest immediate impact on the contemporary self-understanding in the context of the current Baroque-like culture, the first visual image of the globe from an astronautic vantage point which itself presupposed movement beyond the earth into interplanetary space. Globalisation presupposes a perspectival adjustment in accordance with which the constitution and organisation of society comes to be regarded and engaged with as a multilevel process which opens up the form – or, rather, the different forms – of society. Rather than already having reached its *telos*, as many seem to think, at present the process leaves contemporary society in an intermediate position – called the 'postnational constellation' (Habermas, 2001a) – suspended between the territorially bound national constellation, on the one hand, and a potential planetary cosmopolitan ecological world society, on the other. This intermediate position is fraught with a diverse range of problems and challenges on which hinges the very horizon within which globalisation itself moves.

On the one hand, functional (i.e. economic, political, legal, scientific–technological–industrial and cultural) globalisation processes open up a structured field by generating new opportunities (e.g. investment, planetary technology, production, communication, travel) as well as constraints (e.g. externalities, erosion of cultural, social and personality structures, breakdown of solidarities, marginalisation, exclusion, new social cleavages), thus creating a social vacuum which becomes filled with negative and regressive phenomena (e.g. social fragmentation, right-wing extremism, separatist regionalism, religious fundamentalism, murderous identities, terrorism, privatisation and marketisation of the means of violence, and so forth). On the other hand, processes of communicative globalisation arising from civil society and employing constitutionally rooted political means (i.e. formation of associations, non-governmental organisations (NGOs) and social movements, the making of problems into public and political issues, public argumentation about a variety of issues) run counter to functional accumulation, differentiation and evolution in a corrective move against the negative implications and consequences. In and through this dialectical process of competition, contestation and conflict between the two logics over the structuration and direction of society, a process which very importantly also yields collective learning effects, the constitution and organisation of society is driven forward at a level deeper and more pervasive than regular political and economic conflict. It is of course the case that the process of constituting the world society is rooted in the earth and its natural historical development, but as is confirmed by the fact that our relation to nature is dependent on mediation by signs, the social scientifically relevant medium of this process is public communication taking the form of controversies – or, more formally, discourses – about whatever is at stake in the process.

Despite environmental problems and ecology having been the vehicle for the first unlocking of the global perspective, economic and political actors took advantage of the innovation to become leading globalisation forces. Shifts in perspective and horizon do not necessarily translate immediately into public articulation, so that the time lag can be exploited by dominant forces to give it direction, putting alternative interpretations at a disadvantage. Analysis of competition, contestation and conflict at major levels of globalisation is illuminating.

Neo-liberal economic globalisation, the Anglo-American mode of development, generally regarded as the dominant form of globalisation, leads to a global deregulated capitalist system which is shadowed, however, by an unprecedented level of unequal income distribution and the mounting phenomenon of world poverty which have called forth significant movement mobilisation. It is underpinned by scientific–technological–industrial globalisation which, through the unabated exploitation and overburdening of the planetary ecosphere, has given rise to the 'world risk society' (Beck, 2009). In turn, such globalisation of risk has contributed to an expanding risk consciousness which has now infiltrated virtually all areas, including the international financial system, the oil-based energy order, and so forth.

Political globalisation presents a more complicated picture. The new world order that emerged in the wake of the European Revolution of 1989 conferred the status of hyper-power on the United States which needed little encouragement to embark on the neo-conservative 'Project for a New American Century', including a globalisation war in the Middle East. The resulting 'split of the West' (Habermas, 2004), which left the shared US–EU value community in tatters, was further exacerbated by America's spreading unilateralist tentacles. Disparaging of the European commitment to multilateralism and multilevel democratic global governance, it lies behind the spectre of world government which has been surfacing time and again over the past decade and a half, from the G7 proposal for a new kind of geopolitical governance in 1995, via the neo-conservative vision of the United States, United Kindom and Australia taking the lead, to the Washington Junta's Schmittian 'total war on terror'. In view of the unification of Europe, the rise of China and India and the recovery of Russia, however, the realisation of such a twenty-first-century version of the right-wing dream of 'sovereignty' (Schmitt, 1985) seems highly unlikely. Moreover, the United Nations has gained addition authority and power since 1989 and has weathered the American onslaught under George W. Bush quite well.

As regards the politics of ecological and risk globalisation, approaches have become much more clearly defined. Since the first half of the 1980s, stimulated by the Organisation for Economic Cooperation and Development (OECD), the United Nations Environment Programme

(UNEP) and the Brundtland Commission, ecological modernisation theorists to this day defend a widely accepted programme of environmental restructuring, now upgraded to the global level, aimed at reconciling the competing values of ecology and economy in such a way that the latter is seen as not only good for but actually essential to the former (Mol, 2003; Spaargaren, Mol and Buttel, 2006). Taking the assumptions underlying ecological modernisation to the extreme, the functionalist response in the face of increasing complexity is to recommend the multiplication and intensified exploitation of risk taking (Luhmann, 1986) and, where necessary, the exertion of independent administrative power (Willke, 1992). The governmentality approach takes such independence as the only and in fact already realised option (Dean, 1999). Stressing the urgent need to meet the global warming threat, ecologist GAIA theory, inspired by a decisionistic ecological model comparable to Carl Schmitt's political theology, urges decisive unilateral intervention in this exceptional situation by an advanced nation on behalf of all (Lovelock, 2006). Deliberative democratic theory differs sharply from all these positions in that it avoids not only the reification of systemic logics but also sovereign ecological decisionism by adopting a radical democratic stance which ascribes a vital role to civil society and the public sphere and recognises the historical differentiation of sovereignty. At the centre of attention is the realisation of the system of rights and, hence, constitutionalisation, which is aimed at the establishment of a 'politically constituted pluralistic world society' concerned with 'global domestic politics without world government' (Habermas, 2005: 326; 2001b: 7) in which cosmopolitan law and rights prevail and which is ecologically safeguarded.

The globalisation of law, dating back to the 'legal big bang' (Dezalay, 1994) of 1986, is driven by equally contradictory forces. Under the banner of 'legal pluralism', a proliferation of independent self-willed regimes has led to the massive production of commercial and private law without the involvement of states, so-called 'global law without the state' (Teubner, 1997), which typically lays claim to being in accord with citizenship or even constitutionalism. Critical analysis backed by mobilisation shows, however, that such law comes into being not merely without political input, but also shorn of any adequate representation of the interests of those potentially affected and, ironically, that constitutionalisation is increasingly cast in the form of private law production (Brunkhorst, 2005). As regards international law, positive trends are to be observed at different levels, especially since 1989, despite many-sided opposition from the United States which seeks to prevent an effective global legal order. With the revival of the law of the UN Charter and the promotion of the idea of the latter as 'the constitution of mankind' (Tomuschat, 1997), the Westphalian-based law of states has irreversibly entered the protracted process of being transformed into cosmopolitan law. It is complemented by the more recent redefinition of the concept of the 'international community' (Lukashuk, 1997), established in 1969 in accordance with the Vienna Convention, as referring no longer simply to the community of states, but rather to the global human community, including all individuals to whom now falls the duty of actively participating in local and global processes of legitimacy generation. These advances are underpinned by the current shift, inaugurated by the Vienna Declaration and Action Programme of 1993, from international human rights, concerning such matters as stateless, refugee and asylum status, to world citizenship or cosmopolitan rights. While this departure harbours the promise of the very nature of world society's social and political structure being determined by human rights (Donnelly, 1998; Habermas, 2001a), the reality is that such rights are regularly instrumentalised for the purposes of economic and political globalisation and, even more seriously, that there is a tendency toward their inflation into strong moral imperatives for which legal recognition and enforcement is absent since they are not afforded the appropriate form (Brunkhorst, 2005). Nevertheless, like such concerns as ecology and democracy, mentioned above, the emergence of a global rights culture is one of the most significant phenomena characterising the process of cultural globalisation today.

It is the emerging collective definition of issues through the competition, contestation and conflict between those driving globalisation forward, particularly between the functional and communicative logics, that has led to the cosmopolitan discourse of the past decade and a half.

Cosmopolitan discourse

Considering that the transition from the globalisation to the cosmopolitan discourse involved a further augmentation of perspective which was conditioned by the discursive interrelation of the participants, an adequate grasp of cosmopolitanism requires a change from observing and describing globalisation in terms of an external perspective to considering it internally with reference to the learning processes undergone by those actively involved in the process and the cultural models of world openness they phenomenologically construct in that context. In the wake of the process of globalisation as the vehicle for the opening up of the different forms of society, the cosmopolitan discourse concerns the very sense of the openness of the world. Rather than being caused by globalisation, however, this multilevel culture of openness has roots through learning processes going back to the eighteenth century and even late antiquity.

Globalisation is generated and carried by a plurality of actors and agents who are guided by their own interpretations or particular world models and, accordingly, seek to realise their own distinct visions of the world of which they become increasingly conscious through their relations with each other. Taking cues from the current process of construction of a global society, they include corporations, states, international institutions, civil society actors such as NGOs and social movements, and so forth. Through competition, contestation and conflict, but also intercultural and transcivilisational communication and cooperation, they get embroiled in intersubjective communicative and discursive contexts in which a variety of learning processes (Trenz and Eder, 2004; Strydom, 2008; see also Miller, 2002) take place on which the formation of the emerging society feeds. Such learning processes are guided and directed by different cultural models of world openness and thus give rise to distinct types of cosmopolitanism.

Among the learning process there are at least five relevant types. Aggregative learning renders individuals (e.g. business executives, bureaucrats, lawyers) and institutions or organisations (e.g. corporations, states, law firms) able to pursue their own interests more effectively. Institutional learning allows institutions or organisations to fulfil their particular missions to their clients, customers or the citizens. Associational learning makes possible the formation of voluntary groupings and social movements as collective actors. The more complex double contingency learning is a type through which, for example, corporations and/or states on the one hand conflict with social movements on the other, leading to accommodation between the parties. Finally, the most complex type, triple contingency learning, is a discursive form of societal learning, made possible by the emergence of personalities capable of intercultural and transcivilisational communication, discourses, public spheres and publics capable of observing, evaluating, judging, forming opinion and commentary, in which the competing protagonists take account of each other via a reference to the public who has constitutive significance for the emergent, jointly constructed social reality (Strydom, 1999b). In this latter type of learning, transformative moments of discovery and transcendence – truly 'cosmopolitan moment[s]' (Delanty, 2006: 38) – occur through the unforeseeable and unexpected creative combination of forces, cognitive structures and symbolic forms. It is undoubtedly the most improbable kind of learning, which is what makes it also the most promising and interesting, but many examples of it actually occurring are available.

To aggregative learning corresponds an elitist corporate, bureaucratic and professional type of cosmopolitanism, whether in an economic, political or legal guise, which follows models of freedom or the unencumbered self constructed in relation to cosmopolitan citizenship. The contemporary phenomenon of 'the class consciousness of frequent travellers' (Calhoun, 2003; see also Featherstone, 2002) is a good example. In the case of institutional learning, which often goes hand in glove with aggregative learning, a form of corporate or institutional cosmopolitanism prevails which is articulated through a variety of models. Economically, global cosmopolitan – including corporate – citizenship is directed and guided by such models as free trade, mobile production facilities, globally recognised brands and consumerism. Politically, the focus on collective goods is oriented by a number of contradictory and even conflicting cultural models, among which the most prominent are a world state or world government, global governance, cosmopolitan democracy and a 'politically constituted world society without world government' (Habermas, 2005: 329). Legally, finally, the concern with regulative regimes is pursued today according to conflicting models, one being 'legal pluralism' (Teubner, 1997) which is closely related to the neo-liberal capitalist imaginary, and cosmopolitan law in the sense of a global legal order which, however, itself admits of either an authoritarian (Zolo, 1997) or a democratic (Habermas, 2001a) interpretation. The moral cosmopolitan model of the universal human community, which is opposed to the currently ascending model of a closed theocratic community, contains a normative thrust – that is, cosmopolitan and environmental justice – that is at work not only in some of the political and legal models just mentioned, but also in civil societal models mentioned below.

The civic cosmopolitanism related to associational learning takes a variety of contradictory or even conflicting forms, judging by the models constructed here. On the neo-liberal and legal pluralist side, the model of a global private law society (Teubner, 1997) is prominent. Those opposing it invoke the model of a global civil society which is interpreted differently, depending on whether it is regarded as being made up of global institutions such as a reformed United Nations, international governmental organisations, international NGOs, citizens' groups and social movements, or whether it is seen as communicatively constituted, spanned by a public sphere and remaining rooted in civic communities (Delanty, 2000).

To dual processes of learning through confrontation corresponds syncretic cosmopolitanism. Much discussed contemporary phenomena such as societal pluralisation, networks, hybridity or multiple modernities all contain suggestive pointers toward the models of world openness constituting this type of cosmopolitanism. Obviously, different, contradictory and even conflicting models can be entertained by two interrelated parties, such as coordination, accommodation, complementarity, mutual advantage, dependency and so forth, or equally different interpretations can be attached to these models. By contrast, discursive cosmopolitanism generated by triple contingency learning relates to norm formation at a higher level. It therefore typically involves models of world openness that have a bearing on norms which are more or less significantly effective in regulation at the global level. Norms securing ecosystems (environmental accords, sustainability), guaranteeing respect and protection for the individual (human rights) and regulating the protection of the human species (global population and health norms) are the most conspicuous ones today (Held *et al.*, 1999; Therborn, 2000; Habermas, 2001a). As against legal pluralism, there is also evidence that a global or 'universal code of legality' (Günther, 2001: 542) is emerging today.

The articulation of these different cosmopolitan cultures underlines the guiding role the cosmopolitan discourse is playing in the process of globalising: opening up driven by collective learning which brings the nascent twenty-first-century world society into being. This society has already begun to discursively describe itself, its own new sense of worldhood, at both the global and local levels in terms of a selective combination of these cosmopolitan models. Such a discursively attained practical synthesis is reflexively maintained with reference to engagement with reality. It thus retains an inherent flexibility within a horizon of currently pressing problems and challenges. However, such a combination of cognitive structures is not entirely divorced from – indeed, derives from and strikes roots in – the natural historical process. Global cosmopolitan worldhood is intimately intertwined with the new planetary sense of earthiness, thus generating the characteristic contemporary imaginary of global cosmopolitan being in a cared-for planetary biosocial ecosphere.

But this points beyond the cosmopolitan discourse to the communicative form of society.

A cosmopolitan planetary home?

Communication society

The various discourses analysed above are all manifestations of the communicative form of society. Ours is a communication and discourse society. It is reflexively constituted and organised on the basis of the institutionalisation of discourse and corresponding forms of communication allowing possibilities of access to the generation of different kinds of appropriate reasons – e.g. relating to risk, ecology, globalisation or cosmopolitanism – which themselves could become part of the structuring of social relations as such and in relation to nature. And what is more, society itself has over an extended period increasingly become organised according to the rules of communication. Starting with the early modern communication revolution (Strydom, 2000), society constituted and organised itself through a series of historical discourses which allowed the practical resolution of serious issues by means of new institutional arrangements – for instance, political domination through civil rights and constitutionalisation, and economic exploitation through welfare and democratisation. The gains made there, which went beyond mere problem solving toward world creation, left a broadened basis of cultural, social, political and other relevant conditions for the current set of discourses. This set, focused as it is on the currently predominant issue of risk which has penetrated all spheres of life to such an extent that it needs to be addressed ecologically and cosmopolitically right up to the global level, is therefore in a position to exercise a stronger communicative structuring effect on the emerging society.

The constitution of society involves an ongoing, fragmentary, contradictory and conflict-ridden process taking place on a number of different levels, each of which develops at its own pace, yet nevertheless is characterised by identification, collective learning, coordination, cooperation, joint problem solving and world creation. The outcome of this process, society, is not something positively given but an always incomplete phenomenon that emerges from lived experience, the historical development of expanding societal relations and conditions within the horizon of the future – hence from the tension between the real and the possible. On the one hand, then, the process of societal constitution is communicatively mediated through a variety of overlapping and interpenetrating discourses which, while depending on the cognitive import of natural historical developments, articulate the ecological, economic, political, legal and civil societal forms of society. As for society, on the other hand, its most important form, the one making possible societal learning and hence carrying the promise of a reasonable realisation of its potentials, is to be found in its communicative form.

A contrast and comparison of different interpretations of the process of societal constitution and organisation could shed light on the matter.

Cosmomorphism, functionalism and critical theory

A traditionally widely accepted interpretation proceeds from the cosmomorphic model which could be based on either naturalistic or idealistic assumptions. According to it, the process of constitution leads to and culminates, or will culminate, in a single, all-embracing, all-powerful form of global or world society. Most frequently, this form is regarded as coinciding either with a world state or government or with a global legal order, but it is alternatively also identified with a capitalist market society, a global private law society, a global civil society, or a culturally based world society, and so forth.

An opposed interpretation is offered by Luhmannian functionalist systems theory which, like the theoretical position adopted in this chapter, stresses the communicative form of society and thus correctly contests the cosmomorphic assumptions of linearity, necessity and inevitability. It regards world society as already in existence, yet only in the sense of the planetary extension of society's internal functional differentiation – which means, as the 'innumerable multiplicity of simultaneously ongoing communications' considered purely as 'operations' selected in terms of possibilities or 'expectations' (Schütz, 1997: 283). The basic limitation of autopoietic systemism, however, is that it presupposes the adoption of a cybernetically and biologically inspired external perspective from which society appears as a process in the flow of which no acknowledgement, recognition, identification and self-understanding is possible or could make any sense. The strategic point of this approach is to portray society as completely beyond intervention and control. From this viewpoint, it would be misguided, utopian in a disparaging sense of the word, to strive towards and work for the realisation of the possibility of the society disclosed through the destructive potential of the atom bomb and the global phenomenon of risk which threatens not only the biotic but also the social ecosphere.

The critical communication and discourse theory of society adopted here leads to an understanding different from both the extremes of cosmomorphism and functionalism. It has implications for both social scientific practice and political engagement. If the process is not a matter of necessity, is it not one of fatalism either. As Kant's still relevant justification of the possibility of human progress makes clear, a moral demand compels us as members of a series of human generations to make it our duty to conceive of a hypothetical and thus fallible yet actually possible advancement in history, and to conduct ourselves in such a way, including remaining open to the cognitive input from nature, that we contribute to its realisation to the extent possible under current conditions (Kant, 1980; Apel, 1997). Given the communicative form of society, this could be stated a little more carefully (Peirce, 1958; Apel, 1981). Since cognition (including becoming aware and consciousness) and hence knowledge production and employment is a process in which signs mediate between reality and those who interpret signs and engage with reality, signs are not merely imaginary figments of the mind but rather an essential element in the very process of the evolution of nature and society. It is incumbent on us, the sign interpreters, therefore, to use signs correctly and appropriately, and to learn to do so is to acquire the ability to participate responsibly in the process of evolution, both natural and social. In the wake of the failure of the Communist experiment, the unresolved problems of moral responsibility in respect of the ecological crisis and global social injustice have become glaringly obvious, even to those who all along have been benefiting directly from the activities generating these conditions (Apel, 1987).

From this it follows that it is possible to discern the direction of contemporary developments or, at least, the normative criteria guiding it.

Direction and prospects

The epoch-making world disclosure of the mid-twentieth century brought about a change in cognitive structures that gave prominence to the contemporary ecological planetary cosmology and cosmopolitan world model which are refracted through the safety and danger schema of perception and interpretation giving priority to risk on a global scale. The mode of engagement with reality and reading the signs of the times made possible by this reconfiguration of the cognitive order gave rise to a series of overlapping and interpenetrating discourses in which the problems of risk, ecology, globalisation and cosmopolitanism are thematised. These discourses enabled inner-worldly learning processes, particularly norm forming societal learning, which reflexively generated a new view on both world and earth and a new self-understanding, the characteristic cosmopolitan ecological consciousness of our time. In so far as we take seriously the responsibility our cognition assigns to us today – for instance, recognising that we need to follow a course which we would not readily adopt by choice – we have the opportunity to participate in a new spurt in the constitution and organisation of society and, by the same token, in the evolution of nature.

For those who are reading the signs correctly and appropriately and accordingly engage with reality – and an increasing number, although not nearly enough, are in fact doing so – two normative reference points generated by norm forming learning processes stand out. The first is the new understanding of the earth, the planetary ecosphere in the sense of the biosocial system embracing all living beings on earth as their only and indispensable organic foundation of life and health. The second is the new understanding of our world, a global society of cosmopolitan rights, democracy, justice and peace. Taken together, these two form an imaginary allowing us to envisage not only the direction of the process of social and natural development, but also the criterion with which long-term human goals should and must be reconciled through identity formation. As such, it represents the basis for both social scientifically and politically relevant critical judgements about contemporary states of affairs and engaging responsibly with reality in support of appropriate identification processes.

The contemporary symbol of this imagined global cosmopolitan being in a cared-for planetary biosocial ecosphere is the most characteristic visual image of our time, the 'Blue Planet'. Far from a nihilistic rootless homelessness, it symbolises the unavoidability and meaningfulness of our responsible commitment to bringing our new cosmopolitan planetary home into being.

Notes

1 This chapter has been written from the viewpoint of a cognitive communication and discourse version of critical theory which, due to lack of space, remains below the surface in terms of both explication and references. It should be pointed out, however, that the conceptual pair of earth and world basic to the analysis is informed by the weak naturalistic ontology and pragmatic realist epistemology underpinning this version (Strydom, 2002, 2007).
2 The well-known full image of earth taken from Apollo on 11 December 1972 was actually the second photograph, the first being the partially eclipsed image known as the 'Earth Rise', shot on Christmas Eve 1968.

References

Apel, K.-O. (1979) *Die Erklären-Verstehen Kontroverse in transzendental-pragmatisher Sicht* (Frankfurt: Suhrkamp).

Apel, K.-O. (1981) *Charles S. Peirce* (Amherst, MA: University of Massachusetts Press).

Apel, K.-O. (1987) 'The Problem of a Macroethic of Responsibility to the Future in the Crisis of Technological Civilization: An Attempt to Come to Terms with Hans Jonas's "Principle of Responsibility"', *Man and World*, 20, 3–40.

Apel, K.-O. (1997) 'Kant's "Toward Perpetual Peace" as Historical Prognosis from the Point of View of Moral Duty', in J. Bohman and M. Lutz-Bachmann (eds.), *Perpetual Peace* (Cambridge, MA: MIT Press).

Beck, U. (2009) *World at Risk* (Cambridge: Polity).

Brunkhorst, H. (2005) *Solidarity: from Civic Friendship to a Global Legal Community* (Cambridge, MA: MIT Press).

Calhoun, C. (2003) 'The Class Consciousness of Frequent Travellers: Towards a Critique of Actually Existing Cosmopolitanism', in D. Archibugi (ed.), *Debating Cosmopolitics* (London: Verso).

Dean, M. (1999) *Governmentality* (London: Sage).

Delanty, G. (2000) *Citizenship in a Global Age* (Buckingham: Open University Press).

Delanty, G. (2006) 'The Cosmopolitan Imagination: Critical Cosmopolitanism and Social Theory', *The British Journal of Sociology*, 57(1), 25–47.

Dezalay, Y. (1994) 'The Big Bang and the Law', in M. Featherstone (ed.), *Global Culture* (London: Sage).

Donnelly, J. (1998) *International Human Rights* (Boulder, CO: Westview).

Featherstone, M. (2002) 'Cosmopolis: An Introduction', *Theory, Culture and Society*, 19(1/2), 1–16.

Günther, K. (2001) 'Rechtspluralismus und universaler Code der Legalität: Globalisierung als rechtstheoretisches Problem', in L. Wingert and K. Günther (eds.), *Die Öffentlichkeit der Vernunft und die Vernunft der Öffentlichkeit* (Frankfurt: Suhrkamp).

Habermas, J. (1976) *Legitimation Crisis* (London: Heinemann; Boston, MA: Beacon Press).

Habermas, J. (2001a) *The Postnational Constellation* (Cambridge: Polity).

Habermas, J. (2001b) *Zeit des Übergänge* (Frankfurt: Suhrkamp).

Habermas, J. (2004) *Der gespaltene Westen* (Frankfurt: Suhrkamp).

Habermas, J. (2005) *Zwischen Naturalismus und Religion* (Frankfurt: Suhrkamp).

Heidegger, M. (1977) *The Question Concerning Technology and Other Essays* (New York: HarperRow).

Held, D., A. McGrew, D. Goldblatt and J. Perraton (1999) *Global Transformations* (Cambridge: Polity).

Jonas, H. (1973) 'Technology and Responsibility', *Social Research*, 40(1), 31–54.

Kant, I. (1980) *On History* (Indianapolis, IN: Bobbs-Merrill).

Lovelock, J. (2006) *The Revenge of GAIA* (London: Allen Lane).

Luhmann, N. (1986) *Ecological Communication* (Cambridge: Polity).

Lukashuk, I. (1997) 'The Law of the International Community', in International Law Commission (ed.), *International Law on the Eve of the Twenty-First Century* (New York: United Nations).

Miller, M. (2002) 'Some Theoretical Aspects of Systemic (Discursive) Learning', *Sozialer Sinn*, 3, 379–421.

Mol, A. P. J. (2003) *Globalisation and Environmental Reform* (Cambridge, MA: MIT Press).

Peirce, C. S. (1958) *Collected Papers, Vol. VIII* (Cambridge, MA: Harvard University Press).

Schmitt, C. (1985) *Political Theology* (Cambridge, MA: MIT Press).

Schütz, A. (1997) 'The Twilight of the Global "Polis": On Losing Paradigms, Environing Systems and Observing World Society', in G. Teubner (ed.), *Global Law Without a State* (Dartmouth, MA: Ashgate).

Simpson, R. (1996) 'Neither Clear nor Present: The Social Construction of Safety and Danger', *Sociological Forum*, 11(3), 549–62.

Spaargaren, G., A. P. J. Mol and F. H. Buttel (eds.) (2006) *Governing Environmental Flows* (Cambridge, MA: MIT Press).

Strydom, P. (1999a) 'The Challenge of Responsibility for Sociology', *Current Sociology*, 47(3), 65–82.

Strydom, P. (1999b) 'Triple Contingency: The Theoretical Problem of the Public in Communication Societies', *Philosophy and Social Criticism*, 25(1), 1–25.

Strydom, P. (2000) *Discourse and Knowledge* (Liverpool: Liverpool University Press).

Strydom, P. (2002) *Risk, Environment and Society: Ongoing Debates, Current Issues and Future Prospects* (Buckingham: Open University Press).

Strydom, P. (2007) 'A Cartography of Contemporary Cognitive Sociology', Special Issue, *European Journal of Social Theory*, 10(3), 339–56, guest editor, Piet Strydom.

Strydom, P. (2008) 'Risk Communication: World Creation through Collective Learning under Complex Contingent Conditions', *Journal of Risk Research* 11(1–2), 5–22.

Teubner, G. (ed.) (1997) *Global Law Without a State* (Dartmouth, MA: Ashgate).

Therborn, G. (2000) 'Globalisations: Dimensions, Historical Waves, Regional Effects, Normative Governance', *International Sociology*, 15(1), 151–79.

Tomuschat, C. (1997) 'International Law as the Constitution of Mankind', in International Law Commission (ed.), *International Law on the Eve of the Twenty-First Century* (New York: United Nations).

Trenz, H. J. and K. Eder (2004) 'The Democratizing Dynamics of a European Public Sphere', *European Journal of Social Theory*, 7(1), 5–25.

Willke, H. (1992) *Ironie des Staates* (Frankfurt: Suhrkamp).

Zolo, D. (1997) *Cosmopolis: Prospects for World Government* (Cambridge: Polity).

2

Discourses of transition to sustainability in Ireland: outlines of a green republican strategy

John Barry

Introduction

Ireland as an island community (that is, understood as including both the Republic and Northern Ireland) is uniquely vulnerable to ecological changes, especially those around energy security and the transition to a low-carbon economy and climate change: 95 per cent of the island's energy comes from imported fossil fuels, particularly oil and natural gas. Ireland has the third highest oil consumption *per capita* in the European Union, arising from its use in transport and electricity generation. The Republic of Ireland's much-vaunted status as the most globalised economy in the world which, in the 'Celtic Tiger' years, was to bring much wealth and prosperity (however badly distributed), has also, in terms of energy, left it extremely exposed to the vicissitudes of geopolitical events which negatively effect resource flows in energy-supplier countries such as Russia and Iraq.[1] That the brief period of unprecedented orthodox economic growth was literally fuelled by plentiful supplies of cheap hydrocarbons is only slowly dawning on the architects of that phenomenal success within the dominant political, economic and media class, and even more slowly (and reluctantly) beginning to dawn on that generation of Irish people, The Pope's Children (McWilliams, 2005), who gained most from that period, and who now have to wake up to the hangover of the decade before and face up to making the transition to a sustainable, low-carbon economy, the challenge of the twenty-first century. As the Green Party TD and Minister for Communications, Energy and Natural Resources, Eamon Ryan, noted in the Dáil in a debate in early July 2008:

> We bought bigger cars for the status that it gave. We built bigger houses with X number of bedrooms and bathrooms, regardless of how we were going to heat these massive properties. We flew to New York in a way that turned Madison Avenue into our latest Grafton Street ... Let us be

honest with ourselves that is the phenomenon that occurred ... In the last decade China and India started to produce our goods for us at a fraction of the cost. That brought down inflation in the developed world and allowed the central banks to lower interests internationally, which led to easy lending, bad lending. (*Irish Times*, 11 July 2008)

It is perhaps more than telling that it was a Green Party *Minster,* not just an elected member of the Dáil, who was brave (or foolish) enough to hold a mirror to the debt and fossil-fuelled unsustainability of Ireland's 'three planet living'. And he did so in the Dáil, the apex of the Irish representative democratic system, not in a blog or local Green Party constituency meeting. Is this an intimation of a 'tipping point' (to use an increasingly salient concept within green politics and the politics of sustainability) within Ireland? Or is an illustration of 'green rhetoric', a simulative exercise (Blühdorn and Welsh, 2007) making it appear that our political leaders were 'leading', 'telling us like it is' and preparing citizens for a new political and economic reality, and by extension to allow the public also to simulate concern but then continue happily consuming?

At the time of writing, the Republic of Ireland had witnessed its first year of the Green Party in coalition government, the restoration of the devolved Assembly in Northern Ireland (and the election of the first Green member to that Assembly in March 2007), and therefore the beginnings of a new chapter in all-island politics. Unfortunately, this same period (2007–8) also witnessed the doubling of the price of oil and consequent increase in energy prices, food price increases, a global 'credit crunch', major contraction of the housing boom and a global economic recession which spells the end of the 'Celtic Tiger' phenomenon. Just as the post-conflict dispensation was beginning to bed down in Northern Ireland, heralding a new era in North–South relations, this fragile all-island political dynamic is faced with major energy, climate and economic downturns.

Does this appear to herald new possibilities for the environmental movement in Ireland? Do socio-political conditions – above all, growing media coverage, and cultural receptivity to issues such as climate change, peak oil, energy security and low-carbon energy futures – suggest a movement whose time has come? However, the environmental movement in Ireland has long been labelled 'exceptional', characterised as resolutely localist, populist and nationalist in orientation (Tovey, 1993; Leonard, 2006). Generally, it does not conform to patterns of green movement development typical of other parts of Europe, particularly in its preference for being non-confrontational and not seeking widespread structural transformation (Garavan, 2007). As a putative 'environmentalism of place' rather than of 'planet', the environmental movement in Ireland is, as Baker noted two decades ago, closer to environmentalism in so-called 'developing' and post-colonial world than the 'post-industrialism' and 'post-materialism' which is held to typify 'western/European environmentalism' (Baker, 1990; Kelly, Faughnan and Tovey, 2003). A question that arises from this is: What will be the cultural and political impact of a green movement with these historical characteristics on the island of Ireland? Is such a movement likely to align with the contemporary tendency to frame green concerns as 'sustainable development' rather than as a more far-reaching 'environmental' issue that brings into focus the general human relation to nature (Barry, 2008a)?

This chapter will seek to explore the issues affecting the political and cultural impact and influence of the environmental movement in Ireland through examining some of the discursive cultural resources available to it, specifically in relation to a 'green republican discourse'. Commencing in the next section below, the idea of green republicanism is examined both normatively and practically with respect to its generative potential as a mobilising discourse in the transition towards sustainability in Ireland.

Green republicanism: rationale

The language of civic republicanism has been largely absent from debates within green politics and theories of the politics and ethics of sustainability, unlike the conferences, edited books and monographs dedicated to exploring the relationship between green politics and feminism (Salleh, 1997), liberalism (Barry and Wissenburg, 2001), socialism (Kovel, 2002), conservatism (Gray, 1993), or neo-liberalism (Lomborg, 2001). This absence is remarkable given the compatibility of core republican ideas with key principles of green politics, particularly its overarching goal of sustainable development. For example, key features of green politics, include, *inter alia*, active citizenship, understood in part as a form of ecological stewardship, in which duties as well as rights are central; a democratised and decentralised state seen as a necessary institution to promote the common good of sustainability (particularly in relation to regulating the free market); and a sense of justice and connection between past, present and future generations. All of these key features of green politics, and others, are remarkably close to a republican political vision. Emphasising the republican strains native to the political cultures of Western liberal democracies could help to create a political environment more conducive to green politics and policy, and allows greens to offer an 'immanent critique' of the current unsustainable development paths being followed by Western societies in a language comprehensible to the majority of its citizens (Barry and Smith, 2008). Many studies now show that the numerous scientific reports documenting growing unsustainability and environmental degradation and prescribing remedying policies, are failing to mobilise citizens to change their behaviour. In that context, having a familiar, broadly shared political (and ethical) language to communicate and debate sustainability concerns is pivotal. This language should also acknowledge and valorise the ethical plurality of modern societies. The development of such a language is a pressing need for the promotion of social learning and collective problem solving processes. This language should facilitate the meaningful interplay of ethical claims, scientific and epistemological arguments, political strategies and publicly sanctioned policies needed for the transition to low-carbon, sustainability societies. The republican claim of valuing 'contestation over consensus' (Pettit, 1997) fits well with standard green political claims linking democracy and the politics of sustainability as it views democratic politics and decision making as plurality-enhancing and plurality-dependent forms of social learning.

Furthermore, given the prominence of republicanism in Irish history and in contemporary politics in Ireland, encompassing both Northern Ireland and the Republic, it is also interesting to note the absence of research into the relationship between green politics and the claims of sustainability and republicanism in Ireland. This chapter suggests that central features of republicanism can inform green politics, focusing on its understanding of the human condition, the implications of that understanding for politics and citizenship, and its conception of political time and the problem of sustainability. It is therefore feasible to argue that there is a case to be made for 'republicanising' green politics in general, given the programmatic compatibility between green political goals and those of civic republicanism, and on the island of Ireland in particular given the place and role of republicanism in Irish politics and history even if this is contested, complicated and not always positive.[2]

Theorising green republicanism: resilience, vulnerability and citizenship

In contrast to the dominant versions of liberalism and conservatism, both of which emphasise an individualistic conception of freedom as non-interference – either with personal lifestyle choices, rationalised economic behaviour, or 'tradition' – and an optimistic view of humans' ability to transcend their limits, republicanism emphasises the duties of citizenship and the individual's dependence on a specific historical community *as it is embedded in a particular natural environment*. Indeed, civic republicanism is vitally concerned with the key challenge of sustainability – how to extend the life of a specific historical community and its cherished and hard-won values and practices, especially freedom, in a world ruled by forces beyond full human control. The republican conception of the human condition is, in key respects, the same as the green conception: it acknowledges humans' complex relations of dependence on natural forces outside our control, our limited understanding of those relationships and forces that form the (relatively) fixed socio-ecological limits within which human society can flourish.

Republicans, like greens, begin from a recognition of the defining features of our human condition, ones that, as Alistair Macintyre notes (Macintyre, 1999) are absent from dominant forms of liberal political thinking: namely our vulnerability and dependency. Human vulnerability permeates republican thought; as Aristotle reminds us, we are neither beasts nor gods: we cannot survive alone in the wilderness and retain our distinctive humanity. Rousseau, another important source for republicans, argues in *A Discourse on Inequality* that humans' relative weakness, our vulnerability to natural dangers, makes us not just dependent creatures, but interdependent. Interdependence in turn creates the possibility of domination – which is particularly troublesome for republicans, who understand liberty as non-domination. Because we depend on one another for survival and prospering in a dangerous and uncontrollable world, we need political institutions to order our common life so as to preserve and sustain some measure of equality and civil (if not natural) freedom and equality. This goal of civic freedom permeates republican thought, creating an important counterpoint to its equally strong emphasis on civic duties. The republican project is to create a secure home for free men and women, not for slaves, and this will not occur 'naturally' but only by active citizen political action and the creation of liberty-sustaining practices and institutions, particularly the state and the rule of law – especially constitutional provisions.

That project brings us to the heart of the republic political vision: politics, for republicans, is an attempt to build an enduring home for human lives in a world ruled by contingency and filled with potentially hostile agents, both human and non-human. Political communities and their values – of liberty, honour and the common good – are conventional, human creations, not naturally given; they must be actively created and sustained by collective, conscious human action. And like any construction project, building a city (and its citizens) begins with choosing a site and specifying the needs of the inhabitants. Republican theorists are therefore particularly attentive to the many contingent features of the natural and social environment that will determine a community's political possibilities. Because we face unknown threats from nature and from other actors, we must pay close attention to our natural environment and resource base. After all, the ultimate source of the resources needed to sustain a republic, its common good and valued way/s of life, is not created by humans, but found in nature and transformed by humans. We are utterly dependent upon and are vulnerable to nature and therefore there is a strong reason to be particularly attendant to our relationship to nature.

But resources are relative to needs; a disciplined (and united) people accustomed to frugality and modesty will not make as many demands on its resource base and ecological hinterland. They will also be more unified and so better able to defend their city – and to recover from disaster. This republican concern with promoting healthy, robust and resilient communities thus corresponds well with contemporary empirical research on the conditions which enhance a community's capacity to withstand external shocks and disasters and ability to adapt to significant natural and socio-economic transformations such as climate change, peak oil or major downturns in the global economy. That research typically identifies as critical to resilience certain socioeconomic conditions – principally rough socio-economic equality, equal access to political power, robust but not extensive social capital networks, and concrete and embodied practices of solidarity through active, effective modes of citizen mobilisation and effective civic leadership (Cutter, 2006). These conditions, of course, resemble the key features of community life championed within the civic republican tradition.

Republicanism, unlike liberalism, has always regarded luxury and material wealth with some suspicion (often viewing wealth as leading to the downfall of the republic through exacerbating class divisions and thus undermining the solidarity of the citizenry, and also concerned about the corrosive effects of material comfort on stereotypical male marital virtues). As indicated below, one can find echoes of the corrosive social effects of material wealth in the critiques of the 'Celtic Tiger' years from the Green Party and Green Party ministers – uncomfortable and inconvenient truths which are not often popularly received. Leadership therefore is another key component of the republican perspective. Green republicanism not only offers a critique of excessive wealth creation and its misdistribution, but equally importantly sets its face against 'green consumerism' as a solution or viable path of transition away from unsustainability. A green republican position does not accept that the cause of and therefore solution to unsustainability can be found in simply 'correcting' individual behaviour through becoming greener consumers and promoting green consumption. In this way a green republican approach resists what Maniates calls the 'individualisation of responsibility' which leaves 'little room to ponder institutions, the nature and exercise of political power, or ways of collectively changing the distribution of power and influence in society' (Maniates, 2002: 45). A green republican vision regards the crisis of unsustainability as a collective, cultural and political crisis and therefore to do with political power, institutions, policy making and political economy, all of which need to placed front and foremost in the necessary public deliberations about unsustainability and any paths or strategies to transition to sustainability decided upon. In short, green republicanism focuses on (public, political) *citizen* and not (private, economic) *consumer* identities and practices (Barry, 2005).

As a corollary to a focus on citizenship, a republican approach to green politics also leads one to issues of political leadership, a concern notably absent from green political theorising but arguably one of the most pressing 'gaps' in contemporary green politics and the politics of transition to sustainability. Greens typically eschew discussion of leadership on the (false) grounds that leadership is inimical to a green vision of participatory, grassroots democracy. Engagement with republicanism can help overcome this deficiency in green political thinking and strategy. Republicanism reminds us that facilitative and inspiring political leadership is not necessarily a danger to even radical forms of democratic politics, and is undoubtedly essential for the transition to sustainability (the key aim of green politics). Leaders, however, can do only so much. Politics is ultimately in the hands of citizens, and citizenship for republicans is an identity and practice. Citizens as well as cities are made, not born. Here debates within green politics on citizenship (Dobson, 2003: Dobson and Bell, 2005) are illustrative of the potential for engagement between green politics and republicanism, particularly those (Barry, 2005) that have defended distinctly 'republican' notions of green citizenship, including proposing provocative ideas such as compulsory 'sustainability service' for all citizens, that can be defended on green principles of achieving sustainability and that are also liberty-supporting and can contribute to the social and economic 'bottom lines' of sustainability.

A republican sensibility is not romantic; it is resolutely based in '*Realpolitik*' – hence its 'tough' and often 'austere' character – and an empirical/scientific assessment of the dangers and challenges facing the republic and its free citizens. Like republicanism, green politics takes a realistic and empirically informed view of the challenges facing human societies, and of the possibilities for progressive social transformation towards creating sustainable societies (Barry, 2008b). It is thus a politics of hope, though not neglecting in some Panglossian fashion those very real and looming threats we face, the foregrounding of which often means that green politics is presented as a reactionary 'doom and gloom' form of 'fear-mongering'. The 'fear' that animates green politics is not some reactionary Malthusian concern with non-negotiable 'scarcity' – the standard critique of green politics from the liberal left as found in authors such as Anthony Giddens (Barry, 2007) who fundamentally misunderstand green politics. Rather, green politics can be viewed as a progressive, 'concrete utopian' mode of political thought. As concrete utopianism, it offers a vision to guide social reform that is not divorced from the ineliminable 'hard facts' of social–environmental relations – particularly the facts of social relations which delimit the effective range – *but do not determine or dictate* – social choice (Diamond, 2005).

Contestation not consensus: green republicanism, pluralism, and democratic problem solving

According to Pettit (1997) republicanism is a form of politics in which public dialogue, debate and contestation are central, and which must be conducted in an idiom and language which is understandable by citizens. That is, a political language and cause which is incomprehensible to citizens (or a significant proportion of them) is one which will not have much chance of gaining support, or will be significantly deficient in terms of persuading citizens to support it. This is something Pettit highlights as a serious problem for green politics. As he puts it, 'radical environmentalism, according to which the state should be shaped with a view to non-human as well as human interests, does not itself offer a language of grievance and claim that has any chance of reaching the ears of those outside the green movement' (Pettit, 1997: 136). Now, lest I am misunderstood on this point, I *do not* agree with Pettit's point that the anthropocentrism of republicanism (Pettit, 1997: 134, 135) is such that non-anthropocentric or ecocentric claims and interests cannot be coherently expressed within a 'green republican' language. Pettit's point about the centrality of expressing one's political claims in a language and mode which extends one's audience beyond the 'converted' is extremely important. This has been an issue which has gained particular saliency within green political theorising, not least in relation to the huge gap between the public knowledge of growing trends in unsustainability and the lack of a discernable shift in public opinion towards greater support for sustainability policies or large-scale change in behaviour.

Pettit's stress on the republican necessity for pragmatism in politics, and the need to speak in a language acceptable to most citizens, is well made and one to which green politics needs to pay attention. As Pettit puts it, 'The pragmatism required may not appeal to purists, but apart from being ineffective, the purist attitude is also exceedingly precious. Why should devotees of a certain cause shrink from presenting that cause in terms that have general appeal, on the grounds that the cause appeals to them in different, more particular ways?' (1997: 136). While in the main this is a sound point to make, there are a number of reasons for qualifying this and allowing for the legitimacy (even if it has little strategic or persuasive effect) of articulating one's claims or grievances in an ethical or political language which is not immediately or universally accepted. Greens can deploy arguments against presenting their claims in a language or manner which systematically misrepresents, and indeed corrupts, important aspects of the moral import of their claims. Specifically, a long-standing green critique has been of economic modes of articulating sustainability dilemmas, especially contingent valuation techniques of cost-benefit analysis (CBA)(O'Neill, 1993; Barry, 1999). Simply put, green political theory holds the position that moral claims on behalf of nature – or, indeed, non-economic valuations of the environment – should not be forced to be publicly articulated in a language of economic valuation (which does in Pettit's terms have broad 'general appeal' given the ubiquity of the basic logic of 'cost-benefit analysis'). Here, I stand with green 'purists' (to use Pettit's term) who refuse to translate their ethical commitments into an economic language, even though by so doing they do engage in forms of political communication which seem out of step in comparison with widely held and familiar political idioms.

Nevertheless, this may not be what Pettit has in mind in advancing his critique, since an unqualified endorsement of his principle that 'political pragmatism' requires presenting a cause in terms that have general appeal could mean that anti-slavery advocates within a predominantly slave-owning political culture have to express and translate their political into a language which is, to put it mildly, not 'fit for purpose'. Here of course Pettit may accept that this is not what his principle demands. To the contrary, American and British abolitionists in the nineteenth century took recourse to an innovative ethical and political language. This emphasised individual rights and the dignity of the person, as well as a re-interpretation of the Bible, which was different from and a challenge to the dominant political language and idioms of a slave-owning political culture though it was not entirely novel. Likewise green advocates have recourse to a new (though also old) language of the intrinsic value of nature or some other enlightened anthropocentric position which, while it may be a minority ('purist') position, is nevertheless comprehensible to the majority, even if it represents a challenge to the dominant political culture and dominant and shared views of the 'good life'.

A good example here is the political discourse of 'animal rights' and the use of the discourse of 'interspecies justice'. The use of 'rights' in this way alongside the associated language of 'justice' between humans and non-humans represents a novel and minority position, whether in the form of ecocentric arguments for 'biospheric egalitarianism' as in the early articulation of 'deep ecology' (Naess, 1973), Peter Singer's 'animal rights' (Singer, 1990), or more recent developments within green political theory on interspecies 'ecological justice' such as that of Brian Baxter (2004). Regardless of whether one finds their premises compelling or not, the use of the language of 'rights' and 'justice' does serve an important communicative function, and one which Pettit's overdetermined notion of 'pragmatism' omits. This communicative force of the use of the language of justice and rights is that, *ceteris paribus*, the claims expressed in this idiom are not only recognisable as ethical or political claims but also that the audience which so understands the claims can, at the very least, see that they are serious claims insofar as those who articulate them are concerned. Notice that this communication of moral seriousness does not mean that the audience/ listener shares the interlocutor's/speaker's view of the veracity or priority of the claim (or its premise). All that is meant by seriousness being communicated is that the listener acknowledges that the speaker holds that what they are saying is morally and politically serious and non-trivial and therefore demanding of their attention and fit for discussion in the public sphere in relation to the governing principles of public institutions.

Here, and in keeping with Pettit's republican insistence on the need to decide on political issues within a pluralist framework not in the abstract but in the particular context within and from which they arise, one can say that this issue of the choice of language/idiom within which to express one's claims must allow for flexibility and manoeuvre about the following three options:

- When and when not to adopt a dominant common political language (such as conventional uses of the language of 'social or distributive justice', 'democratic equality', 'rights', or even the utilitarian-cum-economic language of 'cost-benefit analysis').
- When and when not to seek to use that common language in new ways (such as extending justice to 'ecological justice', or expanding the rights discourse to encompass 'animal rights' or religious-based notions of 'stewardship' re-cast as forms of 'green citizenship').
- When and when not to seek to articulate their views and claims in a relatively new or unconventional or not widely used political language and discourse (such as the 'intrinsic value' of nature, or non-humanity, or the sacredness of 'mother nature').

There is another issue that Pettit raises which is also extremely important. It is the question of whether green politics demands not only that certain actions be done or behaviours changed (more recycling, greater civic participation, reducing energy use, paying taxes or other measures to decrease socio-economic inequality or other actions demanded of a 'triple bottom line' understanding of sustainable development), but that these actions be done for the 'right' reasons. Here, one can only agree with Pettit and the republican position of not expecting each political agreement for action or policy to be motivated or based on the same or similar set of ethical or other reasons. The pragmatic position of both Pettit and others such as Dryzek (1987) can be taken – that it is more important to convince people to do the 'right' environmental action rather than insist they must also do this for the 'right' reason. Here of course we part ways with a significant body of green political theory and environmental ethics that holds the view that behavioural change without an underlying change in values or consciousness in a 'green' direction is either morally less valuable or practically self-defeating, in the sense that action or behavioural change not based on appropriate green value positions leaves green action vulnerable (Dobson, 2007). We take the more pragmatic, *Realpolitik*, republican view that what matters most – particularly in the face of urgent and pressing ecological, economic and political challenges – is action and behavioural change in a sustainable direction, not that that change necessarily be motivated by green concerns.

In sum, republican theorists remind us that our vulnerability to natural disasters and our ultimate dependence on the natural world – and our concomitant dependence on one another – is the starting point for *any* sort of politics. This *is* the fundamental political problem. Any political strategy which not only fails to articulate this but also sees it as a foundational principle is seriously deficient as a realistic account of our current political condition and a guide to shaping our future.

Discourses of transition: an 'environmental war economy', green new deal, transition towns and green republicanism

Evidence of a shift or evolution of green politics towards republican forms can be seen in the emergence of more 'hard-headed' and prag-matic discourses of sustainability. Over the last couple of years (although one can suggest that it was always present within environmentalism) one can see the rise in arguments indicating that the mobilisation for the transition away from unsustainable development and towards a less unsustainable future will be based on a similar cultural and political experience to that many countries went through during and after the Second World War. This can be expressed as a form of 'Green Keyne-sianism' (George, 2007; Green New Deal Group 2008) or more pro-vocatively as an 'environmental war economy' (Simms, 2001; Brown, 2008).[3] While the latter may be said to be directed mainly at the nation-state level (and sometimes the EU level), it is complemented at the micro local level by a growth in grassroots, collective initiatives such as 'Tran-sition Towns' (Hopkins, 2008; Quilley and Barry, 2008). Both could be regarded as representative of contemporary green republican prac-tices and as signalling a step-change in environmental/green thinking and politics in a more discernable republican direction.

Consider the following statements from Andrew Simms, head of research at the well-known and respected London-based green think-tank, the new economics foundation:

> The situation in the global environmental war economy is not so different from the dilemma that faced individuals in Britain's war economy. As Hugh Dalton, president of the Board of Trade, put it in 1943, 'there can be no equality of sacrifice in this war. Some must lose their lives and limbs, others only the turn-ups on their trousers.' Impacts may differ, in other words, but the acknowledgement of a shared need remains and unifies ... *Faced with a crisis in which individuals are asked to subordinate personal goals to a common good, they can, and do, respond.* This is the lesson of the British and other war economies and it may also prove the rallying cry of a new environmental war economy. (Simms, 2001: 32–3, emphasis added)

Or these from Lester Brown of the Worldwatch Institute, writing about the wartime restructuring and re-prioritising of the American economy:

In addition to a ban on the production and sale of cars for private use, residential and highway construction was halted, and driving for pleasure was banned. Strategic goods – including tires, gasoline, fuel oil, and sugar – were rationed beginning in 1942. Cutting back on private consumption of these goods freed up material resources that were vital to the war effort ... This mobilisation of resources within a matter of months demonstrates that a country and, indeed, the world can restructure the economy quickly if convinced of the need to do so. Many people – although not yet the majority – are already convinced of the need for a wholesale economic restructuring. (Brown, 2008: 279–80)

The contemporary lessons Brown draws from his examination of the 're-directing' of the American economy towards war is to do the same today but directed towards meeting the sustainability challenges. As he puts it, 'The challenge is to build a new economy and to do it at wartime speed before we miss so many of nature's deadlines that the economic system begins to unravel' (Brown, 2008: 22). This discourse can also be found at the EU level. For example, Stavros Dimas, Commissioner for the Environment, in a speech in January 2007, stated that:

Damaged economies, refugees, political instability, and the loss of life are typically the results of war. But they will also be the results of unchecked climate change. *It is like a war because to reduce emissions something very like a war economy is needed.* All sectors – transport, energy, agriculture and foreign policy – must work closely together to meet a common objective. And it is a world war because every country in the world will be affected by the results of climate change – although it will be the poorest who are hit hardest. (Dimas, 2007: 2, emphasis added)

Dimas went on to conclude: 'I am convinced that protecting the environment – and in particular tackling climate change – will be at the very heart of the European project over the next 50 years. The alternative is to surrender in the war against climate change ... and that is really no alternative at all' (Dimas, 2007: 6). The point here is that in this harking back to and learning from the wartime experiences of America and Britain, what is being communicated and proposed is a distinctly republican form of green politics/environmentalism. What makes these recent articulations of green politics republican is that they are based on, *inter alia*: forms of collective mobilisation (whether local, as in Transition Towns (TTs), or more nationally conceived); a stress on duties and active citizenship, including shared sacrifice and practices such as rationing; a more regulatory and interventionist state (especially in relation to disciplining the market and a more planned approach to the economy, especially energy); explicit 'demand management' policies (i.e. not simply 'greening' production and consumption but reducing production and consumption, especially energy);[4] a shared vision of transformation for a particular purpose and securing of a common good (sustainability instead of war in this case), with often less clearly outlined notions of justice and empowered democratic political leadership and new relations of power and decision making between the (nation-) state, (global) market and civil society.[5]

A 'Green Keynesian' example of this more republican form of environmentalism can be found in another new economics foundation report, this time from the recently established Green New Deal Group. Its 2008 report explicitly makes reference to the prewar and postwar American experience:

> Drawing our inspiration from Franklin D. Roosevelt's courageous programme launched in the wake of the Great Crash of 1929, we believe that a positive course of action can pull the world back from economic and environmental meltdown. The Green New Deal that we are proposing consists of two main strands. First, it outlines a structural transformation of the regulation of national and international financial systems, and major changes to taxation systems. And, second, it calls for a sustained programme to invest in and deploy energy conservation and renewable energies, coupled with effective demand management. (Green New Deal Group, 2008: 2)

The report goes on to point out that 'There is a growing consensus that climate change demands an economic mobilisation of clean-energy technology, and other anti-greenhouse measures, on a scale to rival war time' (Green New Deal Group, 2008: 17). The stress on mobilisation and sense of urgency which permeates this report (features that of course, it shares with other environmentalist/sustainability reports and documents) echoes the wartime call for citizens to enlist and support the war effort within an explicitly 'Green Keynesianism':

> In our living memory, the scale of economic re-engineering needed to prevent catastrophic climate change has only been witnessed in a wide range of countries during wartime. No other approach looks remotely capable of delivering the necessary volume of emissions reductions in the time needed. In that light, we can learn from wartime experiences, positively and negatively. The best of those lessons can then be translated into our contemporary circumstances. As Churchill said, it is not enough that we try our best: we have to do what is necessary. (Green New Deal Group, 2008: 41)

The growing sense of crisis and urgency of what the Green New Deal Group call the 'triple crunch' of the credit crisis, climate change and high oil prices in many respects heralds a return of an older and more established green discourse of 'limits to growth' from the late 1960s and early 1970s, but this time in a new and improved formula. As discussed further below, this return of 'limits to growth' (if green republicanism can be so described) represents a major challenge to the plausibility of the discourse and practices of ecological modernisation delivering sustainable development. Ecological modernisation has gained salience in European countries because it promises to overcome the negative zero-sum logic of limits to growth (environment versus economy), by holding that technological innovation can enable economic growth to continue by being greened and more eco-efficient (Barry, 2003). But these more recent green republican discourses, acting, in typical republican fashions, as a *Realpolitik* Strengths, Weaknesses, Opportunities and Threats (SWOT) analysis (combining scientific knowledge, ethical commitment and political vision in a dynamic and potentially powerful manner), highlight the weakness of the ecological modernisation thesis that technological fixes are sufficient to enable the transition to a less unsustainable development path.

A more local-level instance of green republicanism can be found in the rapidly growing Transition Town (TT) movement in the United Kingdom and Ireland. The TT movement is an interesting innovation within environmentalism, in that while it explicitly begins from the twin challenges 'peak oil' and 'climate change' (two issues which it shares with most other parts of the environmental movement) it is also resolutely practical and pragmatic in orientation. It cannot be described (as yet) as overtly ideologically focused in terms of challenging globalisation, for example, or articulating an oppositional form of green political activism. The Green New Deal Group makes an explicit link from their macro-level analysis to the local level of a TT. Their report states that:

> There is a sense already in British society that there is a 'gathering storm': over one hundred Transition Town organisations have arisen from the grass roots in towns, villages and cities across Britain. These are essentially self-help organisations seeking to assist their communities to reduce their dependence on fossil fuels and increase their economic resilience. They are preparing in practical ways for the 'power down' entailed in the coming energy crunch and the low-carbon living needed to fight climate change. Anyone who has attended a Transition Town meeting can report on the spirit that exists to face up to the triple crunch. (Green New Deal Group, 2008: 34)

There is an Irish connection to the TT movement in that it traces its origins to Kinsale, Co. Cork as the first Transition Town, and there are TTs in both Northern Ireland and the Republic. TTs draw broadly on the peak oil discourse and an ecological – economic preoccupation with energy and material flows and geophysical 'limits to growth'. It is also firmly rooted in the philosophy and politics of permaculture (Quilley and Barry, 2008). In some respects the Transition perspective makes a virtue of necessity (not just that 'small is beautiful' but that 'small is inevitable') as local communities prepare for 'power down', for a post-oil/low-carbon energy future. As well as individual TTs in Ireland, other sources of this political discourse and practice include the Green Party (in and outside government), think-tanks such as Feasta and organisations such as the Cultivate Centre in Dublin and environmental NGOs such as Friends of the Earth. Particularly significant is the alignment of the aims of the TT movement with those of the sustainable food sector – especially those promoting local and organic food, farmers' markets, organic agriculture and the Slow Food movement. The TT movement therefore builds upon a much broader current of agitation and cultural engagement around food production and consumption and related developments such as the rise in farmers' markets around the country.

The positive post-oil future promoted by the TT movement is characterised as 'an abundant future ... energy lean, time rich, less stressful, healthier and happier' (Hopkins, 2008: 94). The TT movement eschews outright political confrontation with any clearly identified opposition and the 'targets' of TT practice seem more abstract – perceived collective vulnerability in the face of impending climate change, declining fossil fuel sources, ecological crisis and socio-economic disorder. But the objectives are not abstract in that the TT movement seeks to inspire and empower local communities to re-skill and educate themselves so that community resilience is enhanced to be able to deal with the 'shocks' of declining oil and climate change. The TT movement is first and foremost about enhancing personal, family and community resilience by changing individual and group social, ecological and economic behaviour and relationships within a particular place. If we take Garavan's perspective concerning the non-confrontational character of significant parts of the localised Irish environmental movement (Garavan, 2007), then the solutions-focused, practically orientated objectives of the TT movement is, *ceteris paribus*, likely to find a very convivial and accommodating political and cultural reception, especially in rural or semi-rural contexts characterised by what Leonard calls 'agrarian nationalism' (Leonard, 2006). Also significant here is that what the TT movement represents would be recognisable to republican thinkers such as Thomas Jefferson, and modern green Jeffersonian republicans such as Wendell Berry (Berry, 2004) in terms of its stress on community self-reliance, the localised focus on resilience and (relative) independence from the state, the connection to an awareness of the land (and, by extension, wider ecological relations) and, most importantly, the strong sense of community solidarity and shared work towards providing the material and energy wherewithal to sustain the community in a low-carbon future.

Conclusion: Planning for power down in Ireland: grassroots mobilisation and political leadership

One of the main aims of this chapter has been to sketch out a 'new' green discourse – that of 'green republicanism' – that both exists already within environmentalism on the island of Ireland, but also has the capacity to develop as a more overarching frame for the politics of transition towards sustainability. It is not claimed that green republicanism will become *a* or *the* dominant green discourse in Ireland, only that there are normative, theoretical and practical political reasons (from a strategic perspective) that one can make for its attractiveness and coherence. It is therefore generative and suggestive and at the moment only fully articulated within elements of the environmental and sustainability movement, and is not shared widely within the population as a whole.

Some of the practical attractions of this green republicanism include, *inter alia*, a stress on planning, an acute awareness of human vulnerability and dependence, a focus on the need for both inspiring and clear leadership as well as active and empowered citizen action and its hard-headed *Realpolitik* character in terms of its concern with community/social resilience and ability to 'cope with' environmental contingencies and problems rather than 'solve' them (Barry, 1999). As a discourse it therefore fits the bill well in terms of preparing the people of this island for the transition to a carbon-constrained economy and society, and for the necessary planning for 'powering down'.

As the Green New Deal Group puts it (in relation to the United Kingdom): 'The first thing that Government will need to do is put in place a national plan for a low-energy future and its provision on the ground. There is no such plan at present: no risk analysis of the peak-oil threat and no contingency plan for what would happen if oil and/or gas supplies collapsed rapidly' (Green New Deal Group, 2008: 38). The only environmental contingency plan the Irish government has is in the event of major disaster at the Sellafield nuclear power plant in Cumbria, and plans for its impacts on the east coast of Ireland and elsewhere. However, evidence that the Green Party is articulating elements of this green republican preparedness, a little-noticed aspect of the Programme for Government agreed between Fianna Fáil and the Green Party, is the following under the Energy section, which states that the Government will 'mitigate the impact of any energy supply disruptions by ensuring that contingency measures are in place' (Green Party, Fianna Fáil, Progressive Democrats, 2007: 17). So there is some – albeit unsubstantiated in terms of detail, scale, resources, etc. – indication of contingency planning in the context of energy supply collapse. However, it is clear that the Green Minister for Energy, Eamon Ryan, is committed to promoting Irish energy security by de-carbonising the electricity supply and promoting renewables as quickly as possible. Minister Ryan speaks of the 'urgency with which we have to prepare our country for peak oil and climate change' (Ryan, 2008a). Ryan has also spoken about the 'common sense' of carbon rationing while acknowledging the political difficulties, and has pointed out how the assumption of cheap oil underpinning modern economics makes the economy more vulnerable (Ryan, 2007). Ryan is the first Western Energy Minister to acknowledge 'peak oil' and has made energy security central to how he is re-designing the Republic's energy system as outlined in the agreed Programme for Government (Green Party, Fianna Fáil, Progressive Democrats, 2007) and in public speeches in 2008 (Ryan, 2008b, 2008c). It is perhaps no coincidence that within the first year of the Green Party being in government the Electricity Supply Board (ESB) has committed to become a carbon neutral company by 2035. This is a major and challenging commitment and demonstrates the reality of the need to make the transition to a low-carbon economy. At the same time we can find in the public speeches and policy initiatives of the Green Party in government a sense of preparing people for the transition. Concepts such as 'food in/ security' are used frequently by Green Party Minister of State for Horticulture, Trevor Sargent, to frame and contextualise his public speeches (Sargent, 2007, 2008), though whether these concepts will permeate into actual policy making around food and agriculture remains to be seen.

In these statements, the agreed Programme for Government and the policy initiatives of the new government – not least the commitment to introduce a carbon tax within the lifetime of the government – one can find indications of sustainability leadership. Equally important are the statements by Green Ministers such as Ryan in pointing up the cultural and consumerist values which have underpinned the unsustainability of the 'Celtic Tiger' economic boom (*Irish Times*, 11 July 2008). Rob Hopkins, founder of the TTs movement, assessed Minister Ryan's contribution to the sixth Association for the Study of Peak Oil (ASPO) conference in September 2007 in the following terms:

I have never been around many politicians who can hold a hall so well, who speak from passion and conviction; I was reminded of Collins and De Valera, perhaps in the same way that they were so pivotal in Ireland's transition from a colonial outpost to a Republic with self-belief, perhaps he will be the politician that will help Ireland through the energy transition with the kind of political leadership such a transition will so desperately require. (Hopkins, 2007)

In the days, months and years ahead, perhaps we will see Ryan and other politicians, not all of them from the Green Party, using either in full or in part a section of FDR's inaugural Presidential Address of 1933 as part of leading and preparing citizens on this island for the inevitable transition to sustainability:

This is pre-eminently the time to speak the truth, the whole truth, frankly and boldly. Nor need we shrink from honestly facing conditions in our country today. This great Nation will endure as it has endured, will revive and will prosper. So, first of all, let me assert my firm belief that the only thing we have to fear is fear itself – nameless, unreasoning, unjustified terror which paralyzes needed efforts to convert retreat into advance. In every dark hour of our national life a leadership of frankness and vigor has met with that understanding and support of the people themselves which is essential to victory. I am convinced that you will again give that support to leadership in these critical days. (Roosevelt, 1933)

The question a green republican perspective asks is: The republic is threatened. Who will stand by the republic? How this is answered will shape the economy, polity and indeed culture of this island in the decades of transition ahead.

Notes

1 One of the many reports documenting Ireland's unsustainability is Earth Summit Ireland's report *Telling it Like it is*, produced in advance of the 2002 Johannesburg World Summit on Sustainable Development (Earth Summit Ireland, 2002).

2 Because of this connection between republicanism and Irish nationalist politics, the 'greening' of republicanism or the 'republicanising' of green politics in Ireland requires green politics to engage both theoretically and practically with the claims of Irish nationalism and political reactions against it. Here, although properly another study, it is clear that the internationalist (and non-violent) principles of green politics cannot rest on the narrow existing nationalist interpretation/s of republicanism in Ireland.

3 A full explication of the 'environmental war economy' and 'Green Keynesianism' would require looking at how they relate to more discourses of 'environmental security' which re-cast environmental and climate change challenges as 'national security' issues. For reasons of space, an examination of 'environmental security' is not attempted here.
4 A sustainability defence of rationing based on the Second World War experience and also how 'demand management' and the reduction (not just 'greening' of material consumption) can have positive benefits in both physical health (for example, in relation to reducing food consumption and a reduction of obesity and heart disease, to name but two) and quality of life/well-being (Green New Deal Group, 2008: 32).
5 An excellent example of the leadership rhetoric which accompanies green republicanism can be found in the speeches of former US Vice-President Al Gore. For example, in a speech in Aspen he explicitly linked the current climate change challenge to the challenge of defeating fascism during the Second World War but also the establishing of the Marshall Plan and United Nations and other international institutions in the aftermath of the war (Gore, 2007).

References

Baker, S. (1990) 'The Evolution of the Irish Ecology Movement', in W. Rudig (ed.), *Green Politics One* (Edinburgh: Edinburgh University Press).
Barry, J. (1999) *Rethinking Green Politics: Nature, Virtue and Progress* (London: Sage).
Barry, J. (2003) 'Ecological Modernisation', in J. Proops and E. Page (eds.), *Environmental Thought* (London: Edward Elgar).
Barry, J. (2005) 'Resistance is Fertile: From Environmental to Sustainability Citizenship', in A. Dobson and D. Bell (eds.), *Environment and Citizenship* (Cambridge, MA: MIT Press).
Barry, J. (2007) *Environment and Social Theory*, 2nd edn. (London: Routledge).
Barry, J. (2008a) 'Environmental Movements in Ireland: North and South', in J. McDonagh, T. Varley and S. Shortall (eds.), *A Living Countryside? The Politics of Sustainable Development in Rural Ireland* (Aldershot: Ashgate).
Barry, J. (2008b) 'Towards a Green Republicanism, Constitutionalism, Political Economy and the Green State', *Journal of Political Economy of the Good Society*, 17(2), 1–12.
Barry, J. and K. Smith (2008) 'Civic Republicanism and Green Politics', in D. Leighton and S. White (eds.), *Building a Citizen Society: The Emerging Politics of Republican Democracy* (London: Lawrence & Wishart).
Barry, J. and M. Wissenburg (eds.) (2001) *Sustaining Liberal Democracy* (Basingstoke: Palgrave).
Baxter, B. (2004) *A Theory of Ecological Justice* (London & New York: Routledge).

Berry, W. (2004) *Citizenship Papers: Essays* (Berkeley, CA: Shoemaker & Hoard).

Blühdorn, I. and I. Welsh (2007) 'Eco-Politics beyond the Paradigm of Sustainability: A Conceptual Framework and Research Agenda', *Environmental Politics*, 16(2), 185–205.

Brown, L. (2008), *Plan B 3.0: Mobilizing to Save Civilization* (New York: W.W. Norton).

Cutter, S. (2006) *Hazards, Vulnerability and Environmental Justice* (London: Earthscan).

Diamond, J. (2005) *Collapse: How Societies Choose to Fail or Succeed* (New York: Penguin).

Dimas, S. (2007) 'Climate Change: Why a Global Response Needs European Leadership', Speech at the Launch Event of the European Commission and the All Party Parliamentary Group on Climate Change Co-operation, London, 11 January 2007, available at: http://europa.eu/rapid/pressReleasesAction. do?reference=SPEECH/07/8&format=HTML&aged=0&language=EN&gui Language=en (accessed 12 July 2008).

Dobson, A. (2003) *Citizenship and the Environment* (Oxford: Oxford University Press).

Dobson, A. (2007) 'A Politics of Global Warming: The Social-Science Resource', *Open Democracy*, available at: www.opendemocracy.net/globalisation-climate_change_debate/politics_4486.jsp (accessed 10 December 2007).

Dobson, A. and D. Bell (eds.) (2005) *Environment and Citizenship* (Cambridge, MA: MIT Press).

Dryzek, J. (1987), *Rational Ecology: Environment and Political Economy* (Oxford: Blackwell).

Earth Summit Ireland (2002) *Telling it Like it is: 10 years of Unsustainable Development in Ireland* (Dublin: Ecoprint).

Garavan, M. (2007) 'Resisting the Costs of "Development": Local Environmental Activism in Ireland', *Environmental Politics*, 17(5), 844–63.

George, S. (2007) *Of Capitalism, Crisis, Conversion & Collapse: The Keynesian Alternative*, available at: www.ifg.org/programs/Energy/triple_crisis_av/ panel7/5susan-v.htm (accessed 10 July 2008).

Gore, A. (2007) *Global Warming*, available at: http://minnesota.publicradio. org/display/web/2007/08/09/midday2/ (accessed 11 July 2008).

Gray, J. (1993) *Beyond the New Right* (London: Routledge).

Green New Deal Group (2008) *A Green New Deal: Joined-Up Policies to Solve the Triple Crunch of the Credit Crisis, Climate Change and High Oil Prices* (London: new economics foundation).

Green Party, Fianna Fáil, Progressive Democrats (2007) *Agreed Programme for Government 2007–12*, available at: www.greenparty.ie/government/agreed_ programme_for_government/agreed_programme_for_government (accessed 10 May 2008).

Hopkins, R. (2007) *ASPO 6: In Praise of Eamon Ryan*, available at: http://transitionculture.org/2007/09/26/aspo-6-in-praise-of-5-eamon-ryan/ (accessed 29 July 2008).

Hopkins, R. (2008) *The Transition Handbook: From Oil Dependency to Local Resilience* (Totnes: Green Books).

Irish Times (11 July 2008) *We Revelled in it ... and no one Shouted Stop*, available at: www.irishtimes.com/newspaper/ireland/2008/0711/1215725793485. html (accessed 15 July 2008).

Kelly, M. P. Faughnan and H. Tovey (2003) 'Cultural Sources of Support upon which Environmental Attitudes Draw', 2nd *Report of National Survey Data*, available at: www.ucd.ie/environ/reports/envirattitudessecondrept. pdf#search='environmental%20attitudes%20in%20Ireland (accessed 6 April 2006).

Kovel, J. (2002) *The Enemy of Nature* (London: Zed Books).

Leonard, L. (2006) *Green Nation: The Irish Environmental Movement from Carnsore Point to the Rossport Five* (Drogheda: Greenhouse Press).

Lomborg, B. (2001) *The Skeptical Environmentalist: Measuring the Real State of the World* (Cambridge: Cambridge University Press).

Macintyre, A. (1999) *Dependent Rational Animals: Why Human Beings Need the Virtues* (London: Duckworth).

Maniates, M. (2002) 'Individualisation: Plant a Tree, Buy a Bike, Save the World?', in T. Princen, M. Maniates and K. Conca (eds.), *Confronting Consumption* (Cambridge, MA: MIT Press).

McWilliams, D. (2005) *The Pope's Children: Ireland's New Elite* (Dublin: Gill & Macmillan).

Naess, A. (1973) 'The Shallow and the Deep, Long-Range Ecology Movement: A Summary', *Inquiry*, 16, 95–100.

Norton, B. (1991) *Toward Unity Among Environmentalists* (Oxford: Oxford University Press).

O'Neill, J. (1993) *Ecology, Policy and Politics* (London: Routledge).

Pettit, P. (1997) *Republicanism: A Theory of Freedom and Government* (Oxford: Oxford University Press).

Quilley, S. and J. Barry (2008) 'Transition Towns: "Survival", "Resilience" and the Elusive Paradigm Shift in Sustainable Living', *ecopolitics online*, 1(2), available at: www.ecopoliticsonline.com (accessed 2 July 2008).

Roosevelt, F. D. (1933) 'The Only Thing We Have to Fear Is Fear Itself': *FDR's First Inaugural Address*, available at: http://historymatters.gmu.edu/d/5057/ (accessed 26 July 2008).

Rousseau, J.-J. (1984) *A Discourse on Inequality* (London: Penguin).

Ryan, E. (2007) *Interview with Eamon Ryan*, available at: www.davidstrahan. com/audio/lastoilshock.com-eamon-ryan-18.9.07.mp3 (accessed 26 July 2008).

Ryan, E. (2008a) *Address to Green Party Convention*, April 2008, available at: www.greenparty.ie (accessed 10 July 2008).

Ryan, E. (2008b) *Minister Ryan addresses IBEC Carbon Footprint Conference*, 28 May 2008, available at: www.dcmnr.gov.ie/Corporate+Units/Virtual+ Press+Room/Speeches/Minister+Ryan+addresses+IBEC+Carbon+Footprint+ Conference+28th+May+2008.htm (accessed 26 July 08).

Ryan, E. (2008c) *Speech by Minister Eamon Ryan at the Energy Ireland Conference*, available at: www.dcmnr.gov.ie/Corporate+Units/Virtual+Press+Room/Speeches/Speech+by+Minister+Eamon+Ryan+at+the+Energy+Ireland+Conference.htm (accessed 26 July 2008).

Salleh, A. (1997) *Ecofeminism as Politics: Nature, Marx and the Postmodern* (London: Zed Books).

Sargent, T. (2007) *Address by Mr. Trevor Sargent TD, Minister for State at the Department Agriculture, Fisheries and Foods, Ireland on the Occasion of the 34th Session of the FAO conference*, Rome, 17–24 November 2007, available at: www.agriculture.gov.ie/index.jsp?file=ministerspeeches/sargent/2007/FAOconf_241107.xml (accessed 1 July 2008).

Sargent, T. (2008) *Quarter of a Million Children Challenged to Potato Growing Contest*, available at: www.greenparty.ie/en/news/latest_news/quarter_of_a_million_children_challenged_to_potato_growing_contest (accessed 1 July 2008).

Simms, A. (2001) *An Environmental War Economy: The Lessons of Ecological Debt and Global Warming* (London: new economics foundation).

Singer, P. (1990) *Animal Liberation*, 2nd edn. (London: Jonathan Cape).

Tovey, H. (1993) 'Environmentalism in Ireland: Two Versions of Development and Modernity', *International Sociology*, 8, 413–30.

3

Communications practices and Irish environmental politics: oral hearings, tribunals, planning and sustainable development

Kieran Keohane

Introduction

Recent years have seen a transformation in Irish environmental politics. Twenty, even ten years ago, environmental politics typically centred on industrial pollution associated with particular factories and their health and environmental impacts. Now the compass is much broader: sustained attention is now being accorded to both urban sprawl and ribbon development and damage to countryside, habitat and heritage; concerns for health have extended from the identification of 'cancer clusters' to domestic sewage groundwater contamination in Galway, and there is greater edge to more diffuse problems of quality of life and well-being such as *anomie* and its association with suicide and substance abuse in new dormitory developments. The targets of environmental protests have also shifted – from multinational corporations (MNCs) (including, most recently, Shell) to 'home-grown' polluters – Irish incinerator operators, for example. In the 1980s and 1990s Irish farmers often featured as the victims of industrial pollution. Now, in the wake of BSE and other problems associated with modern agribusiness, farmers are as often the culprits in environmental problems: fertiliser run-off killing rivers and lakes by increasing biochemical oxygen demand; faecal contamination of drinking water by animal slurry; agrichem-dependent crop production and animal husbandry contaminating the food chain; and antibiotics compromising the human immune system. The local Irish actor has hence come to centre stage in environmental protests. This may take the form of the modern Irish farmer; the builder, operating a quarry or constructing holiday bungalows; the property magnate developing a suburban shopping complex; or indeed the Irish state itself when, at the very cusp of peak oil, it is driving ahead with motorway construction while intercity and suburban mass public transit systems are left underdeveloped.

Accompanying the expanded compass of issues, the proliferation of sites and frontiers of contestation, protest and social antagonism, environmental politics in Ireland has seen a noteworthy institutional development in the form of communicative and deliberative institutions, exemplified by the EPA's Oral Hearings, the Tribunals of Inquiry into political corruption, and the reformation of planning as the profession that very often finds itself standing at the centre or straddling environmental disputes.[1] As sites of formally constituted, concentrated, expansive and protracted deliberation, EPA Oral Hearings and Tribunals of Inquiry have become theatres of Irish environmental politics. EPA Oral Hearings and planning Tribunals are communicative encounters where, in a media-permeated public forum, private developers, public servants, lawyers and administrators, politicians and planners, meet communities and individuals, lobbyists and ecological citizens in power plays and language games that seek to define the situation, frame issues, clarify the truth and to mediate and negotiate the meaning of 'progress', to plan for the future and to control the shape of 'development'.

Do these new communicative institutions – Hearings and Tribunals, professional planning – represent crucibles where environmental disputes are concentrated, distilling a new consensus and resolving conflict, representing a reflexive, post-political 'third way', as social theorists such as Ulrich Beck (1992, 1994, 1998b) and Anthony Giddens (1994, 1998) would argue? Or are these new institutions theatres of conflict, where the terms of polarised environmental disputes are clarified and illuminated, where the identities of antagonists become more sharply defined and where ecological politics is further intensified and expanded, as political theorists such as Chantal Mouffe and Ernesto Laclau (Laclau and Mouffe 1985; Mouffe 2005) would contend? The analysis presented here holds that the apparent opposition between reflexive modernisation and radical democratic politics is a false dichotomy. Hearings, Tribunals, and changes in the planning profession, and the moments of consensus achieved through them and represented by them, are not only the expressions of the institutional development of modernity as shaped by the reflexive unfolding of the internal logic of communicative action. These and similar developments also represent achievements in a hegemonic struggle for interlocutory terrain; not simply granted through consensus to further consensus, but ceded in political conflict and furthering antagonism. In other words, instances approximating ideal speech situations not only represent the achievement of consensus through force of the better argument, but equally and as such they are agonal moments of conflict in ongoing hegemonic language games (Keohane, 1993). As a corollary and extension of this argument, universal pragmatics as clarified and explicated by Habermas' theory of communicative action is a social logic that can help us 'to distinguish within a given regime of truth between those who respect the strategy of argumentation and those who simply want to impose their power' (Mouffe, 1998: 38).

Environmental (and other) politics, in Ireland as elsewhere, is characterised by the simultaneous development of normative consensus on the one hand and at the same time by the intensification and proliferation of social conflict and political antagonism. The 'political' entails both consensus formation, through both the progression of reasoned argument and the struggle for hegemony, as well as the reproduction of oppositional political identities and the perpetuation and intensification of dissent. An institutionalised and emergent normative consensus are relatively stable hegemonies that are constantly challenged, reasserted and reconfigured, and Oral Hearings, Tribunals and the practice of the planning profession, rather than being post-political have in fact become the very loci of contemporary eco-political action.

In order to see the multiple and ambivalent roles that the new institutions play in Irish environmental politics after the communicative turn, this chapter will critically analyse and normatively evaluate these communications theatres of ecological politics. First, it will outline and apply a critical theory and methodology of communicative action to the EPA Oral Hearings, revealing their importance in contemporary Irish environmental politics, but also their serious limitations. It will then relocate the institution of the Oral Hearing in the broader context of the communicative turn and the reflexive modernisation of Irish political culture, of which the Planning Tribunals are the exemplary institution. It will show the ambivalence of the Tribunals, as an amplification of politics but also risking political neutralisation by engendering apathy and boredom, and will finally look at the politicisation of the planning profession, and the increasing importance of its role in Irish environmental politics.

Theoretical and methodological framework

In a series of publications Beck (1992, 1995a, 1998a, 1998b) argues that the dynamics of modernisation turn back upon themselves as unintended consequences of progress and development and become potentially self-destructive. The engines of modern progress – industrial expansion allied to technical innovation and the mastery of nature by science, institutionally integrated by a bureaucratically structured managerial apparatus – generate risks that transcend all geographical and temporal boundaries. The production, containment and disposal of nuclear and toxic chemical wastes, for example, poses risks to a global, not just a local environment, and remain hazardous for many generations. The risks associated with these and similar processes and products, risks generated by the very 'successes' of modern progress, are incalculable. Because of the scale and incalculability of these risks they become generalised and dispersed throughout the social body – global warming and climate change, for example, increasingly impact upon all political–economic and socio-cultural discourses.

Modernity has become 'self-endangering, and self-conscious of its self-endangerment' (Beck, 1997: 15) and thus, 'risk society is by tendency also a self-critical society' (Beck, 1995: 11). Risk society is a 'radicalized modernity ... concerned with its unintended consequences, risks and foundations' (Beck, 1998a: 20). In the risk society, Beck says, 'experts are undercut and deposed by other experts. Politicians encounter the resistance of citizens' groups, and industrial management encounters morally and politically motivated organised consumer boycotts ... Ultimately, even polluter sectors ... must count upon resistance from affected sectors. These ... can be called into question ... monitored and perhaps even corrected' (Beck, 1995: 11).

EPA Oral Hearings provide what appears to be a good example of what Beck is describing as an instance of reflexivity in the risk society. The various concerned parties – the polluters, concerned citizens and the state agency responsible for environmental protection – sit down together and try to come to terms with the risks posed by a development – whether an incinerator, a pipeline, a motorway, or a shopping centre. In such discussions, Beck hypothesises, 'no side gets its way, neither the opponents of power, nor power itself' (Beck, Giddens and Lash, 1994: 23). Instead, Beck argues, what emerge are new configurations, compromises and a working consensus on monitoring and controls, and new principles of sustainable development. In the course of evaluating the EPA Oral Hearing, Beck's hypothesis of the emergence of a self-critical, self-correcting, consensus-building, process of reflexive modernisation in Irish risk society will be tested.

Habermas (1972, 1987, 1990) argues that the ability to direct, control and otherwise shape communication, knowledge and what comes to constitute 'truth' is one of the major axes through which power is expressed. Forester (1987, 1989) derives from Habermas a method for identifying communications that are systematically distorted by power. Forester argues that when people engage in communication oriented to reaching agreement – as they might in a planning dispute, or in an Oral

Hearing, for example, they work towards that agreement by evaluating what they say to one another. Every 'speech act', or instance of communication, raises four claims that can be empirically tested and evaluated. These are:

(a) comprehensibility, or clarity. That is, can everyone understand what is being said, or is the communication made in a way that is difficult for some parties to understand? For example, is the discussion couched in a legalistic jargon, or in scientific and technical terms to which only those with specialised training have access?

(b) Sincerity. That is, are parties honestly representing themselves and their interests, disclosing fully their intentions and their knowledge, or are they professing false concern, obfuscating issues and withholding information, attempting to mislead, or lying?

(c) Legitimacy, or appropriateness. That is, is what is said relevant to the subject of discussion: is this something that ought to be considered, or is it a distraction? Or are there issues, stories and information relevant to the discussion that are not being heard; contexts and histories that ought to be considered but are not?

(d) Truth, factual veracity. Is what is being said factually correct; is there convincing evidence to support claims and statements, or is what is said conjecture, speculation, uninformed opinion, or simply error?

On the basis of these empirically testable claims an 'ideal speech situation' can be postulated: a situation of communication in which all four of these criteria are fulfilled. In an ideal speech situation all the parties learn from one another, and this cognitive development becomes normatively institutionalised as a new collective understanding, an agreement and consensus binding on all parties. The standard of an ideal speech situation serves as a methodology with which actual instances of communication can be evaluated in terms of how closely they live up to, or fail to live up to the ideal model.

Critical theory of communications applied to an empirical analysis of EPA oral hearings

This section explores how EPA Oral Hearings measure up to the standard of an ideal speech situation by applying Habermas' theory and Forester's method to empirical case studies. The empirical data presented here is derived from participant observation and interviews conducted at three EPA Oral Hearings held between the mid-1990s and mid-2000s. All three cases concerned the development of incinerators. One was a proposed incinerator as a further development at a long-established pharmaceuticals plant in the mid-west. The other two Hearings concerned the same proposed development, a large multi-user facility in the southern region, the second Hearing concerning a revised version of an earlier application.

Clarity

Taking criterion (a), of clarity, or 'understandability', an imbalance of power is immediately apparent. The Oral Hearing is a formal and quasi-legalistic institution which favours company managers and their lawyers who are used to this form of interaction, who are at home in formal meetings, who are familiar with rules of procedure, who use a special-ised jargon every working day. Objectors – local residents, mothers, members of the community and other participants who may be unfa-miliar with the rules of such language games – may find it intimidating and are at a distinct disadvantage.

The disadvantage is even more marked when one considers that the discourse of Oral Hearings is predominantly scientific and technical. Directors and management scientists of a multinational corporation (MNC), an incinerator operator, consulting engineers acting for a major developer and the personnel of the EPA, are, for the most part, immersed in the professional culture of science and have command of a specialised language. Objectors are typically people who are not professional sci-entists and, however well informed they are, can be made to appear ignorant, and their side of the story can be made to seem invalid by the weight of expert discourse to which some parties at the public hearing have ready access.

Objectors often participate in Hearings by bringing in scientists and medical experts who sometimes provide their services out of a sense of civic responsibility, at their own expense as objectors typically have scarce resources to pay for independent expertise. The EPA and private corporations, by contrast, have their experts 'in house'. They are paid to represent their employers at Hearings. And because they have enor-mous resources to draw on, state bodies and corporations can pay for the best legal counsel and expert consultants. Objectors and their experts have to take time off from their jobs. Nobody pays them or picks up their expenses.

On the other hand the understandability of the Hearing is not con-trolled entirely by the EPA, managers and scientists. Objectors can also engage in discursive strategies and rhetorical tactics that are relatively inaccessible and incomprehensible. Objectors can refuse to engage in the hegemonic technical discourse, and insist instead that this is a moral discourse. Managers and scientists' assurances of the minimisation of risk by the 'best available technology not entailing excessive cost' are countered by mothers who demand recognition of the rights to a clean environment for their children. Rural dwellers demand recognition of the right to traditional livelihoods; conservationists argue about cultural and natural heritage endangered by development. Arguments for the profitability of the factory, the jobs and economic dividends to the local economy, are countered by arguments based on post-materialistic values: that 'development', 'progress' and 'quality of life' should be understood in terms that are not simply economic and materialistic.

For example, at one point during one of the Hearings studied, a community spokesperson was being cross-examined by legal counsel for the developer. The spokesperson broke the counsel's line of questioning, saying, 'But look, Gerry. I don't know the first thing about b.o.d.s and kgs. That's not what I'm talking about at all.' The Senior Counsel momentarily had the wind taken out of his sails. He was conducting himself from within the adversarial conventions of the courtroom. By calling him by the familiar 'Gerry', the community representative was attempting to reclaim the hearing as a conversation among (supposedly) equal parties oriented towards achieving consensus. The tactic revealed the enmity to consensus-building in this formal, aggressive adversarial form of interlocution. The contrast achieved by this rhetorical tactic revealed that the developer was not oriented toward reaching consensus, but was simply concerned with beating the opposition. By admitting that she knew nothing whatsoever of the technicalities of an Environmental Impact Assessment (EIA) she stymied the barrister's line of attack on her and the defence of his client; and by insisting that she was talking about something else altogether, something higher and unquantifiable, she attempted to make the developer appear ignorant, callous and inhumane.

But such counter-hegemonic articulatory practices that seek to reshape the communications process of the Hearing, to shift the terms of the discourse onto grounds on which managers and scientists are less certain, are momentary rather than systematic.

Sincerity

The private interests of a corporation and its shareholders are the maximisation of profits and the minimisation of costs by the strategic planning and organisation of the corporation as a global concern. There is no uncertainty or ambivalence about these risks. Incalculability, uncertainty and ambivalence are precisely what corporate strategists seek to eliminate, reduce, and manage. It is precisely because it *can* be calculated that, as well as paying corporate tax at 12 per cent compared with 28 per cent, environmental controls and monitoring will be less rigorous and community opposition less organised in Ireland than, say, in Germany, that a bulk pharmaceuticals plant is located in Cork harbour and not in Cologne.

Beck argues that in the emerging risk society everybody is equally at risk. This is true of the chronic risks of industrial society when considered abstractly and globally. But it is much less the case when considering the acute, immediate and specific risks of particular developments. Toxic fallout from the incinerator stack of a bulk chemicals manufacturing plant affects people living in the vicinity in ways that it doesn't affect people living in the vicinity of a shipping and distribution facility, or the corporate offices. For Beck's hypothesis of the equalisation of risk and responsibility to become valid would require the development of discursive practices that articulate the links between the global and the local, the chronic and the acute, and the generalised and the particular. At present such hegemonic articulatory practices are still at the margins of political life – or, insofar as they are being effectively raised as 'inconvenient truths', they remain stubbornly remote from mass public consciousness and mainstream politics. What must be borne in mind in the meantime is that a corporation's claim to share a public concern about the environment, globally or locally, should be treated sceptically.[2]

A private interest's claim to be a good corporate citizen notwithstanding, it cannot but operate according to laws of the marketplace. As Weber says, a business interest 'is identical with the pursuit of profit, and forever renewed profit by means of continuous, rational, capitalistic enterprise. Enterprise, and indeed the entrepreneur who does not take advantage of all possible opportunities for profit cannot succeed or prosper' (Weber, 1976: 17). The basic ethic according to which all business must operate is that of the unprincipled principle of the marketplace, namely an 'absolute and conscious ruthlessness in acquisition' and the conduct of business 'without regard for persons' (ibid.: 58).

Within the terms of Weber's formulation of the principles that underpin modern business, a private interest is not interested in future generations, whether in California or in Cork. It is concerned with the profit margin for the fiscal year, or the fiscal year in five, or ten, or possibly twenty-five years' time. But it is not concerned with the world our children and our children's children will inherit. The EPA, by contrast, *ought* to be concerned with this. As a state body this is precisely the responsibility entrusted to it by Irish citizens. The EPA is answerable to the Irish public, and this is exactly what a public Oral Hearing is supposed to accomplish. Given the state of underdevelopment of the political institutions of a global public, one might hope to see the institutionalisation of reflexive modernisation making its appearance first in the already existing agencies of government, such as the EPA.

In the cases studied, however, members of the public doubted the EPA's sincerity. Participants at one Hearing were alarmed to discover that there was to be no transcript of the proceedings, nor even minutes recorded, despite the otherwise formal and legalistic format. Instead, the Chair undertook to summarise the proceedings. Given the number of witnesses, the complexity of the arguments and the duration of the Hearing, they doubted the adequacy of this method and were sceptical of the quality of what recommendations could result. These doubts were voiced to the EPA Chair at the Hearing, and in the national media covering the hearing, but to no avail. Several participants interviewed said that the inadequacy of this aspect of the Hearing was so blatant as to be an insult to the intelligence of the participants. They took it to be an indication of gratuitous insincerity on the EPA's part. They felt that the EPA was not interested in serving their interests; that it was paying lip service to the idea of a Hearing. Far from this being an instantiation of self-critical reflexivity and consensus-building, the Hearing was a cynical exercise in public deception, a sham designed to give the *appearance* of a sincere discussion.

The issue at stake with regard to the recording of the evidence at the Hearing is not so much its inadequacy, but rather the meanings that the participants attributed to this. The legitimation of the Hearing, and of the authority of the EPA as convener and arbiter, was grounded in the trust placed by the participants in the EPA as a sincere actor. If the EPA was not perceived to be sincere, then other participants could not trust it, and the legitimacy of its authority was jeopardised. Thus, the point is not whether or not the EPA was *in fact* a sincere interlocutor in the communications at the hearing, but rather that doubt as to its sincerity was raised and that this doubt was not removed. The result was that the EPA was perceived as being insincere and untrustworthy, and thereby the legitimacy of the Hearing and moral authority of EPA were fatally undermined.

The same issue of the sincerity (criterion (b)) of the key actor, the EPA, arose at another Hearing, some years later, where participants had an entirely opposite but equally problematic experience. This time everything was recorded – meticulously, systematically and tediously. A comprehensive report would be issued, but many months afterwards. The Hearing was conducted in so rigorously proceduralist a manner as to drag every session on for hours and so extend the proceedings for several weeks. Respondents interpreted this as a 'deliberate tactic', a 'war of attrition' on the part of the organisers, as it greatly increased the demands on the time and the interest of the public in attending and participating. And, of course, attending the protracted Hearing became very costly to members of the public, whereas corporate personnel and their legal teams were being paid to be there. After several days the number of the public attending dwindled as it interfered with their working lives and other commitments. Even journalists from national and local media who had been assigned to cover the Hearing left after a few days. One journalist commented afterwards that the Hearing 'seemed to be designed to kill anything that might be newsworthy'.

Legitimacy

An evaluation of the Hearings in terms of criterion (c) of ideal speech, legitimacy, or the 'relevance' of the communications compounds the problem of insincerity. Here the issue is not so much what is communicated to the Hearing, but what is *not* communicated – or, more precisely, in what is prohibited from being communicated. For example, in one case, the format of the Hearing, as determined by the EPA Chair, was that the objectors would present their case first. Next, the developer could cross-examine and offer a counter-argument. The Chair prohibited any cross-examination, giving the developers the last word. Under strenuous protest against what amounted to a prohibition on argument, two days into a three-day Hearing the Chair reversed his ruling, but by then the opportunity for cross-examination had largely been lost. In a later Hearing objectors wanted to discuss the poor record of companies that a proposed incinerator would serve, to present information on specific instances of pollution and breaches of previous and existing emission limits. This information is obviously relevant to the discussion, but the Chair ruled it could not be heard.

The EPA presents itself as an office neither of the Department of the Environment nor of the Department of Industry and Energy, but operates at arm's length from the political system, and can thus arbitrate between the diverse agendas of state Departments, agencies such as the Industrial Development Authority (IDA), and Local Authorities. None of these interests was represented at the first Hearing studied. The EPA did not invite them, and when asked why they were not represented the

Chair stated that the interests they represented were irrelevant to the terms of the Hearing. Thus, state policy on the environment, and on industrial development, could not be discussed, nor could the policies and practices of the several state economic and industrial development agencies. All of these are relevant to a meaningful discussion of industry and its associated risks, but they were systematically excluded from the communications process.

In a subsequent Oral Hearing, by complete contrast, representatives from all of these state agencies, and more, were fully represented. In this instance they were each given a substantial amount of time to present their respective briefs to the public, and the public had the opportunity to engage them in dialogue. But to many observers this seemed to be an unnecessarily exhaustive – and exhausting – exercise. Their presentations were seen as 'bland' and 'innocuous,' 'spin' by 'the PR men'. 'It's very hard to object to what these people are saying, because in fact they're saying nothing really!' one respondent observed. 'I suppose they think that they can bore us into going home', said another.

Rather than indicating institutional reflexivity in the policy making arena, on the contrary, the structural distance of the EPA from the key state Departments, and from economic and industrial development policy making bodies, serves precisely to *prevent* any reflexive institutional development. The evidence in the Irish case suggests that rather than exemplifying Beck's and Giddens' post-political 'third way', the role of the EPA more closely resembles what Offe (1984) identifies as a 'filter mechanism' designed to disburden the state of claims and thus ease its chronic legitimation problems. Offe argues that to ease the legitimation deficit and claims overload the state establishes agencies that operate at some distance from central state apparatuses. The EPA is deployed to draw fire and take the flak in the political conflict between environmentalists, industry and the public. The EPA suffers a legitimation crisis while the Departments of the Environment and of Industry and Energy, and their respective ministers, are insulated from controversy.

Truth

The problems of clarity, sincerity and legitimacy of communications in the EPA Hearings become even more pronounced when evaluated in terms of criterion (d) of ideal speech, namely truth: the factual veracity of communications. Given that the hegemonic discourse of Hearings is scientific and technical, argument hinges crucially around matters of 'fact', scientifically proven or refuted. In this context it is relatively easy for developers to discredit and devalue submissions made by objectors; to question the qualifications of presenters; to undermine their arguments by arguing that as non-experts they could 'merely' voice an 'opinion', whereas they, the experts, commanded the 'facts'.

But science is not nearly as much in control of a world of 'objective facts' as people commonly think. This is especially so in fields where many branches of science overlap. When considering the effects which a chemical compound, or combination of compounds, may have on a complex ecosystem, the number of species, flora and fauna that may be affected, the range of possible effects, the levels at which these effects take place – molecular/genetic/chromosomal/endocrinal/neurological/organic/systemic – the time and space over which effects becomes observable, and the interdependence of the species of an ecosystem upon one another and upon other factors, means that scientists, whether industrial chemists, biochemists, toxicologists, epidemiologists, or from any other disciplinary specialty or field of expertise, readily acknowledge that their knowledge is always partial and incomplete.[3] In EPA Hearings, objectors, in good faith, ask that expert scientists speak in support of their case. But all that is necessary to undermine expert witness is for the objectors to disclose the foundations of uncertainty and partial knowledge upon which the expert scientists' case necessarily and unavoidably rests. There is always 'a factor that hasn't been considered', 'a study published in an equally reputable journal which shows otherwise', and the speaker for the objectors, as a good scientist, will readily admit, that, yes, in fact, some uncertainty exists.

One of the conditions of the risk society, according to Beck, is that scientism is losing its hold over the collective conscience. We are becoming increasingly sceptical of scientific certitudes and assurances, and it is common knowledge that expert opinion is highly relativised and can be countered by a contrary expert opinion. But despite what some analysts see as a generalised crisis in the modern scientific worldview, science is still hegemonic at EPA Hearings. In the cases studied, the relativism of scientific evidence and its limited role in moral practical discourse was never raised, and where it might have been raised it was systematically contained. Giving the developers the structural position in the Hearing of making the counter-argument to the objectors ensured that they were always in the position of being able to introduce doubt and uncertainty concerning the testimony of the objector's expert witnesses. Not being able to cross-examine counter-argument ensured that the objectors were seldom able to demonstrate the partiality of developers' claims to control over the facts, and to pursue the argument on the basis of the balance of probability.

On the penultimate day of the first Hearing, when the Chair had relented to the objectors and permitted cross-examination, objectors availed themselves of the opportunity to reveal the partiality of expertise with devastating effect. The developer had introduced on their behalf the testimony of an expert witness, the world's foremost authority on the toxicology of dioxins in milk. Under cross-examination by the objectors, the witness readily acknowledged that his expertise was as an organic chemist, not as a toxicologist, and thus his opinion was significantly qualified. In a similar instance, cross-examination revealed that a bird count, cited as authoritative in an Environmental Impact Survey, had in fact been conducted on a one-off basis by an amateur bird watcher with no qualifications whatsoever in ornithology. But, again, it must be stressed that these were isolated moments, moments that might be read as harbingers of a relativisation of scientific authority, but as yet they were merely chinks in the armour of hegemonic technocratic discourse.

Contrary to Beck's thesis of reflexivity pointing towards a 'third way', a consensus 'beyond left and right', a critical analysis of the EPA Oral Hearings reveals them to be sharply polarised between oppositional parties. We should expect no more from corporations then that they utilise whatever powers are at their disposal to ruthlessly pursue their private interests. This is what corporations do to succeed in the marketplace. But we are entitled to expect more of public servants in state bodies. The role of the EPA is precisely to protect the public from the harmful consequences of the unfettered pursuit of private interests, and to mediate between such interests and collective public interests in the common good. Instead, the evidence presented above from EPA Hearings to date suggests that the EPA acts as the choreographer in a power play enacted to deceive those whom it is supposed to serve, and to corrupt one of the institutions of democracy.

From Oral Hearings to the Planning Tribunals

While the emergence and evolution of the EPA and communicative forums like the Oral Hearing, on the one hand, represents an important development of environmental politics, it is also one that is deeply problematic. Rationalisation of discourse and deliberative practices that might achieve consensus and normatively binding agreement are, unfortunately, appropriated and turned against this very end. Hearings

assume the appearance of an ideal speech situation, but this is used
to mask continuing systematically distorted communications. Parties
cannot object to this because in terms of procedure the process seems
to be 'reasonable' and in accordance with the standards environmentalists have themselves asked for. This leads to a deepening cynicism
among all parties to the discourse, not only among those whom many
already suspect of deliberate cynicism, but also among those highly
principled and committed idealistic actors, who now find themselves
'going through the motions too' as one such person informed me. 'Its
just a game to these people', he said. 'We have to play too. If we com-
plain about the process they say, well, you asked for this process, but
if we don't show up its like we give them a walkover.' 'But its not over
yet' the same individual went on to say. 'The Tribunals have made these
Hearings redundant anyway.'

The Tribunals emerged initially when, in July 1995, Michael Smith,
a former chairman of heritage group *An Taisce* and barrister Colm Mac
Eochaidh, co-sponsored a £10,000 reward for information leading to
convictions for planning corruption. As allegations of serious corruption
involving public servants, politicians and major developers began to
filter into the public sphere through the national media, the government
was forced to establish investigative Tribunals, presided over by senior
members of the judiciary. Though arguably lacking an adequate statutory basis, limiting criminal prosecution and punishment (Corcoran and
White, 2000) the Tribunals none the less have very considerable powers,
and compared with EPA Hearings their potential to reform the institutions and practices of Irish political culture is of a quantum degree.
Whereas EPA Hearings when subjected to critical analysis turn out to
be a pseudo-legal charade of an ideal speech situation, Tribunals are
much closer to the model. The Tribunals are conducted within standard
modern legal–rational conventions, with rules of evidence, procedures
of examination and cross-examination of witness' sworn testimony by
senior counsel, and so on. Tribunals have painstakingly subjected the
speech acts and communications of those called to give evidence in
terms of criteria of clarity, sincerity, legitimacy and veracity. Furthermore, with a wide and unconstrained brief, open to interested members
of the public to approach them with any information relevant to the
terms of inquiry, with proceedings reported, analysed and interpreted
by serious journalists and public intellectuals in the newspapers
and other mass media, the Tribunals have been moving steadily and
inexorably towards revealing corruption among developers and their
lobbyists, senior local authority officials and elected representatives,
up to and including ministers and former and sitting *Taoisigh* (prime

ministers). While only a small number of individuals have been criminally prosecuted for corruption, and some others for obstructing the work of the Tribunals by obfuscation and perjury, others, very senior politicians, have clearly been implicated in corrupt financial/ political transactions, re-zoning land against good planning in favour of developers' private interests. One former *Taoiseach* had his corruption thoroughly exposed by the Tribunals and ended his career in utter disgrace; a second, his protégée, was forced to resign in light of ongoing investigations and with further revelations pending. On the other hand, the Tribunals may not prove to be as effective as one might hope in reforming Irish political culture. A limitation, similar to that of the EPA Hearings, is that while the intention is to make progress by rational discourse approximating an ideal speech act, Tribunals have negative unintended consequences of juridification and exhausting proceduralism and risk engendering 'Tribunal fatigue'; and as the exposure of more and more corruption to a degree where it may seem to be 'typical', even 'normal practice' in the relationship between public representatives and private developers, Tribunals ironically may contribute to a cynical debasing of politics and local government. For example, the *Taoiseach* who was most recently forced to resign, far from being a pariah, remains one of the most popular and respected public figures in the country.[4]

The ongoing work of the Tribunals has been played out against a backdrop of accelerated transformation under conditions of globalisation, wherein dramatic economic growth has generated development on a scale previously unimagined in Ireland, and the state, through the local authority, has experienced a substantial expansion in its planning responsibilities, ranging from major infrastructural developments to a prolonged surge in the growth and renovation of the private housing stock. As well as providing fertile ground for speculation and corruption, as developers lobby politicians to have their lands zoned for development and to influence planning decisions, accelerated economic growth from the mid-1990s through to 2007–8 has had major consequences for the quality of life and well-being. Ireland's cities have seen unprecedented expansion, and dispersed settlement and commuter villages transforming the rural landscape. The population is increasing rapidly, comprising both returning emigrants and new immigrants. These structural and demographic changes increase demand for services and infrastructure, in transportation, education, housing and health care, services that had been previously underdeveloped and poorly resourced. These changes also put pressures on life-world resources to accommodate, absorb and assimilate cultural differences, to make normative adjustments and become more multicultural and cosmopolitan, while maintaining collective identity coherence and integrity.

At the centre of the constellation of economic growth, environmental impact, social justice, collective well-being and quality of life, more general and transcendent questions of values and ideas – namely, the question of 'the good life' – arise more and more frequently. Irish environmental politics after the communicative turn are becoming increasingly normatively oriented. Transcendent questions of values and ideals are necessarily provoked in the context of particular problems, and very frequently these appear in the first instance as 'planning problems', for example: the major public health challenges of our time – heart disease, obesity and type II diabetes – are directly related to patterns of development that are inimical to a healthy lifestyle and well-being; changing demographics, an aging population and associated gerontological problems raise specific needs for care for the elderly and health services delivery systems that are planned so as to be both integrated and socially integrating; mental health, particularly depression, *anomie*, alcohol, substance abuse and suicide, are directly related to patterns of dispersed settlement and dormer communities. Patterns of development that exacerbate and amplify inequality and social exclusion in terms of lack of access to or inadequate provision of services and facilities are directly related to problems of quality of life and well-being. This is especially so for children; thus, poor, or corrupted planning and unsustainable development have lifelong consequences that are extremely difficult to correct retroactively and that are enormously expensive going forward. Less tangible and generalised issues are also planning problems, such as degradation of the environment, both natural and social: pollution, corruption of the food-chain and damage to the genome; anti-social possessive individualism, unrestrained consumerism and distortions of the communicative competencies and interpretative frameworks upon which ecological consciousness and environmental citizenship depend. The Tribunals, by revealing how planning has been corrupted by short-term ends of private profiteering at the expense of long-term public interests of the common good have directly and indirectly raised all of these questions, and more, thereby broadening and politicising planning in Ireland as never before, and simultaneously and recursively bringing planning and environmental politics into conversation with one another, with broader politics of social justice, democracy and social policy, and with perennial transcendent questions concerning the good life.

Conclusion: the normative repositioning of planning and sustainable development and the intensification of Irish environmental politics

The normative repositioning of planning at the centre of Irish environmental politics is most fundamentally represented by the centrality given to 'Sustainable Development' in the Irish Planning & Development Act 2000. This institutional development in Ireland is to be comprehended as a local and national expression of a much broader cultural, political and institutional process of ongoing transformation taking place at a European – and, indeed, at a global level, i.e. the institutionalisation of the discourse of sustainable development. The normative ideal of 'sustainable development' was generated from the anti-war/anti-nuclear and other radical green and eco-political social movements of the 1970s and 1980s, and came into mainstream usage through the work of the Brundtland Commission[5] expressing growing concern 'about the accelerating deterioration of the human environment and natural resources and the consequences of that deterioration for economic and social development'. Emerging from the Commission and its report was a recognition by the UN General Assembly that 'Our Common Future' depends upon all nations developing policies of sustainable development – that is, development that meets the needs of the present generation without compromising the ability of future generations to meet their own needs. A great deal has happened since – the worsening of global warming, peak oil, the widening and deepening of global and local divisions between rich and poor. But now, and increasingly, we see the intensification of conflicts not only over territory and resources but these conflicts made much more complex by their being intimately bound up with issues of racial and ethnic identity and with clashes of religious and cultural values. Planning and sustainable development must now take all of this complexity of social and political antagonism into account.

The net result of the planning Tribunals and the Planning & Development Act 2000 has been a gradual but decisive transformation in the planning profession and the discourse of planning and sustainable development in Ireland. In the past planning was predominantly a technical and administrative/managerial profession, conventionally underpinned by the academic discipline of engineering, framed by legal and statutory instruments and located within a political culture with deeply engrained residual traditionalist practices of clientelism and brokerage, allied with the interests of modern financial power elites, notably in the construction industry. Planning has now to be re-conceived of as a thoroughly politicised activity, conducted in a social field cross-cut with antagonism and contestation. Planning's communicative practices have become concerned with mediating diverse substantive values in a social field of unequal power relations and political contestations in the wider context of post-national and global influences. In other words, the epistemology of planning as an academic discipline resting on a body of knowledge, and the value basis of planning as a professional practice, are being transformed. Professional objectivity and technical competency must now be reconciled with normative demands for sustainable development arising from reformed political cultural institutions and mediated through the political public sphere.

The collective understanding that the Tribunals and the Planning & Development Act are institutionalising is that multiple and oppositional social actors and contexts define the issues of planning. These actors and contexts are saturated by money, political and institutional power, and are cross-cut by numerous social antagonisms: the private interests of developers, the sometimes selfish interests of individuals, the interests and concerns of communities, residents' groups, heritage, environmentalists and other lobbies, all with their own internal fissures and identity – defining constitutive outsides. Planning is a profession practised in a field of power, a profession defined by communicative practices and normativity and struggles for political hegemony as much as by polymath administrative and technical competencies. The task of planning, in the first and in the last instance, is to seek to elucidate these diverse actors and their social positions, to bring them into conversation with one another, and with local authorities, architects, entrepreneurs and developers, local politicians, public representatives and community leaders, with the aim of clarifying – and, where possible, harmonising – views, anticipating difficulties and mediating conflict in the interests of the common good. This is the new shape of Irish environmental politics.

But, as we have seen, as often as not there is no harmonisation and agreement. While some parties to planning deliberations may respect the process of rational argument and become normatively bound to ensuing agreement, other parties have no such interest, and simply wish to impose their power and ruthlessly pursue their interests at the expense of the common good. The exposure of EPA Oral Hearings as cynical charades and power games, the re-emergence of radical confrontational environmental politics (the Shell protests) and the revelations of corruption by the contemporary theatres of communicative rationality (the Tribunals), all evidence the proliferation and diversification of sites of contestation and the broadening, deepening and often radicalisation of theatres of democratic politics. The diversification and intensification of political antagonism shows not just the emergence of consensus around new normative ideals such as sustainable development, and reasoned agreement through communication and reflexivity, but also, and simultaneously, the disagreement over the meaning of 'sustainable development'. There has been splitting, dissent and contestation, the emergence of new fronts and divisions corresponding to the new formations of power and gulfs of social inequality that the forces of globalisation have wrought, and the emergence of new alliances and political configurations that contest the hegemony of the neo-liberal consensus, both locally and globally. This simultaneous development and institutionalisation of nodal points of normative consensus – even if they are regarded (as they should be) as contingent hegemonic achievements, and subject to competing hegemonic articulatory practices – coinciding with the multiplication of sites of antagonism and dissent is by no means contradictory, or a weakness of Irish environmental politics after the communicative turn. On the contrary, this ambivalence evidences an antagonism that is constitutive and formative of the political as such as intractable and inexhaustible.

Notes

1 The EPA and the Tribunals were established in 1992 and 1995, respectively.
2 Such claims, always implicit, are made explicit by corporate spokespersons at Oral Hearings who, for example, claim that senior management live locally, and thus share the same concerns as the local communities, and they are made explicit by industry associations, such as the Irish Pharmaceuticals and Chemicals Manufacturers' Federation who, during the course of one high-profile Oral Hearing, ran an expensive promotional feature in the national media, entitled 'Responsible Care in Ireland's Chemical Industry' (*Sunday Tribune*, 29 September 1996), communicating to the public the 'good news' about the industry: its contribution to employment; its concern for the health and safety of its workforce; and its concern to protect the environment from pollution.
3 The best available knowledge can always only demonstrate correlations of research data and offer inferences, interpretations and hypotheses based on statistical probability. The Supreme Court judgment on the Hanrahan case against Merck Sharp & Dohme hinged upon an understanding of this limit to science in the risk society. Merck's defence was that it could not be proven as a certain fact that its toxic emissions caused the deaths on the Hanrahan farm. The Supreme Court ruled on the basis of 'inferring from the balance

of probabilities' (O'Callaghan, 1992) which, in fact, is actually the register and the currency of science. (See also Chapter 6.)

4 For an elaboration of this critique of the Tribunals see Keohane and Kuhling (2007).

5 The United Nations World Commission on Environment and Development, 1983–7.

References

Allen, R. and T. Jones (1990) *Guests of the Nation: People of Ireland versus the Multinationals* (London: Earthscan).

Beck, U. (1992) *Risk Society: Towards a New Modernity* (London: Sage).

Beck, U. (1995) *Ecological Politics in an Age of Risk* (Cambridge: Polity).

Beck, U. (1997) *The Reinvention of Politics* (Cambridge: Polity).

Beck, U. (1998a) 'Politics of Risk Society', in J. Franklin (ed.), *The Politics of Risk Society* (Cambridge: Polity).

Beck U. (1998b) 'Misunderstanding Reflexivity: The Controversy on Reflexive Modernization', in U. Beck, *Democracy Without Enemies* (Cambridge: Polity).

Beck, U., A. Giddens and S. Lash (1994) *Reflexive Modernization* (Cambridge: Polity).

Corcoran, M. and A. White (2000) 'Irish Democracy and the Tribunals of Inquiry', in E. Slater and M. Pellion (eds.), *Memories of the Present: A Sociological Chronicle of Ireland 1997–98* (Dublin: IPA Press).

Forester, J. (ed.) (1987) *Critical Theory and Public Life* (Cambridge, MA: MIT Press).

Forester, J. (1989) *Planning in the Face of Power* (Berkeley, CA: University of California Press).

Giddens, A. (1994) *Beyond Left and Right* (Cambridge: Polity).

Giddens, A. (1998) *The Third Way* (Cambridge: Polity).

Habermas, J. (1976) *Legitimation Crisis* (London: Heinemann and Boston, MA: Beacon Press).

Habermas, J. (1972) *Communication and the Evolution of Society* (Boston, MA: Beacon Press).

Habermas, J. (1987) *Theory of Communicative Action, Vol. II* (Boston, MA: Beacon Press).

Habermas, J. (1990) *Moral Consciousness and Communicative Action* (Cambridge, MA: MIT Press).

Harding, S. (1991) *Whose Science, Whose Knowledge?* (Milton Keynes: Open University Press).

Keohane, K. (1993) 'Central Problems in the Philosophy of the Social Sciences after Postmodernism: Reconciling Consensus and Hegemonic Theories of Epistemology and Political Ethics', *Philosophy & Social Criticism*, 19(2), 145–69.

Keohane, K. and C. Kuhling (2007) *Cosmopolitan Ireland? Globalisation and Quality of Life* (London: Pluto Press).

Laclau, E. and C. Mouffe (1985) *Hegemony and Socialist Strategy: Towards a Radical Democratic Politics* (London: Verso).

Lash, S. (1994) 'Expert Systems or Situated Interpretation? Culture and Institutions in Disorganised Capitalism', in U. Beck, A. Giddens and S. Lash *Reflexive Modernization* (Cambridge: Polity).

Mouffe, C. (1998) 'Radical Democracy: Modern or Postmodern?', in A. Ross (ed.), *Universal Abandon? The Politics of Postmodernism* (Minneapolis, MN: University of Minnesota Press).

Mouffe, C. (2005) *On The Political* (London: Routledge).

O'Callaghan, J. (1992) *The Red Book: The Hanrahan case against Merck Sharp & Dhome* (Dublin: Poolbeg).

Offe, C. (1984) 'Ungovernability: On the Renaissance of Conservative Theories of Crisis', in J. Habermas (ed.), *Observations on the Spiritual Situation of the Age* (Cambridge, MA: MIT Press).

Postman, N. (1992) 'Scientism', in N. Rostman, *Technopoly: The Surrender of a Culture to Technology* (Toronto: Knopf).

Sunday Tribune (1996) 'Responsible Care in Ireland's Chemical Industry', 29 September.

Weber, M. (1919) 'Politics as a Vocation', in W. Runciman (ed.), *Weber: Selections in Translation* (Cambridge: Cambridge University Press).

Weber, M. (1976) *The Protestant Ethic and the Spirit of Capitalism* (London, Macmillan).

4

Social positions and dynamics within the cognitive order of Irish environmental discourse

Patrick O'Mahony[1]

Introduction

This chapter empirically explores the manner in which communication in multiple settings of political participation leads to ongoing change in political norms and identities. Such norms and identities, including ideas of citizenship, should be viewed both as relatively fixed in political cultures and constitutional orders and subject to innovation through communication processes. The relative volatility of norms and identities derives from the fact that the beliefs, classifying practices and discourses that hold them in place change more often than is conventionally supposed. Participants in communication processes thereby enact, and sometimes re-define, institutionalised political norms and identities by means of cognitive practices of classification and communication.

This perspective will be developed by analysing 'social positions' within the empirical setting of political discourse on genetically modified (GM) crops in the Republic of Ireland at the peak of this controversy between 1998 and 2003. This interest will be pursued within a cognitive approach of the kind described by Strydom (Strydom, Chapter 1, 2007; O'Mahony, 2009). Such a cognitive approach views culture as composed of dynamic and relatively stable components; the cognitive component is dynamic and takes the form of communication practices of classification and argumentation that result in either the maintenance or transformation of the components of culture, beliefs, norms and identities. This relation is understood as the essence of the communicative turn in the social sciences and philosophy, subverting the assumption of the 'natural' evolution of norms and values.

The different kinds of interpretive schema that guide communication processes, leading to the validation or unbinding of norms and identities, are positioned on different social levels. On a transsubjective macro-cultural level are located broad-ranging *cultural models* such as philosophies of justice or responsibility. On the micro-level of individual or collective joint commitments, the mental models of actors take the form of *cognitive models*. The latter involve constructions of or perspectives on broader macro-level cultural models. These two levels of the cognitive – macro and micro – provide two of the levels; the third is provided by the meso-level of the interaction order (Goffman, 1983; Eder, 2007). Here, the interplay of cognitive models makes cultural models 'live' in dynamic communicative settings.

Conventionally in the interactionist literature, such communicative settings are assumed to be co-present ones between actors. However, this can only be one dimension of a sociological approach, which is also concerned with non-co-present interaction on wider planes such as the mass-mediated public sphere or within extended interorganisational settings. These latter settings of discourse make clear how central is the macro-dimension of culture to all communication, as it provides a supra-local shared horizon that is collectively reproduced and reconstructed and that is 'interactive' on a variety of temporal and spatial scales (Habermas, 2006; Strydom, 2006).

In the following chapter, which will develop the above framework empirically, a first step will provide necessary contextual information on the GM plants issue as it manifested itself in the Republic of Ireland between 1998 and 2003. A second step will provide a short outline of the cognitive–discursive methodology used in the analysis of interviews with key actors in the political arena. The micro-levels of the cognitive models of these actors will then be analysed as they manifest themselves through distinctive social positions, the meso-level of the interaction order and the macro-level of constraint and innovation in societal cultural models. This three-level circuit is assumed to constitute a dynamic interpretive system that regulates stability and change in political norms and identities.[2] In conclusion, some short reflections will be offered on the value of the exercise.

The legal–political context of the Irish GM plants controversy

At a general level in Europe, the GM food debate divides into two camps with opposing standpoints. On the one hand, it is claimed that public opposition to the introduction of GM foods will lead to European countries losing out on a significant new 'growth engine' industry and falling behind the United States and other countries in a key technology sector. On the other, it is claimed that the overhasty introduction of GM foods means that health and environmental risks are being unnecessarily generated. The official government position in Ireland broadly falls in line with the first standpoint. The importance attached by the Irish government to the biotechnology sector in general is very high, though food biotechnology lags behind some other sectors in terms of scientific infrastructure and competence. Government policy, reflected in policy statements and voting in relevant EU debates and procedures, is designed to create conditions for the introduction of plant genetically modified organisms (GMOs) within what is described as a 'precautionary' approach that would continuously monitor possible damage to human health and the environment.

However, such a precautionary emphasis differs quite significantly from the way in which the precautionary *principle* is used in other European countries to allow for the importance in decision making of *hypothetical* as opposed to *demonstrated* risks. Such hypothetical risks are regarded as capable of generating significant hazards in certain circumstances. However, these hazards are considered so serious in their implications that it follows that certain innovations should not be pursued until more evidence of absence of hazard can be accumulated. The Irish policy climate, by contrast, is oriented more by a 'sound science' approach that emphasises scientifically demonstrable risk rather than by the precautionary principle in its customary sense.

Food biotechnology is a potential growth sector with high attraction for the country. It builds from an existing and strong agricultural sector and there are some bases of scientific expertise in higher education, which are significantly supported by the government research support programme, Science Foundation Ireland (Barry, 2008). This attraction is further accentuated by the pro-business climate in Ireland. Achieving economic growth by correctly choosing and investing in the 'industries of the future' is given high political importance, especially if these industries are knowledge-based and high up the 'value chain' within globally expanding and competitive markets. The prominence or antici-pated prominence in the Irish case of the food biotechnology industry has also seen the emergence of a loose pro-GM industrial lobby, chiefly composed of scientists, sections of the business community and some journalists. However, farming associations, who have considerable public prominence and influence, have generally stayed on the sidelines on the issue, reflecting divisions in the farming community and the fear of loss of European markets given the negative public attitude to the innovation.

The opposition to food biotechnology in Ireland is composed mainly of NGOs in the environmental and development fields. The most active of them, Genetic Concern, failed in a court case taken against the EPA and Monsanto in 1998 and has since disbanded (see Skillington, Chapter 5 and Sage, Chapter 6). The success of the anti-GM coalition in Europe, and in the neighbouring United Kingdom, in turning GM foods into a contentious political issue, together with their own actions, has given the anti-GM cause in Ireland greater institutional and public standing than most protest campaigns in the country.

Much of this enhanced public standing derives from widespread public disquiet concerning the possible introduction of GM plants. This public disquiet is in part a product of the resonance of the messages emanating from the anti-GM side, especially the apparent risk considered against the unclear benefits for consumers. Similar campaign tactics are used in Ireland and the United Kingdom, taking the form of vociferous symbolic politics, largely conducted through the media, and also direct action in the form of the trashing of fields planted with GM crops. Field trial experiments were brought to a halt by sabotage and the state of public opinion. Hence, in the period of the research that underpins this article (2001–04) there were no new applications for licences for field trials. The anti-GM campaign received additional impetus by the decision of major supermarket chains in Ireland not to stock products with GM ingredients.

The 1998 High Court case of Watson versus the Environmental Protection Agency and Monsanto was important to the development of the Irish controversy (see Skillington, Chapter 5). The case is illustrative of the claimed difficulty of environmentalists and other protestors of entering what they regard as meaningful public participation though, in line with the EU legislation, there were opportunities offered to the public to comment on licences for GM field trials. The perceived inability to enter meaningful participation through the licensing procedure escalated into seeking redress before the law.

The case arose from an application by a member of Genetic Concern to seek judicial review of the conformance of the Irish EPA to its own statutes and procedures in granting a licence to Monsanto to conduct sugar beet trials. The application was not granted and the conflictual lines of the evolution of the controversy were firmly set. These lines of conflict were further manifested by the withdrawal of anti-GM NGOs from the second day of a consultation forum organised by the Irish Government in 1999, claiming that the agenda and general ethos of the procedure did not adequately reflect the risk issues.

In the subsequent five years, there were no significant attempts made to open up further participatory initiatives, or to break the logjam. The political debate continued via an ongoing media debate and by ad hoc public meetings. The failure to agree on a way forward at a European level led to an effective moratorium on the commercialisation of GM foods in European countries in the early years of the new century.

A cognitive sociological methodology for the analysis of political discourse

The in-depth expert interviews, conducted with leading figures in the national GM debate and policy networks in 2003, are the research focus of the current chapter. They partly address the re-contextualisation of issues germane to the lines of conflict sketched above, first taking form in the crucible years of 1998–9, in the opinions of actors offered nearly five years later in 2003. They also address broader dimensions of self–other characterisations, views on citizenship, accounts of the experience of participation, risk and its assessment and judgements on the value of the technology. The interviews were long enough and the participants pivotal enough to enable the reconstruction of central dimensions of the respective *social positions* of the actors in the wider context of the GM issue and political culture.

These social positions refer, respectively, to the cognitive models of the various collective actors – administration, industry, science, environmentalist and concerned citizen; to the manner in which such cognitive models are embedded in broader societal cultural models; and to the manner in which the normal outcomes of the mutual constitution of the actor and the broader culture in the interplay of micro-models and macro-orders is either reproduced or challenged in communication processes (Hausendorf and Bora, 2006).

The results of the interview analysis presented below unfold in three steps that correspond with the above positions. In the first step, actors' cognitive models are reconstructed by analysing various aspects of how they reveal a position, first, in relation to identity issues, views of self and others and, secondly, in relation to their evaluations of what is the case and what needs to be done. In the circumstances of a contested issue of this kind, these dimensions may respectively be understood as the presentation – in this case, highly conflictual – of actors' conceptualisations of 'good' and 'bad' identities and norms.

In the second step, the manner in which these cognitive models relate to one another in communication is examined. This dimension of the analysis explores how an interaction order is constructed. Here is revealed something of the complexity of normative and identity issues when the public sphere is fully mobilised and when differentials of power are not sufficient to result in the simple imposition of one or other preferred position.

The communicative relations between actors continue to generate an interaction order even when real interaction is weak or non-existent, as it is here. In this instance, instead of operating as a communicative context in which interactor learning is possible, it becomes instead an interaction order characterised by power and behind-the-scenes communication – and also simply miscommunication arising from misunderstanding.

The absence of manifest communication should not therefore be equated with the absence of interaction. Sometimes, as here, it indicates how incompatible cognitive structures – for example, economic or moral – that constitute wider cultural models have been activated. These incompatible cognitive structures are capable of blocking one another due to their respective wider resonance among the public and other actors.

To address a general objection often made against this kind of approach, it is not a presupposition of the analysis that consensual, reciprocal learning between positions is the only desirable outcome; often the teleological and inescapably evaluative dimension comes into play with respect to which position constitutes the better outcome for society in the short or long term. It is here that the analyst must make arguments rather than merely reflecting the state of play between the contending positions.

Social positioning in Irish environmental discourse

Cognitive models

In line with the methodology sketched above, the cognitive models of five actor types that were prominent in the Irish discourse and were the subject of extensive interviews and other contextual research will now be outlined. The reconstruction of cognitive models is, however, almost exclusively text-immanent – that is to say, it begins with what the actors actually said or could be reasonably inferred to have intended in the interviews.

The description of cognitive models can take many forms. For present purposes, consistent with the overall approach of this exercise in cognitive sociology, two essential aspects will be concentrated on: the construction of identity by actors in interaction processes achieved through activities of *self-* and *other-positioning* and the taking of a normative position on issue-specific political affairs by sketching the broader *ideological positioning* of the actors with respect to actual or preferred states of affairs. The analysis begins with the policy actor who is a senior official in the Department of the Environment.

Cognitive model of the policy actor

The policy actor's *self-positioning* has two facets. On the one hand, he presents himself as reasonable, consistent and obliged to serve the public and, on the other, as frustrated by the tactics and positions of environmental opponents and a public prone to generalisation. For the first, the tenor of his self-characterisations is most evident in the legislative genre that he utilises. This legislative genre emphasises the 'interests' of the people that responsible legislators should protect against too literal a notion of the 'fundamental rights' of citizens. The distinction between the actor's comfort with 'interests' and discomfort with the assertion of certain kinds of rights suggests that his political philosophy is a variation on a 'realist' liberal pluralism rather than any kind of deontological rights liberalism – as, for example, Rawlsianism.

For the second, expressed within a critical genre, it is one of the policy making self as transparent and genuine, trying to get things done and to broker a reasonable position. The actor uses very few direct self-ascriptions; rather, he speaks *ex officio*. The representation of self rather appears in the combination of the communicative tasks he sets himself – legislatively rational, implicit criticism of the irrationalism of the anti-GM side, corrective of questions that imply excessive normative commitment to ideals of citizenship, but the latter perhaps done with the self-understanding of protecting these citizens' rights as consumers.

The only consistently used self-category in the interview is the 'regulatory self', consistently with the use of the pronoun 'we'. Identification with the collective plural in this instance often occurs in relation to the EU level. It often takes modal forms such as 'can we', which partly relates to the uncertainty of success given public recalcitrance and differences between the various EU countries. This is somewhat at variance with the emphatic import of the active verbs the actor often uses in giving assurance to the public of the safety of GM innovations. The difference can be explained by the uncertainty over whether the public will accept the assurances and also by the extent to which policy makers should give hostages to fortune by making unequivocal commitments to policy innovations. Notwithstanding the limited range of self-ascriptions the actor uses, the regular use of appositives – for example, 'Well' is often used at the beginning of answers – and the generalised pronoun 'you' keeps a sense of the subjectivity of the speaker in play.

In relation to *others*, the actor is more forthcoming. This is most clear in his insinuation that others have agendas that are not consistent with honest and transparent communication. Here, NGOs receive pre-dominantly negative mention and scientists and economic actors pre-dominantly positive, though the latter are criticised for their deficient pro-GM tactics. This is not entirely surprising as the actor favours the cautious commercialisation of GM products within the strengthened regulatory process.

There is a consistent implication that communicating with others – who are either presumed to have agendas or to be prone to ungrounded generalisation – is not productive and that consequently the actor has tired of extensive public participation. The theme of the difficulty of working with people who have agendas or covert interests also occurs in relation to the law case, where it is suggested that it was brought to delay Monsanto field trials in Ireland.

His view of the public as other is circumscribed to that of recipients of communication rather than communicators *per se*, though they are ascribed valid grounds for their objections to GM crops being intro-duced in the first place. However, his commitment to the script of the 'real issues' – i.e. the actual existence in his view of adequate procedures to ensure safety – suggests that any public opposition is seen as arising through misunderstanding rather than as properly grounded in either facts or appropriate evaluations. Indeed, the actor sees the public's consultative role as fraught and regards the public as prone to being manipulated by those acting according to unacknowledged self-interest or with deficient rationality.

In relation to *ideological positioning* the actor speaks at considerable length about the nature of legislative procedures using a descriptive rhetorical mode. The adequacy and transparency of these procedures, especially with the advent of the replacement EU Directive on GM Crop Releases in 2001 (2001/18/EC), is set against the recalcitrance of a public that is in need of persuasion. The nature of public beliefs, largely seen as unsatisfactory in relation to the issue, and the equally unsatisfac-tory mechanisms whereby they arrived at them – the manipulation of others and deficient knowledge of science – fill in a further large part of the actor's ideological reading.

Cognitive model of the economic actor

The economic actor is a senior employee of a major multinational cor-poration (MNC), which plans to commercialise GM plants and to conduct field trials in Ireland and elsewhere. The self-ascriptions of the economic actor are not very explicit, similar to the policy actor. In general, he assigns himself both the role of a scientist – he was formerly one – and also as publicly concerned – though not explicitly from the standpoint of being a citizen. The self-ascription as a scientist fits in extremely well with the 'other' characterisations made of scientists by the policy actor. The aura of authority deriving from scientific practice is contrasted with the communication of oppositional public actors. The latter is represented as floating free from scientific grounding and tending towards the irrational.

The economic actor provides another variation on this theme in which he combines a self- and other-perspective. The self-perspective he adopts is the persona of the perspicacious self. He achieves this in part through the use of active, visual verbs such as 'we saw' that indicate his ability to ascertain beneath-the-surface views. He uses this principally with respect to opponents. The metaphor of 'seeing' is used, for example, in relation to the court case brought by Genetic Concern, which is dismissed as a 'standard tactic'. Here, the lexical choice 'tactic' suggests that the case was brought for extrinsic reasons to do with delaying the field trials, but it also indicates that the position he represents does not engage in the use of strategic rationality or tactics. It rather represents clearly stated interests.

The economic actor's other characterisations generally appear most intensely in the communicative task of discrediting. Characterising the other as self-interested allows for a wide variety of positioning. Through the device of positional inversion, the anti-GM critique that the economic actor's own organisation is profit-oriented and irresponsible is transferred to the opposing parties in the debate. The actor claims that a key environmental protest actor also has a self-interested motive and therefore should not try to claim the moral high ground.

The technique of positional inversion is also used in relation to the regulatory process. Here, the actor uses the dog-and-tail metaphor to emphasise how ungrounded fears, deriving from the nature of public debate, drive this process. In the act of symbolically discrediting an important opponent, the actor also has an explanation for how some, potentially more 'rational', anti-GM campaigners are 'duped' and 'misled' by other actors on the anti-GM side into a fundamentalist position.

The extent of public opposition is also explained by the influence of these misleading communicative activities on the general public. In many instances, the style is revelatory, with the actor strategically re-contextualising conversations that reveal the hidden motives of others or seeing beneath the surface to the deeper reasons that motivate action.

In general, the actor engages in personalised, ethical critique to illustrate the flawed and dubious foundations of the others' arguments. This often takes the form of factual critique of opponents' arguments and ethical critique of their unwillingness to change them. Language use is generally unambiguous, with the actor favouring outright critique rather than the more circumlocutory tactics of the policy maker – based on his confidence and authoritative position as a scientist and also his status as a 'player', a senior actor in an MNC.

In relation to ideological positioning, the economic actor makes much play of his certainty about the safety of GM products; a safety claim that is given added rhetorical force by his own background as a scientist. In addition, he expresses concern about the consequences of covert interests in public communication. The actor's opinions are nonetheless of a purposive–rational nature connected with the realisation of 'normal' commercial opportunity, and he does not engage in extended reflection on wider implications of a political and ethical kind – that is, anything that goes beyond the speech acts of the anti-GM campaigners. Indeed, his whole style and activities of positioning suggests scepticism about the value of such wider reflection. His idea of solving political problems appears as honest argument between different interests framed by an underlying agreement on the importance of 'real' benefits.

Cognitive model of the scientific actor

The self-positioning of the scientist, a leading researcher in the field, is as reasonable, rational and progress-oriented, but also as frustrated and angry at the Luddism and bad faith of others. His primary self-position is to present himself as a scientist who brings a detached, methodical rationality to the issue. He is completely convinced of the safety of GM foods and while as a citizen he regards himself as having the right to object to them, he would also regard it as 'silly' to do so in the light of the available evidence. He therefore can present himself as a formal defender of certain political freedoms, while criticising the judgement on which such rights might be exercised in this case.

The above is yet another example of how in highly charged controversies, positive self-categories are often placed beside negative other categories. The strategy in this case continues the juxtaposition of rational/irrational in the symbolic coding of the issue outlined above for the economic actor, in this case invoking the authority of science to negatively depict the scientific rationality of the opponent.

The actor is frustrated by his own inability to make the 'rational' argument more effectively. As a scientist concerned with research issues, he regards himself as not adequately equipped with the skills of communicating through the media. This modest self-characterisation indicates the extent to which the actor believes that if the case were made 'properly' for GM plants the public would be relatively easily convinced, hence echoing certain positions in the debate over the public understanding of science.

His other positions are largely consistent with the public administrator and the scientist. He is broadly happy with the regulatory situation, which is tough but fair. MNCs like Monsanto are, however, regarded as 'bad guys' by the public and this opens up an opportunity to assert that publicly funded science is more trusted. Hence, even though he broadly belongs on the same side as Monsanto and the regulatory authorities on this issue, he believes that 'disinterested' public science is in the best position to address 'trust' issues.

The issue of trust comes back in his scathing account of some NGOs and the organic movement generally. His basic position is, like that of the economic actor, that they cannot be trusted as communication partners because they have hidden interests. His language and tonal emphasis expresses considerable frustration on this issue. He sees the public as having legitimate grounds for 'some' level of disquiet given the scandals affecting the food industry in Ireland in recent years.

However, this disquiet is amplified by the misinformation provided by the anti-side, aided by the media. He is also more generally negative about the role of the media and its propensity for sensationalism as opposed to dealing with underlying issues. As with all the actors on the pro-GM side, the 'real' scientific state of affairs is contrasted with the irrational construction of oppositional and public opinion. Their depiction of others reveals real frustration and even anger at the anti-GM coalition and scepticism about the level of knowledge that the public can manifest on this issue.

The ideological positioning of the actor is that of a public scientist who nonetheless has considerable affinities with private corporations and industry. Science is seen as very much connected to the economic development of the country and acquires its importance from this rather than from the pursuit of knowledge *per se*. This is, of course, a judgement of degree rather than of kind as the actor also sees himself as a disinterested and trustworthy scientist. Yet, the actor clearly understands how the promotion of science in Ireland, and the security of financial support for research, depends on its real or apparent contribution to economic performance. The actor can therefore clearly row with the contemporary international movement favouring a closer relationship between public science and the innovation system.

In keeping with this, the scientist argues for the normality and acceptability of taking risks in many spheres of modern life. This is an argument often used in defending the right to research freedom over perceived attempts to slow or prevent it. In general, across the pro-GM coalition, the level of risk arising from the technology is presented as small and diminishing as the history of what they claim as its 'safe' utilisation becomes more apparent.

The cognitive model of the environmental actor

The most evident self-positioning of the environmental actor, a senior officer in an environmental organisation active on the issue, is to present the environmental movement as communicatively excluded. This occurs in a state of affairs in which 'others' in government are permanently 'not listening'. There is little explicit self-reference, though a we-category of anti-GM NGOs is constructed around the experiences of the Government-organised consultative forum in 1999, especially the establishment of an agenda. NGOs withdrew in protest from the second day of this forum, in protest at what they claimed was the narrowness of the agenda.

Throughout the interview, the actor describes the futility of trying to communicate in circumstances where the other is perceived to be not listening. An elaborate image of self thereby emerges as being both rational and sincere, qualities that may be in some part a response to how some others contrastingly characterise their environmental opponents. Hence, much energy is dedicated to the re-contextualisation of communication episodes in which the actor uses a highly dramatic language to make her point about particular acts of exclusion, with much use of repetition and reported speech.

More generally, the environmental movement is presented as having a weak hand in Ireland, due both to low public interest and governmental disrespect. She contrasts this weak hand with the situation in other European countries, where environmental movements and ideas are much more highly valued. This self-position – and corresponding other position – operates as an explanation of why the environmental movement is weak in Ireland and also why on the specific issue of GM plants that the relationship has become so conflictual between the antagonistic parties.

The predominant other that is constructed for policy makers is as non-communicative, though this characterisation is generally not a moral critique, apart perhaps from the instance where their treatment of the losing plaintiff in the court case is regarded as 'harsh'. Scientists are given different treatment in that they are portrayed as 'arrogant'. Such a characterisation of scientists is precisely the contrary of the policy-actor who generally regards them as 'excellent' communicators.

The actor also portrays the public as excluded in a similar manner to environmental actors. The public is also regarded as lacking in resources to pursue its environmental interests, a theme that is extended to the law case. The treatment of the plaintiff in the law case shows a good understanding of the legal grounds on which the case was lost. In this section of the interview the actor speaks self-confidently from within a legal genre, elsewhere showing the capacity to utilise a legislative genre.

The ideological positioning of the environmental actor is highly concerned with alleged institutional deficiencies in access and voice within the political system for those outside of the dominant economic interest coalition. On a related theme, she also engages in extensive critique of the limitations of public participation and consultation in Ireland as compared with other European countries. The general idea emerges of a cultural climate, a network configuration and institutional arrangements that are inimical to environmental interests. However, this critique is not generally cast in terms of an appeal to a discourse of citizenship on issues of rights and the general status of civil society, but rather more in terms of a critique of the general policy style used by public authorities.

The cognitive model of the citizen actor

The concerned citizen's self-positions revolve around the integrity and quality of food. She presents herself as an opponent of irresponsible risk taking in this regard, which she contrasts with her own more responsible approach. She particularly emphasises the time horizons attending the introduction of the technology, which she regards as far too rapid to allow for proper deliberation on such an important matter. It is these time horizons, rather than the technology *per se* viewed over the longer term that excites her strong opposition. She speaks for certain social interests that share her concerns but are not clearly represented in the debate. Her language use at various points uses clear self-categorising and assigning strategies 'as a cook', 'as a mother'. Part of her self-positioning is constructed in opposition to the ways public officials and scientists respectively try to position her 'as a crank', or as a 'scientific illiterate'.

Her other positioning towards public administration is less overt than for scientists. She claims that public administration does not implement its own regulations as it is committed to the commercialisation of intensive agriculture and, by extension, to the introduction of GM plants. This is all the more serious given the nature of the technology itself, which is not 'precise' and has unknown consequences in terms of both biodiversity and safety. The critical stance towards the biotechnology industry is not directly personalised; rather, it appears as a critique of an unnamed force that is out of control and capable of subverting established values, such as freedom from endangerment, the edible inheritance, even academic freedom.

By contrast, her other position towards scientists is directly personalised. While she has some sympathy with the position of some scientists, who might have reservations about GM but cannot speak out, she describes other scientists as 'arrogant', a view that echoes the position of the environmentalist. In relation to the public, the actor positions herself as a member of the public; her role is in some part to give a voice to the voiceless public who have grave reservations about GM foods but who find difficulty in articulating this position.

She also wishes to promote stronger associational bonds among bodies affected by GM. Her main reference in this regard is the agricultural community. Indeed, both sides of the debate are disappointed by the non-appearance of the agricultural community on their respective platforms. In relation to the court case, she espouses sympathy for the applicant, who faced huge costs as a consequence of losing. She supports peaceful protest only, but understands the frustration of those who feel compelled to take direct action.

As regards the ideological positioning of the concerned citizen, she is very concerned with the trajectory of food production methods – she favours organic production – and also with the need for more active public involvement. She sees a threat emanating from the power of resource-rich biotechnology corporations who are able to establish the rules of the game. They succeed in Ireland in some substantial part because the government is committed to what she considers to be a failing strategy of intensive agriculture and lacks the vision to consider and develop an alternative. Civil society is basically failing to re-orient government priorities, partly because it is resource-poor and partly because the rural community remains both de-politicised and wedded to a system that is not delivering for them.

Looking at a general level across the various actors, the environmental actor adopts a moral–normative frame of reference as part of her self-image as a defender of environmental interests on behalf of wider society, future generations and general ecological well-being. This is instanced in relation to the characterisations of the science–society interface, where she claims, with considerable rhetorical flourish, that scientific trajectories should be subordinate to societal need. The concerned citizen adopts a similar position. Both actors adopt a critical–normative style that often leans towards moralised critique. Such critique is accentuated when the distance to feasible alternative arrangements for political participation appears to be great, or when other parties appear to be adopting attitudes that frustrate this desired direction.

By contrast, the policy actor is suspicious of too much broadening out of the agenda in this way, and sticks to a legislative rationality. He sees his role as contributing to the establishment of regulatory instruments that would advance the policy goal of commercialisation with precautionary safeguards. This illustrates a desire to follow instituted norms and procedures. He wants 'closure' and is not interested in significantly expanding policy consultation.

The economic actor in his own arguments quite closely follows the policy actor, perhaps more closely and less critically than he would do if the issue were not so politicised and he had wider interests in diminished regulatory surveillance. However, he is more direct and combative than the policy actor, in part reflecting his greater freedom in this respect. Much the same might be said of the science actor as of the economic actor. He is perhaps even more inclined to moralised argument and less politically pragmatic than the economic actor. His moral standpoint is quite opposite to that of the opposing actors, in that his view is that the institutionalised capacities exist in Ireland to deliver the good society, with science and GM food technology playing its part, but for the Luddism that currently inhibits this trajectory of development.

Apart from considerations of strategy and rationality, the broader cultural context – what resonates in the Irish setting – also shapes the communicative stances of the actors. The economic actor knows that to appear genuine allows much latitude for the critique of others' positions and that successful positional inversion – reversing the direction of critique – has much value. The economic actor speaks more from his own milieu, but this milieu of progress and economic development through science and technology has much currency and underpins his trenchant, unambiguous 'progressivism'. The policy actor knows that to appear reasonable and inclusive is a good tactic when closure is the goal. He also knows that it is not necessary to name and shame an opponent directly, given that audiences can be expected to understand the intricacies of insinuation.

The environmental actor knows that detailed portrayal of efforts at genuine involvement is needed to deal with the claim that an actor has been included, even where the actor feels that the terms of inclusion are impossible, a device of incorporation. The concerned citizen knows that to appear a defender of the ordinary counts for much in spite of the risk of the condescension of opponents. None of the actors see much value in extended discussions of principles of citizenship.

Interaction dynamics and cultural change from a cognitive perspective

Direct interaction was not a strong feature of the GM debate in Ireland. The only sustained attempt to promote interaction was the Government forum of 1999. As reported above, the NGO side withdrew on the basis of claims that the agenda was too limited and the format too restrictive. Leaving to one side the decision to withdraw, it is difficult to argue that the agenda was not limited, especially with respect to public involvement by comparison with the British GM Nation or other possible participative forums like the Danish citizen juries.

The court case of 1998, Genetic Concern versus Monsanto and the EPA, was also an example of interaction. This consisted of long submissions by lawyers on rather technical questions of conformance with regulations, though it nonetheless generated sophisticated arguments on the question of risk. It was not designed as debate, rather as a deliberative procedure in the formal setting of a court. Its formality and the inability to immediately respond by the other side – due to the procedural rules of such hearings – meant that direct interaction in the normal sense of the term was hardly operative at all.

If direct interaction hardly characterises the Irish case, it would be a mistake to regard it as exceptional in this respect. It is relatively common in periods of extended argument on an issue for involved parties to communicate only indirectly by seeking to influence public will formation (see O'Mahony, Chapter 9). The Irish case, therefore, as outlined in the methodology above, suggests the need for attention to be paid to indirect interaction within the broad forum of the public sphere rather than to direct interaction in formal structures of political or legal participation. Such participation, where it happens in the forum and in the law case, only succeeds in animating antagonistic cultural models, broadly economistic and ecocentric. The real question of interaction generated by the GM debate in Ireland is: Why has interaction proven to be so indirect?

Societal argumentation is frequently characterised by indirect interaction and most politically significant interaction takes both direct and indirect forms. However, this phase of argumentation in many cases evolves into other types of societal coordination – compromise oriented or consensual (see also O'Mahony, Chapter 9), which are animated by moral, ethical and pragmatic learning processes. Rather than moving on this plane of explanation here, it is proposed to briefly return to the self–other characterisations that are outlined above and to explore how they are culturally embedded so as to make interaction difficult.

The most notable feature of the interaction order on GM plants in Ireland is that even significant indirect interaction is manifest in environmental public discourse. It is perhaps the first case, apart from the much earlier issue of nuclear power, in which an environmental issue acquires this status on a national plane.

Even though the pro-GM side is dismissive of the anti-GM arguments, style and even motives, as manifest in the interview analysis presented above, they are forced to admit the existence of opponents who possess influence, even if they stop short of granting any validity to the kind of epistemic and normative claims on which such influence is founded. They are certainly not accustomed to this and generally find the process unpalatable. Their strategy is to wait for another day when normal business is restored, hence preserving cognitive models that in one way or another are committed to a 'strategic' style of decision making based on narrow, rather exclusive, policy coalitions.

This is essentially a manifestation of interactive power. There is absolutely no recognition at any level of the salience of arguments provided by the other side. Their arguments are sustained by the idea of 'sound science' and responsible risk taking within the broader frame of economic rationality and a relatively low estimation of the rationality, and basic scientific literacy, of their opponents and of the general public.

A two-fold position on communicating with citizen 'others' emerges in the interviews with the policy, science and business actors. In the public to private channel of public communication they should be – and normally are – persuadable through the discourse of responsible risk regulation to respect official assurance. In this sense, they are capable of public rationality and assent to the regulatory order.

In relation to the different interaction channel of participation, however, another view of citizenship becomes evident. Here, communicating citizens are on the whole not very rational, do not stick to the point, are susceptible to media and 'special interest group' manipulation and speak in generalisations combining scientific knowledge, risk, ethical and economic claims. Offering opportunities for the performance of citizenship in such settings does not appear very promising. However, the real problem with the public is that irrational arguments have taken hold, chiefly due to their media amplification.

On the other side, it is not that anti-GM actors are content with their new level of recognition. They can clearly see that it is grudgingly given and that it has corresponded with no real change in mentality and no significant participatory innovation. Their cultural models of interaction are frequently reactive to the perception of exclusion and disrespect that appears on the evidence of the interviews to be well grounded. The anti-GM actors know that their symbolic power on this case is rather precarious, depending on the European balance of power on the issue and the moratorium on the commercialisation of GM plants and media allies that may one day change sides.

In relation to public education, what the policy actor regards as legitimate persuasion the environmental actor regards as manipulation. In the wider frame of the environmental actor's standpoint, the criticism of participation arrangements leads into a different, expanded notion of participation as a new kind of representative democratic layer that would decide on complex questions of this kind. Whereas the sequence in the policy actor leads from the institutionally confirming to the absence of viable alternative arrangements, in the case of the environmental actor it leads from institutional critique to the desirability of alternatives. At bottom, totally different assumptions about the rationality of citizens underpin the two examples and these different assessments lead to different views about the need for institutional innovation in a participatory direction.

The interaction order is characterised by a strong sense of emotional conflict behind entrenched differences that have no immediate prospect of mediation, still less of resolution. It is highly emotionally structured, with the bad experiences of the law case and the Government forum supplementing opposing cognitive models. It is also unusually characterised as an environmental issue by the relative advantage of the institutionally weaker environmental side in terms of the symbolic politics of the issue.

Cultural models and cognitive structures

To properly analyse the cognitive structures that characterise environmental communication in Ireland, it is necessary not just to account for the structures themselves but also for how they are actively held in place. This second task will be deferred while the first one is addressed.

The cognitive structures that shape the cognitive models specified above attach primacy to the instrumental values of economic development. Historically, Ireland has struggled to reach a level of economic development to match its near neighbours. Recently, this has begun to change and the country has gained in prosperity, even if currently this prosperity is being rapidly reduced due to the economic crisis. Whatever the vicissitudes of levels of prosperity, economic development goals continue to have exceptional importance.

The degree of this importance, which amounts to near-hegemony on many issues, has to be explained historically. In Ireland, the social welfare state project emphasising redistribution and compensation has always been weak, as it conflicted with the dominant conservatism sponsored by a highly influential Catholic church. Furthermore, partly owing to the cultural authority of conservatism and partly owing to the residual legacy of the British constitutional model, citizenship is largely conceived in passive rather than active terms. Democracy, therefore, has tended to be a strictly representative, clientelistic and elitist form and social projects aimed at deeper social justice have been constrained.

The values arising from these historical experiences have been transferred into the cognitive structures that appear in the issue under current consideration. The pro-GM side in particular is dismissive of protest actors and infuses its judgements with both moral critique and emotional animus. Hence, the critique of the idea of citizenship as something other than legislative paternalism, the attribution of covert interests to environmental protestors, the assertion of economic and epistemically 'rational' values and so on all indicate a form of the kind of liberal political philosophy described by Ferree *et al.* as 'representative elitism' (Ferree, Gamson, Gerhards and Rucht, 2002).

The dominant value of economic progress has been joined in the contemporary period by the new value of scientific innovation in the knowledge economy. Together, they form a hegemonic dyad that is to be applied to the new frontline of environmental issues. The addition of the new value of scientific rationalism attests to the weakening of older religious values and the potential for a different kind of hegemony to be brought into being. Specifically with respect to the environment, the new value complex of science is extensively used to define risk issues, with scientific expertise given pride of place in risk assessment (see Sage, Chapter 6).

The hegemony of science in the definition of environmental issues coincides with generally poor environmental performance on issues such as waste, water quality, air pollution and carbon emissions. Scientific rationalism both structures risk discourse and also makes it difficult for a specifically ecological ethic to emerge (see O'Mahony, Chapter 9). This is the case because an ecological ethic must rest on ecological values to which scientific values would serve as a means rather than a dominant driver.

At this point, the low estimation of such intrinsic ecological values must be instanced. An ecological ethic is weak in Ireland. The values of either conservation or radical ecology have not significantly influenced the general culture. Nature is generally seen as a resource to be exploited rather than as an intrinsic value in itself. Unless specific and significant risks are perceived to be a 'clear and present danger' on a local level, environmental activism is relatively low.

Moreover, given the dominance of a rationalistic nature ethic as described here, environmentalist ideas struggle to find resonance. The idea of nature as an indivisible common good has a poor time of it in a society where distributive economic goods are so highly valued and where civic privatism reflects the historical hegemony of a conservative attachment to family and the private sphere generally. Such civic privatism is also a poor base for the kind of participatory dynamism that environmentalism calls for in institutional innovations such as Local Agenda 21 and more generally.

If these remarks serve as a rough approximation of the cognitive structures that shape Irish nature politics, the question arises of how they are kept in place and why the issue of GM plants reflects an unprecedented challenge. A first and compelling reason why these cognitive structures endure and become transformed into a new kind of functional hegemony by adding scientism to economism is that they have historically enjoyed such preponderance. Without dramatic episodes of collective learning most likely responding to acute crisis, such deeply rooted structures will tend to shape values, norms and general collective perceptions of what is possible, just, responsible and desirable on an ongoing basis.

A second reason is the fact that the interaction order of the public sphere is relatively poorly developed, lacking intellectuality and, following the young Habermas, not characterised by a rational–critical dimension. Epistemic issues and normative directions are often decided outside of the public sphere altogether in elite networks of influence, dominated by political and economic actors – as, for example, revealed in Skillington's analysis of how waste policy was decided in the 1990s (see Skillington, 1997).

The third reason is that the social distribution of cognitive beliefs among the public coincides closely with the semantic dominance of the dominant cognitive structures described here. The social pragmatics of interaction on environmental issues, then, reflects this semantic structure and social distribution. Cognitive models that emphasise an ecological ethic are not extensive or in respect of matters such as citizenship well developed and they generally struggle to find resonance.

What remains to be explained is why the issue of GM plants is so untypical in that the wishes of the dominant science–economy coalition to proceed rapidly to commercialisation have been stymied. The obvious answer, of course, the presence of a transnational governance order on this issue, has already been offered. Ireland cannot proceed alone due to the implications of EU directives that call for unanimity.

This development points to the existence of a real communication community and associated cognitive structures that lie beyond the immediate control of the Irish nation-state. While the politics of the European Union on environmental issues admits of multiple interpretations, some of which are by no means inimical to the dominant Irish cognitive structures, they do introduce a new complexity of multi-level cultural and institutional variation into the equation. The GM plants issues reveal how deeply entrenched are European food cultures that emphasise food quality (see Sage, Chapter 6). Irish cognitive structures and associated normative orders are becoming fused with this wider context.

On environmental issues generally, and in relation to this issue in particular, the enlarged communication community and cognitive order offers new horizons for societal learning in that they dilute the dominant Irish cognitive order. A further phase of development would be initiated if the alternative cognitive models became 'real' and genuine rivals on the structural plane. The way out in that scenario would either be, depending on circumstances and actors' strategies, the restoration of a repressive hegemony that is currently still broadly the case on most environmental issues or the initiation of moral learning processes in the environmental field (see O'Mahony, Chapter 9).

Notes

1 I would like to thank Siobhan O'Sullivan and Tracey Skillington for conducting some of the interviews on which this analysis is based and for their expert research throughout the PARADYS project. The latter transnational research project, coordinated by Alfons Bora and Heiko Hausendorf, was an important and stimulating context for the research. I would also like to express appreciation to Nicholas McMurry for excellent work in transcribing the interviews according to the complex socio-linguistic convention provided in PARADYS.

2 For an extended account of the nature of normative innovation, see O'Mahony (Chapter 9). Also see Skillington (Chapter 5) for a study of challenges to a dominant Catholic cultural model in Ireland.

References

Barry, J. (2008) 'The Environmental Movement in Ireland: North and South', in J. McDonagh, S. Shorthall and T. Varley (eds.), *A Living Countryside?*

The Politics of Sustainable Development in Rural Ireland (Aldershot: Ashgate).

Eder, K. (2007) 'Cognitive Sociology and the Theory of Communicative Action: The Role of Communication and Language in the Making of the Social Bond', *European Journal of Social Theory*, 10(3), 389–408.

Ferree, M., W. A. Gamson, J. Gerhards and D. Rucht (2002) *Shaping Abortion Discourse: Democracy and the Public Sphere in Germany and the United States* (Cambridge: Cambridge University Press).

Goffmann, E. (1983) 'The Interaction Order', *American Sociological Review*, 48, 1–17.

Habermas, J. (2006) 'Political Communication in Media Society: Does Democracy still Enjoy an Epistemic Dimension? The Impact of Normative Theory on Empirical Research', *Communication Theory*, 16, 411–26.

Hausendorf, H. and A. Bora (eds.) (2006) *Analysing Citizenship Talk: Social Positioning in Political and Legal Decision-Making Processes* (Amsterdam: John Benjamins).

O'Mahony, P. (2009) 'Sociological Theory, Discourse and the Cognitive Construction of Participation', *Comparative Sociology*, 8, 490–516.

Skillington, T. (1997) 'Politics and the Struggle to Define: A Discourse Analysis of the Framing Strategies of Competing Actors in a "New" Participatory Forum', *The British Journal of Sociology*, 48(3), 493–513.

Strydom, P. (2006) 'Intersubjectivity – Interactionist or Discursive', *Philosophy and Social Criticism*, 32(2), 155–72.

Strydom, P. (2007) 'A Cartography of Contemporary Cognitive Sociology', Special Issue, *European Journal of Social Theory*, 10(3), 339–56, guest editor, Piet Strydom.

5

Nurturing dissent in the Irish political imagination: the contribution of environmental law to a new civic cosmopolitanism

Tracey Skillington

Suppressing the impulse to praxis

From the standpoint of the social and cultural conditions of belief, understanding and reasoning, a distinctly conservative Catholic moral order continues to exert a powerful influence over the Irish political imagination today. Whilst the state has long ceased to legislate for the collective according to explicitly Catholic social principles (Peillon, 1982), it does, nevertheless, still promote a model of learning that values the vitality of a more adaptive and contemporary 'socio-cultural Catholicism'. With the 'liberalisation' of culture from the 1960s onwards, a significant ontological shift has occurred in the development of a collective moral reasoning on issues of sexuality, gender, family planning, religious practice, etc. Even so, secularisation does not appear to have hindered the ability of a Catholic worldview to find ways of adapting to social change. It thrives at the subterranean level of everyday social consciousness, for instance, where it continues to offer the individual a broad repertoire of meaning representations of right and wrong, or good and evil, with which to negotiate their everyday lives. When assessed from this broader socio-cultural perspective, Catholicism can be shown to still shape the acquisition and collective processing of information on self and other, world interpretations, as well as the context in which such cognitive activity occurs. The type of 'naturalised' reasoning attached to this enduring model of learning and the 'moral grammar' to which it gives rise, continues to shape a distinctly Irish model of socio-cultural and political integration and exerts an impact on popular reactions to current social problems.

Even in the face of the more recent disclosure of widespread political corruption, incidents of child abuse in Irish Catholic religious orders and an institutionalised neglect of psychiatric patients, this model of collective learning propagates a culture of profound non-accountability. Instead of experiencing the healing effects to be had from an engagement in a genuine discourse of self-understanding and 'working through' a sometimes traumatic or painful past, governing authorities revert to more traditional moral reasoning and respond to such revelations with a degree of non-recognition, forcing not only increasing numbers of aggrieved Irish citizens to take legal action against the state, but also prompting Brussels to threaten legal action (O'Carroll, 2003). Such authoritarian cultural tendencies unashamedly express a desire to preserve the existing socio-economic and political order as it is and, if anything, increase its influence. Its exaltations of Ireland's past heroism, its fight for independence or struggle for economic survival, or even its nostalgic remembering of the excessive indulgences of the 'Celtic Tiger' era, eternalise the vicissitudes of this varied past and disconnect them from present-day praxis. When confronted with contemporary economic, political and social crises, it becomes all too apparent just how bereft of meaning such practices of remembrance are and how contrary to the task of real understanding. Borne out of an authoritarian secular Catholic moral order, such practices actively hinder the capacity to grasp the critical import of history and, therefore, interfere with the social imagining of a transformed future. As a consequence, faith in the capacity of human agency to alter Ireland's corrupt present in the image of more utopian possibilities is discouraged, especially when the source of social, political and economic transformation is thought to be controlled by forces located on the outside. Little effort is made to alter this particular mindset by acknowledging the necessity of voluntarism and praxis (action oriented towards social change) to the long-term survival of democracy. Its more conventional political outlook promotes the fatalistic assumption that there is no escape from the determining impact of global economic recession and political turbulence. Publics are encouraged to unite behind their 'common future' as market speculators and respond passively to mystifying, yet profound, social changes sourced elsewhere. In the process, opportunities for critical reflections on the kind of fiscal and socio-economic policies that have led Ireland blindly into the kind of calamitous scenario it currently faces are deliberately passed over, as are those exploring the likely impact severe recession will have on society's more vulnerable citizens, many of whom happen to be children. Such cynicism has decelerated Irish society's movement towards a self-production (Touraine, 1977) over the years, and has also allowed the historical condition to gradually degenerate into a more 'anti-historical' one. The type of historical agency and critical thinking that once brought about nationalist revolutionary changes in this society are no longer celebrated. Instead, there are repeated efforts to suppress the imperative to praxis and exclude the 'otherness' of the critical thinker, thereby allowing more monologic political–moral elements to thrive institutionally.

Relativising the national frame of reference in the struggle for social justice: assessing new sources of historical agency

As an abstracting mechanism used in the symbolic construction of Irish political community, the anti-historical begins with a denial of the real historical subject and promotes quasi-naturalistic assumptions about the course of social change. Such strategies are used to impose a form of social integration based on a principle of exclusion. Given the nature and historical depth of such problems, we may ask whether contemplating Ireland's political future amounts to a staring into a ceaseless void? Perhaps not.

Moral authoritarianism and a thriving socio-political culture of non-accountability have, quite by accident it would seem, also produced a new historical agency among those enraged by the sheer indifference of protagonists of the anti-historical. For those who repeatedly encounter 'moral injury' (Honneth, 2007) under such a regime, solace has been found in a deepening acquaintance with 'the culture of rights' (Berg and Geyer, 2002) and the internationalisation of culture. The emerging 'cosmopolitan imagination' (Delanty, 2006) intensifies the likelihood of collisions between old and new forms of moral reasoning that co-exist in Irish society today. The result to date has been an escalation of tensions between conservative political elements and new actor configurations struggling for recognition. The latter launch a collective assault against the state's attempts to delimit struggles for social justice to a conservative national frame of reference. Actors like Inclusion Ireland, who campaign for full and equal rights for those with an intellectual disability, simultaneously campaign on the national, European (Inclusion Europe) and international (Inclusion International) levels to advance the rights of citizens by evoking context-transcending norms of justice and equality. With its expanding presence in Irish society, the cosmopolitan imagination appears to enhance the propensity towards civic action and activates new formulations of social justice. The impetus to change in this instance arises from the realisation that the conditions of real social progress are not to be found in imitating some global 'outside' but in social action occurring 'inside' the Irish social order.

An 'inner globalisation' (Beck, 2002) and a pluralisation of various knowledge regimes, values, lifestyle choices and identities both within and beyond Irish state borders would appear to be feeding the current crisis in the Irish state's morality of exclusion.

Arguably, law is one of the most important sites where such activism is flourishing today (Bernstein 2001; Pedrianna, 2006). Sociologists of law have for many years argued that legal norms and rules, administrative regulations, statutory texts and judicial rulings are key catalysts to social change (Stryker, 1994; Bernstein, 2001), but it is only in recent years that the exemplary symbolic significance of high-profile legal challenges to a revitalisation of the Irish social and political imagination can be seen. This chapter will focus on the specific High Court challenge of Clare Watson against the Irish EPA and the multinational giant Monsanto in 1998. Arguably, this case was one of the first in Irish society to translate emerging legal political norms of an ecological justice and responsibility into a more 'desublimated pragmatic form' (Habermas, 2008), as well as enduring democratic ideals of accountability into a situated reason. Although a primary point of reference for Watson in this case was international law, this actor also recounted arguments of wrongdoing and victimisation through an empirically grounded reasoning. At all times, Watson's skills of argumentation as well as her identity as a citizen in conflict with both a collective national and an international corporate actor like Monsanto, were translated through the symbolic crucibles of a legally binding world of rights and duties.

The analysis that follows examines the various ways in which Watson, in this legal setting, called into question the exclusive authority of the Irish state to define social justice without respecting wider international norms of ecological democracy. In so doing, this actor, quite radically at the time, opened up a critical space for challenging the anti-historical element in Ireland's conservative institutionalised moral order on environmental issues. In particular, Watson challenged the exclusive authority of the Irish state to define social justice, especially when a transnational reason could be accorded a higher court of appeal for all rights and claims. In so doing, Watson's case came to typify how Irish local and national contexts of action today are being re-defined as a result of their interactions with the global. Watson managed to illustrate how the international can be effectively employed as a component of a legally relevant identity when a bridge is created between emerging global and local definitions of social and ecological justice. In raising concerns about the revisable basis of scientific evidence of risk and evolving interpretations of justice among other things, this court case introduced a new dimension of civic cosmopolitanism into Irish legal–political challenges against the state. In the period since, this has proven to be a serious threat to authoritarian Catholic nationalist dimensions of Irish political imagination. This case thus established new precedents in the legitimation and empowerment of a more reflexive, critical legal capacity and firmly established an ecological justice as a major axis of conflict in the Irish political and legal spheres for years to come.

Such cases attest to the progressive consolidation today of an internationally anchored doctrine of human and ecological rights, one that is likely to pose serious challenges to more traditional arrangements between state, non-state and intra-state actors now and into the future. The intention here is not to deny the ongoing relevance of the state in the enforcement of law but rather to explore, through a specific case study, how a distinctive pattern of 'Europeanisation' of law contributes to an increase in the number of non-state actors shaping the production, interpretation and implementation of international legal norms, both directly and indirectly. The resultant pluralisation of legal justice poses a number of problems for the Irish state, especially in relation to its capacity to impose the more authoritarian elements of its will on others. Watson's legal challenge captured in miniature form the clash that often arises between the growing pressure towards 'world openness' (cosmopolitanism) and Ireland's more traditionalist desire for sovereign closure. Such tensions here are particularly evident today in state responses to public efforts to reinvigorate political trust, civic virtue, accountability and moral–political autonomy in contemporary Irish society.

On the positive side, emerging conflicts between the historical and anti-historical political forces in Irish society today are pushing out the boundaries of both the understanding and practice of democracy, not only in terms of perceptions of rights, duties and responsibilities, but also in terms of social praxis, especially in the sense of communicative action. The protester who communicates about the law on issues relating to the environment, asylum, human rights, discrimination, etc. normatively goes beyond systems thinking and, in the process, makes a strong statement to wider observing publics about the limitations of Irish legislative practices and systematic closure of public administration to new moral–political arguments. Expressions of a civic cosmopolitanism, usually driven by a crisis-led process of social change, uncover the universal in the concrete particulars of Irish political and legal struggles, as the actor attempts to assert its autonomy through universal reason – reflected, for example, in the increasing number of referrals to the European Court of Justice (ECJ) or the European Court of Human Rights (ECHR). In the midst of such struggles, justice becomes embedded at once in the

universal and the particular, as Ireland's anti-historical political imagination is gradually prized open by a new army of critical constitutional
interpreters whose patriotism is not directed towards the nation, but
towards a post-national allegiance to human rights (Brunkhorst, 2003).

Post-national allegiances of this kind inspire a revival of interest in
civil protest and a radical re-interpretation of what Arendt (1990)
describes as the 'right to have rights'. Relying on the gains that have
been made over the last fifty years or more in international law, such
actors re-invigorate the use value of citizenship on a local, national and
international stage by interpreting modernity's culture of rights in a
more open-ended and creative way. The interpretative work of such
actors offers occasional relief from the tensions caused by the blocked
learning capacities of those more conservative elements of Ireland's
institutional order. It also provides welcome opportunities for the articulation of a more 'expansionist democracy' in the form of counter-
interpretations of rights, entitlements, duties and identity formations
beyond the field of Irish parliamentary politics. The legalisation of disputes involving the state, including environmental ones, has created a
vital means of challenging the fatalism and political apathy of the anti-
historical condition. Perhaps the greatest indicator of moral learning in
this instance is the protesters' re-interpretation of Irish democracy as an
incomplete truth, patiently awaiting the 'return of the actor' (Touraine,
1988) for its further realisation.

Law's expansion capacity in this regard stems from the growing
internationalisation of its justificatory basis, now increasingly rooted in
two legalised worlds – 'cosmos' and 'polis'. It is at the interface between
the national and transnational that new opportunities are currently
arising for a more critical exploration of the limits to the Irish state's
democratic potential. The international dispersal of legal norms not
only delimits state sovereignty, but erodes the legal as well as the cultural basis of legitimation for the Irish state's authoritarianism or defensive learning and further weakens its ability to control the sources of
change that affect the lives of its citizens.

Bringing transnational norms of ecological justice to bear on a situated legal conflict

It is only in the context of 'live' legal disputes, such as that studied here,
that this alternative articulatory function of law comes to light. When
such legal cases are assessed in their discourse setting, it is possible to
see how legal symbols and categories can act as essential 'cognitive

lenses' through which economic practices, social and cultural relationships with nature, as well as competing definitions of risk can be subject to an invaluable, critical normative evaluation. On 30 June 1997, a statement of opposition was filed by Clare Watson against the EPA in its decision to grant consent to Monsanto to conduct limited field trials of its new, glyphosate-tolerant sugar beet plant over a four-year period between 1996 and 2000 at the Oak Park Research Centre in Carlow, Ireland. According to Watson, the EPA's decision to grant a licence to Monsanto failed to comply with the requirements of natural and constitutional justice and was thus thought to be 'unconstitutional'. The EPA was also said to have acted in breach of regulation when it delegated the task of granting consensus to a board member, a duty normally performed by the board. Finally, Watson argued that the EPA had failed to apply the 'effectively zero' risks to the environment and human health test established by the 1994 Genetically Modified Organism Regulations. The court considered whether Watson, as the applicant in this case, had the right to seek injunctive relief on the grounds of the above objections. Watson was originally granted permission to comment on Monsanto's notification but when that notification was amended with supplemental material evidence which, Watson claims, radically altered the notification itself, no opportunity was given to her – or, indeed, any other member of the public – to comment on the amended notification. The court asked whether this act was a breach of natural and constitutional justice and a denial of Watson's rights as a citizen.

Arguably, Watson's legal challenge to the EPA's decision to grant a licence to Monsanto to conduct GM field trials was one of the first to shift bioethical and legal disputes on the limits to democracy within the Irish context onto a transnationally relevant legal plane. The applicant in this instance used law to articulate a civic cosmopolitan identity as a defender of human and ecological rights. The grievances thereby expressed translated newly emerging EU norms of ecological justice through a more situated discourse on citizen participation and procedural justice within an Irish policy setting. Together, grievances and assertions of citizenship entitlements gave rise to a 'detranscendentalised' reasoning on democracy and accountability (Habermas, 2008). Internationally relevant idealisations of ecological democracy become imbued with meaning and socio-cultural relevance in such courtroom settings, as conflicting actors attempt to add experiential content and localised understandings to national, as well as transnational legal norms. The key symbolic significance of Watson's legal challenge lay in this actor's ability to move ethical–legal norms from a purely normative–political plane, to one where they became central components of a contested social reality and subject to an intense degree of interpretative work in a 'live' legal setting. The wording of legal texts like the 1990/220/ EEC Council Directive (in particular, Article 4(1)), Genetically Modified Organisms Regulations, 1994 (SI No. 345), as well as various Irish environmental legislation, including the Environmental Protection Agency Act 1992, enacted under Council Directive 1990/220/EEC, became the subject of an intense and protracted debate among competing parties on their precise meaning and application. Indeed, this debate proved highly illustrative of a dialectic occurring more generally today between local and international interpretations of social justice.

Once democratic reason becomes 'detranscendentalised' and transformed from substance (ideals about democracy, freedom and equality) to subject (actor identity) in this manner, critical opportunities are created for a collective recognition and learning as to how transnationally elaborated concepts of risk assessment, responsibility, causation, prevention and ecological justice ought to be both interpreted and applied in specific social settings. Legally enshrined categories like citizenship, participation and justice not only reinforce the protester's juridical status as a bearer of rights and duties, they also inform the actor's identity as a legitimate challenger acting in the name of constitutional democracy. When Clare Watson strategically anchored her framings of the major issues at hand within a broader, historically embedded legal referential system, this actor situated the self in direct line with a wider body of rights and entitlements that defined her perceived victimisation and injuries as a valid or legitimate extension of Western modernity's histories of democracy. At the most general level, Watson began a legal process of interpretation when she questioned previously unquestioned social conditions, when she re-interpreted the 'mundane' as 'problematic' and when she translated unfolding social experiences and events into ethically objectionable acts or injuries with the aid of legal norms, values and frames of meaning. Ten years on, debates on citizenship, environmental justice, liability and risk are now routinely subject to empirical testing in such legal contexts, but in the late 1990s, the Watson High Court challenge, apart from the earlier legal case of Hanrahan Versus Merck, Sharp & Dohme (1988), was one of a few that was breaking new ground at that time.

Self and global 'other' as mutual victims of environmental destruction

Ethically objectionable acts must have their victims and environmental disputes are no different in this regard (Douglas, 1996). All parties to the Watson versus the EPA and Monsanto case struggled to appropriate an identity as a victim of injustice. Framing one's identity as a victim has been central to an Irish mode of politics for many years, especially strong during the conflict transitional phase of Irish independence when nationals saw themselves as discriminated against and denied civil rights and liberties. Diagnostic framing strategies are used to identify precisely who is a victim. Because Watson concentrated on prospective victims of future environmental destruction, the spectacle of suffering she constructed mixed real (scientific evidence of risk and histories of disaster) with fictional scenarios depicting environmental contamination, the likely development of 'super weeds', as well as resistance to antibiotics in humans and animals as just some of the effects of this 'runaway technology'. Watson's choice of 'victims' was interesting, not least because of their proximity to the Irish social imagination and cultural narratives of exploitation – the Irish farmer (a personalised category of victim), a concerned Irish public (a general category of victim), the environment (a general category of victim) and future generations (an abstract category of victim). In relation to the last category of victim, Watson not only defended future generations' right to have rights, but also recognised their legitimate status as relevant members of a legal–political community that extends into the future. This last category of victim was of particular importance to Watson as her definition of risk, to a large extent, rested on an evaluation of likely damage – suffering in the future. As a consequence, the spectacle of the unfortunate and their suffering conveyed by Watson in this instance, was apprehended largely through a 'fictional' rather than a 'realist' mode (Boltanski, 1999), in spite of the heavy presence of counter-scientific opinions to support Watson's claims. The outcome of this framing process depended on Watson's diagnosis of the nature of the spectacle of suffering (the very real risk in the future, according to Watson, of a horizontal gene transfer from plant species to humans: p. 46, document three of the officially recorded Court proceedings), the type of moral reasoning applied ('we would say that the attention to human health issues was improperly superficial in the course of this assessment', Mr. Gordon, acting on behalf of Clare Watson: p. 31, document two of the officially recorded Court proceedings) and their joint relationship to an empirically verifiable reality (counter-scientific evidence and expert testimony presented by Dr Steinbrecher and Mr Dowding among others on the unknown consequences and irreversible damage caused by GM releases).

Watson linked the prospective suffering of all four categories of rights-bearing victims identified above repeatedly to a cosmopolitan ethics of care (Turner, 2006) and to a wider 'politics of recognition' (Fraser and

Honneth, 2003). The foundations of this actor's own civic identity is seen as connected to that of an internationally extended 'other' whose suffering is consistently devalued and ignored. Watson established a relationship of mutuality between self and global 'other', even time-distant 'others' (future generations), in a manner that drew attention to humanity's shared vulnerability to regulatory indiscretion and environmental risks, particularly those posed by GM agriculture today.

However, Watson did not merely wish to contemplate the potential suffering of identified victims. She also attempted to transform sentiment into legal action by balancing victimisation with a strong sense of political agency among a 'very concerned Irish public'. Inspired by the vulnerability of humanity to such new precarious bioagricultural developments and the lack of scientific knowledge on the long-term effects of GM crops on the environment and human health, Watson stressed the significance of the protective security of stringent national and international legal norms and institutions. As the modern equivalent to the 'sacred canopy' (Berger, 1969), modernity's 'juridical shield' – comprised of civil rights, the rule of law, human rights, ecological rights, social rights and so forth – offers citizens like Watson the tools needed to fight back against global capitalism's grand plan to commodify organic nature.

Making ample use of modernity's juridical shield, Watson questioned the EPA's 'rather bland' and 'superficial' attitude towards the environment and appealed to a more engaged sense of collective responsibility inspired by 'very, very stringent regulations throughout the world'. Such regulations, Watson reasoned, ought to proceed on the assumption that risk assessments should occur before a release is made, rather than after. Here Watson explored the underlying political meaning of a risk dramaturgy that promotes acting 'before it is too late'. The basic belief is that GM crops, whose destructive capacities are not yet fully apparent, pose not only a local, but also a global threat to nature. As a rational legal actor, Watson demanded that her citizen's rights to rational accountability be recognised. She consistently maintained that, in terms of procedure, the EPA not only acted in 'breach of Irish constitutional justice', but also European normative obligations which clearly indicate how the EPA must first conduct independent studies testing the truthfulness of Monsanto's claims and, second, record its conclusions and reasons to grant a licence to Monsanto in a report that could be made available to the general public.

In opposition to Watson's case, both Monsanto and the EPA applied their own legal moral reasoning to exonerate their position and construct competing identity categories as victims. The EPA, for instance, advocated a factually based congruence between 'the whole purpose of the European Directive on GM releases' and 'allowing field-testing in the appropriate ecosystems'. According to this state actor, 'an overall concern on the part of the European Council' is that each country should test GM crops in their own ecosystem so that the consequences can be identified. In its references to the need for a 'step-by-step accumulation of GM releases in the interests of both scientific and economic development', the EPA revealed its ideological commitments to the idea of 'society as laboratory' (Strydom, 2002). The EPA protested that it had 'consulted widely and considered in-depth and asked more questions than normally asked in other countries' (p. 4, document six of the officially recorded Court proceedings), while Monsanto claimed that it had been unfairly targeted by 'lawbreakers' and 'objectors' who had unlawfully destroyed their trial crops in the middle of the night. For Monsanto, Watson's legal challenge represented an injustice against both a law-abiding corporate actor and the EPA who, it claimed, had acted in accordance with the regulations and whose reputation was being unduly questioned. To play down its material interests, Monsanto not only emphasised the 'needs of Europe' as well as the 'preferences of the European regulatory regime', but also the contribution it was making to a European-wide data collection scheme that encourages a large number of field trials in other jurisdictions.

All three actors in this legal case adopted their own distinct discourse of denunciation of the persecuting 'other'. What is most evident, however, from the final outcome of this case is how power and vested interests in the Irish legal context act as constraints on a selective ethical recognition of potential suffering. A minimum degree of recognition was granted to Watson's four categories of victim. As the defendant in this case, the EPA challenged Watson's particular construction of the natural environment as a victim. Alternatively, the EPA emphasised the naturalness of risk in this era of global market competitiveness and its sheer necessity to scientific industrial progress in the modern world. Indeed, it was this perceived necessity of risk to modern life which was used as the main justification by the EPA for assessing any risks posed by the release of GM sugar beet after such a release occurred, rather than before.

What becomes apparent is that risk assessment in this instance was not conducted in the interests of nature, but rather in the interests of consumer safety since these 'products', as Monsanto's legal team preferred to call the GM trial crop under review, would eventually be placed on the international consumer market and that, they argued, was 'the scheme of things'. The pragmatism of Monsanto's position was spelled out quite clearly here – innovations in research ought to be implemented insofar as these developments point beyond trials towards the GM supermarket shopping experience. GM agriculture was said to be an impending reality, a techno-scientific component of the present that will, in all likelihood, flourish in the future. The only problems acknowledged in this instance are those of a practical, rather than an ethical nature. A Lockean, liberal tradition of thought shaped this actor's unremitting trust in bioscientific research, one that foregrounds the protection of the individual legal person's freedom of choice against the state in an overall power structure that supports vertical relations between citizens and state (Habermas, 2003). From this liberal perspective, freedom of choice is a sacred creed and a key element of Western liberal interpretations of individual rights that persons maintain against the state.

Relying heavily on a neo-liberal interpretation of such rights, Monsanto asserted that it rather than nature was the main victim in this legal case, as it had been unlawfully victimised by irrational and emotionally driven elements and behaviours like field trashings conducted on its GM crop trials late at night. Monsanto repeatedly referred to the negative effects of this law case on its competitive advantage in the marketplace, resulting in costly delays and additional legal engagements. With such reasons in mind, Monsanto asserted its right to know when it could resume field trials, expressing great impatience for a decision to be made sooner rather than later. This actor also communicated great unease about the possible imposition of a tighter state regulatory control of its operations. For Monsanto, consulting with the 'appropriate experts' on its operations was thought to be sufficient. Judging from the type of arguments it made on the question of risk assessment, regulation and consultation, it would appear that Monsanto at times felt justified in thinking that there was complementarity between legal and economic meanings, evaluations and socio-economic power relations, and for such reasons the court ought to recognise the higher order of justice embodied in global market imperatives.

In many ways, Monsanto's distinct interpretation of freedom, and its construction of the infringement on such freedoms as a form of victimisation, resonated more strongly with a dominant master frame of economic growth at all costs in the Irish political context. Since the early 1980s, the neo-liberal revolution has extended market principles to all social spheres in the Western world. It was not until the late 1980s that the drum roll of this revolution was finally heard in Irish society when the political climate consciously shifted towards a policy of limited state intervention, deregulation of labour and financial markets, greater commitment to free trade, the tighter regulation of state expenditure and a reduction in personal taxation. Such developments were a clear indicator of the arrival of right-wing theories of government as a critical component of neo-liberal world politics. From this emerging ideological framework, evaluations of human and ecological risks were re-interpreted as better left to the spontaneous operations of minimally regulated markets. A gradual 'softening' of regulations that infringe on global corporate interests has followed in the wake of this consensus. This is a direct consequence of their lobbying power and ability to intimidate judicial processes (Edelman, Uggen and Erlanger, 1999). Thus, the neo-liberal revolution may have carefully groomed and nurtured the interests of the global corporate world, but not necessarily the democratic rights of the global citizen.

The ideological system which has accompanied this global neo-liberal revolution has come to firmly establish itself as a series of background assumptions in contemporary Irish political life – a development which actors like Monsanto not only applaud but actively foreground in asserting the pre-eminence of its market position over all other practical and ethical considerations. Indeed, such background assumptions have in general proven themselves to be less open to a process of re-negotiation or critical reflection, explaining why Watson's legal challenge was so significant in the late 1990s. In particular, Watson questioned the implicit logic embedded in the assumption that the Irish state could not afford an overly stringent, protectionist closure of its domestic economy to the operations of such a global giant as Monsanto. Although Watson voiced her complaints against such a climate of intimidation on legal–ethical grounds, there was an insufficient critical distance from this political–moral consensus for her protests to have any real 'narrative fidelity' (Snow and Benford, 2000: 622) in this setting. Added to this was the fact that Irish people in the late 1990s did not in general perceive themselves to be victims but, rather, beneficiaries of an economic boom gaining momentum at that time. Certainly since 2008 the mood of the Irish people has shifted quite dramatically with the deterioration of the economy, soaring unemployment and national debt. Many now see themselves as losers once more in an economic drama, misled by a state that has mismanaged accumulated funds that ought to have been invested in environmental services, health and education. There is thus a renewed predilection for victimhood in Irish political culture. This finding suggests that the frames of meaning actors used to construct an identity during episodes of conflict are the product of a particular convergence of political, cultural and historical forces in a society which may change and evolve over time (McAdam, McCarthy and Zald, 1996; Della Porta and Diani 1999). The rise and fall of particular

symbolic representations of the self indicates how perceptions of grievance and constructions of victimhood are both culturally and socially
conditioned.

A model of social integration without solidarity: exposing a climate of intimidation

Watson consistently drew critical attention to the unethical nature of
the threats being made in this court setting and to the political economy
of citizenship emerging more generally. According to Watson, the full
potential of citizen rights is not being realised institutionally because
the various ways in which multinational giants like Monsanto continue
to intimidate the local legal process is not being addressed. For its part,
Monsanto availed itself of several opportunities to remind the court of
Ireland's vulnerable economic position in a world where the nation-
state has a declining influence over the determination of economic realities. In this globally interdependent phase of late capitalism, Monsanto
implicitly warned, legal authority must concede to the inevitability of
the bioagricultural revolution.

In response to such threats, Watson accused this corporate actor of
deliberately trying to jeopardise the legal process and protesters' rights
to a fair trial. Monsanto, on the other hand, repeatedly stressed the
greater needs of the 'European market', the needs for continued economic growth, product innovation, consumer choice and, of course, 'the
preferences of the European regulatory regime' over and above any
objections being aired in this legal context. It pleaded with the Court
to allow it to resume its field trials immediately, stating that it would
have no choice but to conduct its trials elsewhere where there was a
less strict regulatory regime. In its continuous efforts to objectify the
emergence of GM foods on the European market, regardless of any
objections raised in this court setting, Monsanto sought to trivialise the
importance of this legal process and intimidate its decision making
procedures.

Watson criticised what she perceived to be the EPA's concessions to
the greater power of this global economic actor on the grounds that
this was a blatant attempt to compromise Ireland's own legal authority,
its rights to take a stance and impose its will. Watson condemned the
more general power of MNCs to pressurise state-sponsored regulatory
bodies caught between the often conflicting requirements of social and
environmental policies, on the one side, and the need to foster a sustainable Irish economy, on the other. Critics like Watson see the EPA as

terrorised by the looming threat of capital flight and complicit in the creation of a more deregulatory climate. Certainly, the EPA has played its part in the government's overall plan to improve the relative attractiveness of Ireland's local economic position under conditions of stiff global competition.

Watson reminded the Court that in the light of Monsanto's actions and failure to comply with regulations, behaviour created in the first instance by a policy culture of indifference, the only real alternative internationalising force to the oppressive antics of global economic actors was international law and civic solidarity. Indeed, Watson's legal team drew attention to 'a principle [of public participation] that has been recognised in Europe and acknowledged in other types of cases' but not, it seems, in this case. A selective application of principles of democracy, Watson highlighted, results in a strained, often acrimonious co-habitation of international and national legal standards of environmental justice due to political–corporate pressures. Only a more inclusive, international negotiating system can insist upon the application of ecological justice to industrial activities, and place limitations on the current cost-cutting 'race to the bottom'. Such an authority must have the potential to grant real substance to the regulatory power of a cosmopolitan democracy – or, at the very least, place restraints on the current regulatory power of the global market economy. Solidarity in this instance begins with a genuine commitment to public participation, a principle already established in the 'hard' law of the treaties of the European Union, as Watson pointed out, but also in 'softer' legal agreements such as Europe's Charter of Fundamental Rights, or the internationally agreed Cartagena Protocol on Bio-Safety.

On several occasions throughout the proceedings, Watson reminded the EPA in particular of this internationally recognised principle, as well as the special reference given to 'the involvement of the public' under Section 31(4) of the 1990/220 Directive. The latter, Watson highlighted, was not for fun, but for the public to be heard on the issue of whether a proposed release should occur. Watson also repeatedly referred to those Irish Constitutional requirements said to confer a 'substantive right of public consultation rather than a minimum one' (p. 48, document ten of the officially recorded Court proceedings). In contrast, Monsanto choose to de-emphasise the state's commitment to forms of civic solidarity based on an allegiance to international standards of equality and justice, or any patriotism to human rights expressed by Watson in this instance.

Article 7 of the 1990/220 Directive states that groups shall be consulted on any aspect of a proposed GM release. As Monsanto interpreted this element of the Directive, consultation may be with the appropriate experts and 'competent authorities', rather than any public representatives. Instead of being intrinsic to the wording of the Directive, public participation was interpreted as an additional right (p. 4, document eight of the officially recorded Court proceedings). For Monsanto, the appropriate place for public participation was the editorial pages of newspapers. In making such claims, this actor not only positioned itself argumentatively, but also ideologically, as one committed to a model of limited public participation. While expressing a strong concern for the protection of the economic, and in particular, consuming capacities of the public, Monsanto displayed little or no interest in the civic ideal of a more reflexive, critical public whose beliefs and actions are understood to be inherently political.

Rather than reflecting on Watson's critical point that field trials should not be allowed to proceed when there is little scientific understanding of the risks involved, the EPA chose to refute the rational basis of this actor's claims and the grounds for further public participation on this and similar cases in the future, especially when challengers rest their legal case on such 'unreasonable' claims. Indeed, the EPA went so far as to state: 'the concerns of objectors cannot influence the Agency in determining or carrying out its function under the Regulations.' It was for such reasons that Watson accused the EPA of merely 'paying lip service to the idea of public involvement', thereby highlighting the social distance between transcontextual norms of participation and actual institutional arrangements in the Irish context. It was also a very clear indication of the persisting presence of an authoritarian defensive learning on the part of Irish environmental policy actors.

If nothing else, Watson's case illustrated how law can create vital opportunities for new frames of meaning on victimisation, bioethics, risk, expertise and so forth, to be combined in a new configuration and communicated through legal discourse. Law continues to be a powerful medium for the play of power between competing actors, leading to a re-negotiation of legal meaning systems embedded in the cognitive order over time. Arguably, this case, occurring over a decade ago, helped forge a new understanding among Irish publics as to how law can be made a public mouthpiece for democratic environmental protest. The growing incidence of High Court proceedings against the Irish state since that time on issues as diverse as healthcare and public safety, education, disability, sex abuse, etc. is testimony to this. Also the fact that no GM crops have been grown commercially in Ireland, apart from some herbicide-tolerant GM crop testing, is also interesting in itself.

Conclusion

While law furnishes protest politics with its most resonating symbols of justice, freedom and equality, it may also act as a constraint on actors' efforts to reshape social relations and release blockages to learning in Ireland's more conservative institutional order. Ideally, many voices should contribute to the evaluation and interpretation of the law. However, several factors intervene to shape this decisive process, including political culture, value orientations, institutional logics and decision making procedures. Cumulatively, such factors engender distinct 'societal mentalities' (Tarrow, 1992) that have a conditioning effect on legal outcomes. In the Irish legal context, there is much evidence to suggest that such societal mentalities have facilitated a blurring of the differences between 'common interests' and 'corporate interests', especially in relation to interpretations of 'acceptable' levels of human and environmental risk, as well as issues of responsibility and accountability. In the Watson versus the EPA and Monsanto legal case, there was evidence of a deliberate 'softening' of regulations that could potentially impact negatively upon Monsanto's financial investments in field trials. In a legal–political field that largely favours economic interests over all others, the content and meaning of environmental legislation is in danger of becoming 'endogenous' to just corporate interests. Added to such problems is what Teubner, Falmer and Murphy (1994) describe as a gradual weakening of the causal links between individual acts and ecological damages/risks as well as the political translation of new forms of risk pooling, thereby rendering the attribution of environmental liability to any one actor in a legal dispute extremely difficult. With the 'causes' of environmental damage now increasingly interpreted as multiple and circular, opportunities for a clear demarcation between victims and villains in legal political disputes are lessening, as was clearly apparent in the legal challenge under review here.

Judge Justice O'Sullivan did decide to rule in favour of Monsanto and the EPA, upholding the EPA's decision to grant a licence to Monsanto to conduct field trials in controversial circumstances. While Clare Watson suffered heavy personal expenses as a consequence of her taking on this case, many important developments emerged. For instance, Watson did, at a minimum, stimulate a legal questioning of the communicative dimension to official interpretations of environmental risk – and, indeed, the rationale applied to assessments of such risks. Furthermore, this actor questioned the extent to which Ireland's dependence on multinational investment for continued economic growth is proving detrimental to a more general articulation of freedom and citizenship. She pointed in this instance to the need for citizens to look beyond law's national boundaries. If freedom is understood as the absence of dependence upon the will of another, then any claim on the part of Monsanto that it is an international player, and that the decisions of the Court are insignificant to its global operations, should not have been recognised by the Court, especially in the light of internationally determined standards of justice. In the years that followed this case, there have been a number of high-profile legal challenges against the state or a state-sponsored body. It may be that Watson's heroic efforts did in some way help to stimulate a heightened legal consciousness on environmental issues as well as those pertaining to planning, sex abuse, medical misdiagnosis or malpractice and so forth. Collectively, high-profile legal challenges have helped revitalise the collective social imagination as to how human rights and social justice ought to be respected. The legal victory in the United Kingdom of the 'Kingsnorth Six', who in 2007 broke into a coal-fired power station and shut it down, is testimony to law's occasional role in extending the range of application of ecological justice. The argument presented by these protesters was that the burning of toxic fossil fuels amounted to a crime against the planet and thus constituted a 'worse harm' than that caused to the power station. The court concurred, and the activists involved were acquitted. Here in Ireland, an accumulation of environmental legal challenges, including the ongoing 'Shell to Sea' campaign at Rossport against the construction of a natural gas pipeline through Rossport, County Mayo and a refinery at Bellanaboy intended to refine natural gas from the Corrib gas field, also mobilise resentment against a state largely perceived as being indifferent to the negative consequences arising from the actions of those who have violated internationally recognised standards of justice.

The success of many legal challenges to date attests to the willingness of Irish domestic courts occasionally to engage in a dialogue with international legal norms and foster universally recognised values and principles. In this respect, many Irish judges, like their counterparts in other jurisdictions, have made rulings that potentially damage the reputation of the state and have refused to allow their courtrooms to become mere instruments of national legal–political conservatism. Certainly, the cumulative effect of such bold legal outcomes will undoubtedly help stimulate a more open and responsive Irish public culture, one that increasingly looks to Europe and beyond in its critical translations and evaluations of truth and justice.

References

Arendt, H. (1990) *On Revolution* (London: Penguin).

Beck, U. (2002) 'The Cosmopolitan Society and its Enemies', *Theory, Culture & Society*, 19(1–2), 17–44.

Berg, M. and M. H. Geyer (eds.) (2002) *Two Culture of Rights: The Quest for Inclusion and Participation in Modern America and Germany* (Cambridge: Cambridge University Press).

Berger, P. (1969) *The Sacred Canopy: Elements of a Sociological Theory of Religion* (New York: Anchor Books).

Bernstein, M. (2001) 'Gender, Queer Family Politics and the Limits of Law', in M. Bernstein and R. Reimann (eds.), *Queer Families, Queer Politics: Challenging Culture and the State* (New York: Columbia University Press).

Boltanski, L. (1999) *Distant Suffering: Morality, Media and Politics* (Cambridge: Cambridge University Press).

Brunkhorst, H. (2003) *Solidarity: From Civic Friendship to a Global Legal Community* (Cambridge, MA.: MIT Press).

Delanty, G. (2006) 'The Cosmopolitan Imagination: Critical Cosmopolitanism and Social Theory', *The British Journal of Sociology*, 57(1), 25–47.

Della Porta, D. and M. Diani (1999) *Social Movements: An Introduction* (Cambridge: Blackwell).

Douglas, M. (1996) *Natural Symbols: Explorations in Cosmology* (London: Routledge).

Edelman, L., C. Uggen and H. S. Erlanger (1999) 'The Endogeneity of Legal Regulation: Grievance Procedures as Rational Myth', *American Journal of Sociology*, 105(2), 406–54.

Fraser, N. and A. Honneth (2003) *Redistribution or Recognition: A Political–Philosophical Exchange* (London: Verso).

Habermas, J. (1998) 'Reply to Symposium Participants, Benjamin N. Cardozo School of Law', in M. Rosenfeld and A. Arato (eds.), *Habermas on Law and Democracy: Critical Exchanges* (Berkeley, CA: University of California Press).

Habermas, J. (2003) *The Future of Human Nature* (Cambridge: Polity Press).

Habermas, J. (2008) *Between Naturalism and Religion* (Cambridge: Polity Press).

Honneth, A. (2007) *Disrespect: The Normative Foundations of Critical Theory* (Cambridge: Polity).

McAdam, D., J. McCarthy and M. N. Zald (1996) *Comparative Perspectives on Social Movements: Political Opportunities, Mobilizing Structures and Cultural Framings* (Cambridge: Cambridge University Press).

O'Carroll, P. (2003) 'A Century of Change', in M. P. Corcoran and M. Peillon (eds.), *Ireland Unbound* (Dublin: Institute of Public Administration).

Pedrianna, N. (2006) 'From Protective to Equal Treatment: Legal Framing Processes and Transformation of the Women's Movement in the 1960s', *American Journal of Sociology*, 111(6), 1718–61.

Peillon, M. (1982) *Contemporary Irish Society: An Introduction* (Dublin: Gill & Macmillan).

Snow, D. A. and R. D. Benford (2000) 'Framing Processes and Social Movements: An Overview and Assessment', *Annual Review of Sociology*, 26(6), 1–39.

Strydom, P. (2002) *Risk, Environment and Society: Ongoing Debates, Current Issues and Future Prospects* (Buckingham: Open University Press).

Stryker, R. (1994) 'Rules, Resources, and Legitimacy Processes: Some Implications for Social Order, Conflict and Change', *American Journal of Sociology*, 99, 847–910.

Tarrow, S. (1992) 'Mentalities, Political Cultures and Collective Action Frames: Constructing Meaning through Action', in A. D. Morris and M. C. McClurg (eds.), *New Frontiers in Social Theory* (New Haven, CT and London: Yale University Press).

Teubner, G., L. Falmer and D. Murphy (eds.) (1994) *Environmental Law and Ecological Responsibility: The Concept and Practice of Ecological Self-Organisation* (Chichester: John Wiley).

Touraine, A. (1977) *The Self-Production of Society* (Chicago, IL: University of Chicago Press).

Touraine, A. (1988) *Return of the Actor: Social Theory in Post-industrial Society* (Minneapolis, MN: University of Minnesota Press).

Turner, B. S. (2006) *Vulnerability and Human Rights* (Pennsylvania, PA: Pennsylvania State University Press).

6

Conventions of quality and governance of artisan food: revealing the tyranny of 'sound science' in the regulation of Irish raw milk cheese

Colin Sage

Quality is not natural; rather it is a mode of ordering the natural and the social (Allaire, 2004: 65)

Introduction

It has been suggested that the current economic dynamic is based on an obsession with quality much as the Fordist era was preoccupied with the quantification of production (Raikes, Jensen and Ponte, 2000). A focus upon an economy of qualities (Callon, Méadel and Rabeharisoa, 2002) helps to reveal the dynamics of current economic restructuring (Wilkinson, 1997). It is well established that 'quality' is a complex and contested term carrying a vast array of meanings and socially constructed according to context (Watts and Goodman, 1997; Ilberry and Kneafsey, 2000; Morris and Young, 2004). Yet quality is more than a label to be ascribed by different actors but emerges through tests of qualification designed to evaluate and objectify the robust suitability of the product to a specific quality designation (Callon, Méadel and Rabeharisoa, 2002). Complex social, economic and scientific processes are at work here reflecting the increasingly heterogeneous range of interests (producers, corporate retailers, consumers, the state) engaged in the government of food.

For Marsden (2003) the evidence (ranging from the rise of biotech to the emergence of 'alternative' speciality production) suggests that the post-war model of public policy-led regulation has given way to a more turbulent period of food governance. Private interest regulation, particularly the dominant role played by corporate retailers in controlling the origin and quality of their supply chain, has limited the state's ability to act in the public interest. While it may no longer govern (i.e. 'command and control') the entire food system on behalf of consumers (Marsden

2003) it nevertheless can police the agricultural and rural system using a discourse of 'sound science' in the public interest. Alongside this exist expressions of 'multi-level governance' involving a variety of non-state actors, public and private, competing and collaborating in shifting coalitions across a number of different levels (Hooghe and Marks, 2001; Bulkeley and Betsill, 2003). Clearly, all these actors may have very different views on the meaning of quality in food, with the result that contrasting narratives and rules give rise to moments of considerable contestation.

Efforts to understand the construction of quality have been substantially advanced by the use of concepts developed by the French convention school (Boltanski and Thévenot, 1991, see below). For example, work on global commodity or value chains has drawn attention to the development of measures and standards and to the dominance of process and production methods even over the attributes of the product (Busch, 2000; Raikes, Jensen and Ponte, 2000; Friedberg, 2003; Busch and Bain, 2004; Fold, 2004; Ponte and Gibbon, 2005; Cidell and Alberts, 2006). The proliferation of quality management and monitoring systems in an era of generalised consumer anxiety around food safety illustrates this changing government of food, particularly the rise of private interest regulation displacing command and control-style public policy.

Yet conventions theory has also been used to interrogate aspects of an alternative food sector comprising products of local origin, culinary tradition, regional speciality and gastronomic merit. Across Europe, North America and elsewhere small to medium-sized enterprises (SMEs) engaged in artisan (low-volume) production of foods characterised by their organoleptic properties (taste, smell, appearance), embeddedness in place and tradition and short supply chains has been extensively discussed (Sage, 2003; Renting, Marsden and Banks, 2003; Maye, Kneafsey and Holloway, 2007). Studies informed by conventions theory have drawn attention to the significance of nature (Murdoch, Marsden and Banks, 2000); the importance of place-based labelling (Parrott, Wilson and Murdoch, 2002; Barham, 2003); and the role of aesthetics (Murdoch and Miele, 2004a) and networks (Murdoch and Miele, 2004b). Together, they emphasise the significance of a relational governance of food grounded in personal ties, local attachments, methods of production and trustworthiness.

This artisan speciality sector consequently embraces a more diverse set of criteria of quality that are far from all agreed at international level (as disputes between the United States and European Union over protected designation origin labelling demonstrates (Barham, 2003)), nor even between countries within the European Union. Here it has been noted that there is a sharp contrast between the countries of Southern Europe – where the prevailing associations are with the territorial, social and cultural embeddedness of foods and marked by more benign regulatory arrangements – and the North of Europe – where quality criteria are more strongly oriented toward industrial performance and economic efficiency and where regulation is more strict (Parrott, Wilson and Murdoch, 2002). The Republic of Ireland illustrates this latter approach, with those agencies of the state responsible for governing the food sector strongly committed to the implementation of science-based food safety regulations.

This chapter uses an understanding of conventions to compare the quality designations constructed around one artisan food product: Irish raw cow's milk farmhouse cheese. It is argued that the composition and configuration of these quality conventions constitutes the basis of contrasting governmentalities of this product: a command and controlstyle 'top-down' regulation imposed by a state agency; and a relational, co-responsible form of governance utilised by actors within this food chain. Towards the end of the chapter a case study is used to illustrate the tensions between these two modes of evaluating quality and the way in which their contestation has been addressed in a court of law.

Conventions of quality

As noted above, a focus upon the way qualities are combined and aligned within products and goods has emerged from conventions theory (Boltanski and Thévenot, 1991; Salais and Storper, 1992; Storper and Salais, 1997; Wilkinson, 1997; Thévenot, Moody and Lafaye, 2000; Thévenot, 2001, 2002, 2005). Recurrent situations of production and exchange involving actors within a context of uncertainty and indeterminacy reveal a panoply of practices, routines, agreements, trade-offs and mutual understandings. Unlike mainstream economic theory that considers behaviour to constitute a rational response to an informational universe dominated by price signals, conventions theory acknowledges that individuals may foreclose their subjective interpretations of the world and take their cues from the behaviour of others (Morand, 2006). Thus coordination emerges from common judgement, and far from constituting a fixed and universal understanding of quality it reflects a cognitive approach in which actors are brought together in specific relation to a particular world of justification and evaluation. Naturally, a 'precondition of coordination' is that participants agree to the qualities of products bought or sold, and in the absence of such agreement exchange does not take place (Storper and Salais, 1997: 38).

Put simply, a customer looking for a highly specialised, high-value good is unlikely to be satisfied by vendors of anonymous, mass products produced on the grounds of functionality and low price.

The contribution of convention theory is that it emphasises the inherent qualities of a product as well as its price and quantity; it acknowledges the uncertainty surrounding actor coordination and to which conventions are a strategic response; and it demonstrates the significance of other motivations to production beyond neo–classical profit-maximising rationality (Wilkinson, 1997). Conventions theory is not, however, a theory of consensus where conventions guarantee automatic agreement. Recognising the existence of conflict within and between logics of quality and, in particular, the possible tyranny of an overwhelming worth (and its associated tests of qualification) offers possible avenues of compromise (Morand, 2006).

Boltanski and Thévenot (1991) originally outlined six historically based 'worlds' within the regime of justification. More recently, new conventions have been added (a 'connectionist' order of worth indicating a 'new spirit of capitalism' as well as an order of information worth (Thévenot 2005)). Yet taking as a point of departure the work of Thévenot, Moody and Lafaye (2000) that employs seven categories of conventions in a comparative study of two environmental disputes, these appear to offer the most robust principles each with their own set of qualifications through which to develop the analysis here. Briefly, these comprise:

- Commercial or *market* worth where evaluation is based on price and where the elementary relation is exchange. Qualification rests on competitiveness, with human engagement based on purchasing power and the desire to appropriate, and goods are detached from place.
- In speaking of *domestic* worth evaluation is based on reputation and trust. Here, goods remain attached to a past ('tradition') and to place (locality). It is not used here to encompass attributes owned by brands but to exemplify direct personal connection between people. As shall be seen, this constitutes a very important quality convention for artisan producers.
- Goods inscribed with *industrial* qualities are judged by scientific standards of technical efficiency and reliability (uniformity). Social actors exist here with professional expertise and knowledge is concerned with calculation, measurement and statistics. Science-based narratives of quality place great store on performance in this category.

- In the world of public opinion, objects are signs such as trademarks, brands and packaging. Actors are linked by their cognitive capacity to recognise and understand these signs. The test of public opinion is based on *renown* and reputation.
- *Civic* qualities are concerned with the health and safety of people, their collective welfare. People engage with this world through demands for equality and the protection of rights.
- The quality of *inspiration* involves judgements that draw on passion, emotion and creativity. Here, inspired (or inspiring) individuals can make powerful statements or claims that articulate a common good.
- Finally, a 'green' justification speaks to contemporary concerns for the environment that would be measured by ecosystem health and sustainability. This recent addition to Thévenot's orders of worth echoes Latour's proposal for an *ecological* regime (Latour, 1998).

It has been emphasised that there is no externally determined hierarchy between these different worlds; their legitimation proceeds by internal justification and qualification, and by external negotiation. Yet, because of the existence of heterogeneous logics governing the process by which quality is defined in any situation (Wilkinson, 1997), a plurality of worlds can co-exist. Ponte and Gibbon (2005) note how multiple justifications of action can occur at the same time and different worlds can overlap. Allaire argues that this plurality of conventions coincides with the 'polymorphic world emerging from the "quality turn"' (Allaire, 2004: 89). Yet, despite circumstances where multiple conventions co-exist under a particular logic of quality, elsewhere a singular order of worth might prevail. In the discussion that follows the chapter will draw upon available evidence to argue that the state agency responsible for regulating artisan cheese makers in Ireland has demonstrated an overwhelming interest in the industrial convention of quality and this has resulted in a 'command and control' style of government. This sharply conflicts with alternative constructions of quality comprising a plurality of conventions and which results in an utterly different conception of governance.

Raw milk cheese in Ireland

Approximately 16.5 million tonnes of cheese is produced worldwide annually, of which Europe accounts for just over half (Fox and McSweeney, 2004) and this includes 700,000 tonnes made from raw milk (Grappin and Beuvier, 1997). Cheese is generally a very safe product in which the infrequency of large, cheese-associated outbreaks of human illness is notable, especially when compared to the record for cooked meat products (Donnelly, 2001; Nestle, 2003). However, the microbiological safety of raw milk cheese remains a highly contested issue. In the early 1990s there was debate within the European Union and the Codex Alimentarius Commission for the mandatory pasteurisation of all dairy products (Dixon, 2000) and there remains a powerful scientific discourse opposed to the continued availability of raw milk cheese.

In the countries of Southern Europe national bodies have designated such cheeses as being distinctive products of local origin with clearly defined methods of production and are regarded as cultural assets by their governments. In Northern Europe, however, the landscape is populated by fewer specialist cheese makers who have not only faced overwhelming market competition from industrial standardised production, but regulatory harassment from the food safety authorities (Cunynghame, 2001). It is ironic that while the rural development discourse in Europe is increasingly positive about small food businesses providing the basis of economic regeneration in peripheral areas (Ilberry and Kneafsey, 1999; Ilberry, Maye, Kneafsey, Jenkins and Walkley, 2004), food safety regulations impose significant obstacles to their economic viability.

In Ireland milk and milk products have always fulfilled a significant role in the diet (Sexton, 1998). However, from the seventeenth century decades of political and agrarian upheaval saw the decline of cheese making for local consumption and the development of the provision trade in which Ireland increasingly exported its farm produce in the form of salted beef and salted butter. Although cheese making returned in the early twentieth century as an industrial activity of the large dairy cooperatives, it was only from the 1970s and 1980s that farmhouse cheese reappeared. This was the result of incomers buying small farm holdings in remote rural locations, especially in the west and southwest, and who began making cheese on their kitchen stoves as a way of creating a livelihood by which to survive. The cheeses they created were a diverse range reflecting the personalities and origins of their producers. Gradually their numbers swelled and an association, *Cais*, was created to act as a forum and lobbying body. The artisan nature of the process, involving a hand made element with upper limits on quantities of milk used and volume of cheese produced, has always been an important defining characteristic of the sector.

The introduction into Irish law of Directive 92/46/EEC in January 1997 was to form the cornerstone of food safety regulation in the dairy sector. The legislation governs every aspect of the sector, from the health and hygiene of the dairy herd to the labelling of finished products (FSAI, 2006). Overall, the principal enforcement duties reside with the Department of Agriculture and Food (DAF). Unfortunately it is fair to say that an institutional culture of deep suspicion has existed towards the farmhouse cheese makers, especially those using raw milk. The prevailing view within DAF was that small-scale producers were unconventional, maverick and 'alternative'. This seemed to justify the tighter domestic legislation, which was considerably stricter than the requirements set out in 92/46/EEC.[1] The introduction of the legislation had a big impact on the farmhouse cheese sector; many producers using raw milk felt obliged to introduce pasteurisation, while others left the business altogether, unable to make the level of investments necessary to achieve the standards required. Currently, there are thought to be up to ninety small farmhouse cheese makers in Ireland using cow, goat and ewe's milk, though fewer than fifteen continue to use raw cow's milk, which is the focus of the study here.

Farmhouse cheese makers have formed the backbone of the alternative food network in Ireland, due to their number, their organisation and lobbying, and because of the high regard in which their products are held by food writers, cheesemongers and consumers both within the country and internationally. Though most continue to rely on short food supply chains selling through local, regional and spatially extended networks, some have seized the opportunity to undertake contracts to supply corporate retailers. Despite meeting the strict microbiological audits of retailers, the DAF maintains a close scrutiny of raw milk cheese makers, and in the next section the chapter characterises its evaluation of quality.

A singular view of quality: the government department

Only government food is safe food (Salatin, 2004)

State-led regulation is responsible for the interpretation, implementation and enforcement of international guidelines and directives, although considerable differences in application exist between states, reflecting the particular balance of structural factors and cultural traditions, especially agricultural, culinary and gastronomic. The prevailing feature of recent years, however, has been the rise of a science-based food safety narrative that has dwarfed all other food policy issues (Lang and Rayner, 2003).

The series of food safety crises that spread from the United Kingdom across Europe from the late 1980s introduced far-reaching regulatory and institutional reform involving the creation of food safety authorities at national and at EU level (Van Zwanenberg and Millstone, 2003; Barling, 2004). In an effort to restore consumer confidence in the food supply chain these new and reformed institutions have vociferously embraced a discourse of 'sound science' in their pursuit of food safety. A science-based approach to food safety is principally concerned with risk assessment, which involves the identification of hazards (e.g. microbial infections, pesticide residues, allergens), determining exposure of the population to that hazard and calculating the balance of risk to benefit and cost. This measurable quality of risk is what enables science-based food safety to represent itself as objective and neutral (Nestle, 2003).

As Harvey, McMeekin and Warde (2004) observe, there are many dimensions of concern besides that of safety: nutrition and health; culinary and aesthetic values; animal welfare and other ethical questions about practices in the food chain; as well as environmental damage. Yet science-based decision making and risk assessment have become the dominant and universal discourse across all regulatory levels. Indeed, science appears to have achieved an unassailable platform of authority and influence in relation to policy making, particularly since the hitherto voluntary food safety standards of the Codex Alimentarius Commission have acquired legal status under the World Trade Organisation (WTO) (Busch and Bain, 2004; Buonanno, 2006).

In an era of generalised reflexive anxiety (Beck, 1992, 1995) science not only provides the authoritative reassurance needed to assuage public fears but also serves as a political resource to endorse policy decisions about what constitutes safe food (Van Zwanenberg and Millstone, 2003). Thus emphasis is placed upon the microbiological dangers of food contaminated with pathogens such as *Listeria* or *Salmonella*, but not on the risks presented by genetically modified organisms or on the use of recombinant growth hormones in livestock (Rowell, 2003). Invariably, as Marsden (2003) has observed, the food safety paradigm puts into place, in a highly interventionary and bureaucratic fashion, policies that effectively police the food system in ways that make it seem more hygienic. The basis of such regulation has been generally located in appeals to 'science' as the universally legitimate and politically neutral justification. But science is increasingly challenged by economic, social and political arguments in managing food risks (Mol and Bulkeley, 2002). Ultimately scientific risk assessments involve value judgements – for example, in cost-benefit analyses (CBAs), while there is not always consensus over acceptable limits, tolerances or how test procedures are to be conducted (Khachatourians, 2001).

Thus, with regard to characterising DAF's view of quality, and its putative choice of qualified conventions, it is evident that scientific measurement – with technical performance judged by reference to microbiological, chemical and other standards of safe food – constitutes the most important tests of qualification. This demonstrates the superiority of the industrial order of worth, which also places great store by uniformity and consistency. A food product that changes with the season – reflecting the absence of denaturing processes such as pasteurisation – is invariably viewed with suspicion.

A second test of quality would arguably concern the integrity of values and brands ('renown'), not of the farmhouse cheese producers, but of 'Ireland plc'. This has been a favoured term of DAF functionaries who are anxious to defend the status quo of conventional agriculture and the large agribusiness companies such as Kerry Foods, Glanbia and Avonmore. The message, stated on more than one occasion to farmhouse cheese makers, is that their production methods represent a danger to the reputation of Irish food exports. Clearly this is also closely related to a concern with maintaining economic performance within the commercial world, represented by the market order of worth.

It is recognised that DAF is being used here as the sole competent agency, presented as a rather monolithic entity and without reference to overlapping or competing areas of interest and enforcement involving other institutions of government. Clearly, different state agencies may not always share the same outlook, reflecting their own sectoral interests. For example, Bord Bia, the state-sponsored body responsible for promoting Irish food especially abroad, takes a more positive view of the Irish farmhouse cheese sector. It recognises the high regard in which the cheese is held internationally, and happily uses imagery of artisans labouring against a natural landscape in its efforts to secure large volume sales of beef and other agricommodities into distant markets. Moreover, the creation of the Food Safety Authority of Ireland (FSAI) was heralded as representing a new, science-based and independent organisation capable of delivering a seamless guarantee of food safety from farm to fork. Yet the maintenance of a rather narrow and conservative approach to consumer protection that has resulted in the defence of the mainstream food system noted elsewhere (Barling and Lang, 2003) has not fundamentally altered either the institutional architecture or the prevailing values of risk management by the Irish state (Taylor, 2003). Consequently, the lead agency dealing with the farmhouse cheese sector remains DAF, and it has pursued a 'top-down', command and control-style approach to the sector, expressing little interest in any of the remaining conventions of quality (domestic, inspiration, civic or ecological).[2]

A plurality of conventions and relational governance

It is now well established that alternative food networks, of which Irish raw milk farmhouse cheese producers constitute a significant element, demonstrate a number of critical attributes. First, the food products are associated with particular places and this establishes both their ecologically embedded character ('naturalness') and the reassurance of traceability. Secondly, they are produced using high-quality ingredients with the objective of achieving the best possible aesthetic properties – taste, smell and appearance. Thirdly, the products often move through a network that ties together producers, knowledgeable distributors, committed retailers and informed and conscious consumers united by a sense of social connectivity, trust and mutual regard.

While this would meet the tests of qualification of the domestic order of worth, it is important to note, following Wilkinson, that the qualification of products in turn presupposes the qualification of the producers themselves. Quality control, he argues, 'is guaranteed preferentially through the consolidation of network arrangements and the development of relationships based on trust' (Wilkinson, 1997: 331). In this regard, network arrangements constitute a vital aspect of the logic of quality of artisan food producers. While some attention has been placed upon the 'alternative' character of food networks (Holloway, Kneafsey, Venn, Cox, Dowler and Tuomainen, 2005; Watts, Ilberry and Maye, 2005; Maye, Kneafsey and Holloway, 2007), it is suggested here that a vital property of such networks is their *relational* character, particularly the way in which responsibility is extended in an active form throughout the network.

The emergence of the social concept of risk (Beck, 1992, 1995) gained currency as a means of making sense of human-made disasters involving technology, nature and society. At the same time risk invokes its complement: 'the responsibility that needs to be taken for the collective definition and social organisation of such processes as well as their products and especially their consequences' (Strydom, 1999a: 33). Following the work of Karl-Otto Apel (see Apel, 1996), Strydom (1999b, 2000) uses the notion of co-responsibility as a mobilisable form of responsibility, in which the perception of a problem is framed and communicated in such a way that it is assumed that all those involved equally bear co-responsibility for the consequences and side effects of collective activity. In relation to raw milk cheese this would extend responsibility in a number of directions and to a variety of critical points, objects and actors throughout the entire food chain. The construction of an ethically responsible frame of action, effectively extending from 'farm to fork', begins with the health and feeding practices of milking animals and ends with the way the consumer stores and prepares the food prior to the final act of ingestion. Note that such a relational conception of co-responsibility far exceeds the requirements of a Hazard Analysis and Critical Control Points (HACCP) system[3] and its completion of record sheets; it represents a vigilance and a commitment over the integrity of the entire network.

Recognising the relational properties of food networks, such as that involving raw milk cheese makers, offers some deeper insights into the logic of quality of such producers:

- It underpins the significance of craftsmanship, of the vernacular or tacit knowledge that producers develop by working with their materials over a sustained period of time. Appreciation for other kinds of knowledge other than that represented by an instrumental scientific expertise has been an important lesson from the social construction of science (Wynne, 1996; Eden, 1998). The sense of it being 'well-made' and functionally appropriate (Harvey, McMeeking and Warde, 2004) constitutes an overriding consideration for producers in evaluating quality.
- It reveals the importance that the scientific–industrial outlook attaches to the 'black box' of technology, which has the power to outflank nature, render materials safe and provide for public reassurance. In relation to the case here, the 'black box' is that of pasteurisation, which is believed to rectify all risks arising from dangerous milk (the result of poor animal husbandry, carelessness in the milking parlour and so on). It overlooks the evidence that post-pasteurisation contamination is a significant area of risk in the dairy sector (Nestle, 2003).
- It recovers the esteem of human labour in food production for, unlike industrial plants where a high degree of automation eliminates much of the potential source of contamination from people, farmhouse cheese production involves a large number of manual operations. This requires a high level of vigilance and shared responsibility among all those involved. It also brings into sharper relief the inspirational and creative elements involved in the creation of these foods.

In a very material way co-responsibility extends to the final consumer of the product. Unlike conventional food systems in which the consumer has a negligible engagement beyond selection from a wide range of similar standardised products, consumers who choose to buy raw milk cheese presumes a more conscious act of involvement. Indeed, within face-to-face short supply chains (e.g. farmers' markets), purchase brings with it opportunities for the grant and pursuit of regard (Sage, 2003, 2007; Kirwan, 2004). The extension of co-responsibility to the consumer in such networks represents a more authentic construction of a 'farm to fork' regime than is generally the case with conventional food safety models.

How might this logic of quality inform the selection of suitably qualified conventions? Certainly, it would appear that the 'domestic' qualifies by right as utterly central to the network. Thereafter, however, individual producers place different emphasis on the tests of qualification that motivate them. Arguably, all demonstrate strong 'inspirational' attributes, being passionate about what they do – though for some, official hostility has triggered a discourse of justification rooted in the struggle for equality and the protection of basic rights (civic convention). Others (by no means all) demonstrate strong green credentials – having invested, for example, in the installation of wetland systems for dealing with their liquid waste streams. All enjoy a degree of renown, actively seeking to extend their reputation through national and international peer review (cheese awards) and widen their market. Although their ideology is not market driven, they nevertheless must be mindful of revenue generation in order to maintain the viability of their business and their livelihood. Finally, a statutory requirement to meet industrial tests of qualification (microbiological and other laboratory measures of performance) completes the inclusion of this convention in the hierarchy.

The battlefield of quality and regulation: a case study

In 2002 a small West Cork business making a Swiss-style raw milk cheese ran into considerable difficulty with DAF. Although it had sought to have its supplier herds tested for bovine tuberculosis before the beginning of the cheese making season – as it used only milk from cattle feeding on summer pasture – a test on one key supplier was only finally conducted in mid-August. This revealed a high incidence of positive reactors in the herd and consequently DAF issued a Detention Order, removing the cheese that had been made to that date (about 2 tonnes) from the food chain. WCNC, the business, appealed the order to the District Court, with a final judgement made at Cork Circuit Court in

December 2004. The case revealed the sharp differences in the construction of quality, in the processes of qualification and in their resulting expressions of government ('top-down' regulation versus a relational, co-responsible governance).

From the perspective of DAF, where quality is largely configured around the industrial mode of evaluation, scientific standards are used to establish vital tests of qualification. In this case, the most important was that of the tuberculin test used to establish that the herd was free of bovine TB. Given that the witnesses called by DAF to provide evidence to the courts were heavily weighted toward expertise in animal health, it was notable the degree to which the risk of infection in the cheese was extended from the positive reactor status of the animals. Indeed, it was made clear in court that the inclusion of unpasteurised milk from even one cow infected with *M. bovis* would be sufficient to condemn the entire cheese as unfit for human consumption. The witnesses called by DAF set great store by the claim that an absence of proof was not proof of absence. In other words, even if infection was not found in the animals, the milk, or the cheese it would not mean that it was not present, and therefore it could claim continuing 'reasonable doubt' that the cheese was unsafe.

Indeed, one might note a supreme confidence bordering on arrogance of state agencies proclaiming their commitment to science-based decision making and risk assessment. Armed with the sword of scientific standards and the shield of defending public health, such agencies have sought to police the food system in a highly interventionary and bureaucratic fashion in the pursuit of a hygienist conception of food quality. Unfortunately, their conception of science is beset by significant challenges, as noted earlier: increasingly complex and contested risk assessment process (Khachatourians, 2001); growing disputes around the different ways of evaluating risks, including the weight that should be given to public attitudes (Ansell and Vogel, 2006); and questions about the independence of science and its susceptibility to be compromised by commercial pressures and political agendas (Rowell, 2003; Skogstad, 2006).

Consequently, faced with an argument of reasonable doubt that the cheese was unsafe irrespective of the evidence, it was up to legal counsel for the cheese maker to prove otherwise. This involved:

- Challenging the perception that raw milk was always a dangerous source of pathogens
- Determining the extent of the *M. bovis* disease within the animals and the likelihood of their shedding infection into the milk

• Establishing that the cheese making process rendered the milk safe and yielded a product that was fit for human consumption.

In the course of addressing these points, requiring the presentation of recognised scientific evidence, the significance of a plurality of quality conventions also became apparent. This demonstrated that, far from the application of a narrow range of scientific tests of qualification, an array of issues involving craftsmanship, vigilance, co-responsibility, trust and the pursuit of functionally appropriate best practice characterised this cheese making business and its short supply chain. For example, as the quality of the cheese is only as good as the milk from which it is made, this business, like many artisan cheese makers without their own dairy herd, invests considerable time and effort carefully selecting the most suitable farmers within the vicinity from which to source. These farmers must not only employ high standards of hygiene in their milking parlours, but vigilance in managing all aspects of their dairy herd and the pastures (and supplements) on which they feed.

This contrast in perspective was first illustrated in relation to raw milk. The FSAI had itself published a study reporting on the high level of consumption of unpasteurised milk by farm families with their own dairy herds – 84 per cent of families bring a jug or churn from the milking parlour to the kitchen (FSAI, 2005). Yet, if M. bovis was so widespread (5,000 infected herds nationally) and following the argument that even the milk of one positive reactor animal in a bulk tank would be sufficient to spread the infection, how did this account, asked counsel for the cheese maker, for such a low level of infection within the human population (no more than six cases per year)? The response by witnesses for DAF simply referred to the possibility of dormancy in the human population.

This raised a second issue concerning the degree of development of the disease in the infected herd. Here, the court learned about the contraction of the disease in cattle and the signs of its level of development. This usually begins in the lung with the identification of characteristic lesions and the lymph nodes then progresses through other parts of the body. Given the regime of yearly testing in Ireland (and twice yearly on herds supplying raw milk for cheese making) it was noted by witnesses from both sides that advanced infection is no longer common. Thus, it is unusual to find infection as far as the supermammary glands associated with the udder and the milk secretion capabilities of the animal.[4]

The forty-seven positive reactor animals were slaughtered in late September 2002 and their carcasses examined by a veterinary inspector: there were no signs of generalised TB.[5] Indeed, apart from the head, lung and other minor tissue, all of the carcasses were passed fit for human consumption and entered the food chain. This reveals a striking paradox, commented on by the District Court judge (Judge Finn), that the carcasses of animals infected with TB were passed fit for human consumption and entered the food chain in a raw state; yet the cheese was considered unfit and condemned for destruction. It also reveals a contradiction in a food safety policy that expects consumers to cook the meat thoroughly before eating, yet they are not permitted to buy a product in which the milk from many animals has been biochemically transformed rendering it safe for consumption.

Ultimately, this third area, concerning the microbiology and chemistry of cheese making and whether this effectively killed off any pathogens present in the milk, became the most critically contested issue in the case. This was in part due to the fact that little research has been done on the survival of *M. bovis* in cheese. However, during the court hearings a surrogate measure for *M. bovis* was used – *Mycobacterium avium* subsp. *paratuberculosis* (MAP) – which shows more than 90 per cent similarity except that *M. bovis* is less tolerant of heat and acid. Adversarial exchanges centred largely upon the degree to which the characteristics of MAP could be extended to *M. bovis,* particularly through challenge testing, laboratory-based experiments involving the inoculation of cheeses with a precise number of cells and monitoring their rate of decay. A distinguished Professor of dairy science from the United States who had been brought over to give expert testimony in support of DAF was taken through one of his own published scientific papers that had reported on experimental work in which the combined anti-microbial effects of salt, acid, heat and curing time in a soft cheese eliminated the injected level of MAP within sixty days. When then invited to comment on the conditions in the cheese at issue in the case, which would all point to a more rapid reduction in MAP (or *M. bovis*), he would not be drawn: 'It is extremely hazardous to extrapolate a different organism, different cheese, different production.' When reminded that *M. bovis* was less tolerant than MAP, he responded, 'the chain of evidence is far too weak, all assumptions can be challenged. It is rational to accept the food safety experts rather than a single research paper which can be fallible' (quotations from Court transcripts). In other words, the evidence was too weak to prove the cheese was safe, but incontrovertible through assertion that it was unsafe. It is also revealing how this senior scientist was reluctant to stand over his own research, as well as that conducted by other scientists that had come to similar conclusions regarding the elimination of MAP and instead sought sanctuary in the community of 'food safety experts'.

Judge Finn was swayed by the scientific case presented by counsel for the cheese maker, and in quashing the Detention Order noted that he was convinced both by the quality of the milk and by the antimicrobial effects of the cheese making and maturation process. Yet within days of this ruling the FSAI issued a Prohibition Order against the sale of the cheese. While it initially sought, unsuccessfully, to have Judge Finn disqualify himself from this new hearing, it subsequently failed to contest the case when it came to court, the Order was cancelled and the FSAI were left to pay €30,000 in costs (Table 6.1). When asked by the *Irish Farmers Journal* how it could defend these actions, their reply was 'The FSAI believed that it was acting in the best interests of protecting consumer health' (IFJ, 2005: J2, 5). Following this, DAF then appealed the ruling on the cancellation of the Detention Order to Cork Circuit Court. At the close of the second hearing Judge O'Donnabhain provided his judgement and, in doing so, condemned the scientific credibility of DAF's case:

Table 6.1 Comparing constructions of quality as represented in the court case involving DAF and the West Cork cheese maker

DAF's construction of quality	The artisan food network's construction of quality
Primacy of industrial convention	Plurality of conventions
Unsafe unless proven safe by the producer (using recognised tests of qualification)	Safe unless proven unsafe by recognised authorities (due to relational / co-responsibility safeguards)
Number of positive reactors in herd: one would be sufficient to condemn the cheese regardless	Not the number but the extent of development of the infection in cattle that is important, regular testing and herd management
Pasteurisation of milk: a critical black box to render milk (and cheese) safe.	The complex microbial ecology of cheese (pH, salt, heat, maturation time) is proven as effective
Use of MAP as surrogate measure: cannot extrapolate from one micro-organism to another; trust the food safety experts	Reasonable to extend the behavioural characteristics of one micro-organism to another with a high level of similarity
Absence of proof is not proof of absence	Lack of presence implies absence
Need for command and control-style regulations in the interests of public health	Accountable, transparent and co-responsible self-regulation

I am convinced the Department are moving with a conviction to which all science must bend. There is a considerable gap in their science in what happens with the milk and the cheese making process. The Department's evidence is defective in relation to this cheese making process and is based entirely on speculation and the need to get the science to match the conviction that the cheese is contaminated. I am convinced...that there is no risk to the human population in eating the cheese. (Drawn from transcript of hearing, Cork Circuit Court, 13th December 2004)

Conclusion

The conventions approach recognises the contingent and contested nature of quality as comprising a shifting array of incommensurable characteristics that change according to movement through a food chain. Constructions of quality rely upon processes of qualification to determine particular properties of a product, and the selection of tests reflects the balance of power and authority at different stages in the food supply chain. Understanding a little more about the prevailing logic, mode of evaluation and resulting configuration of quality conventions at each stage reveals the extent and limits of power. For example, Marsden (2004) argues that the rise of corporate retailers has witnessed the development of highly competitive and sophisticated supply chains and food quality criteria, while government authorities restrict themselves to baseline food safety (see also Fulponi, 2006). Meanwhile, alternative, artisan-led short food supply chains develop 'a whole host of new quality conventions and certification systems in defiance of – in many ways in opposition to – the former two' (Marsden, 2004: 151).

The chapter certainly bears out Thévenot's claim that a conventions analysis helps to disclose forms of evaluation which are concealed under governance procedures, indicators pretending to value neutrality and power abuse arising from the tyranny of an overwhelming worth (Thévenot, 2005). In the case of the Irish Department of Agriculture's evaluation of raw milk farmhouse cheese, overwhelming importance is placed on meeting the tests of the industrial convention in the apparent interests of public health ('the power of numbers'), with few other considerations of quality involved. This tyrannical pursuit of 'no-germ' food imposes significant costs of compliance on small producers who, ironically, have been entirely marginal to the causes of the contemporary anxieties around food (Marsden, 2003).

Contrasting configurations of quality conventions provides a valuable insight into the deepening asymmetries of power between state, corporate retailers and artisan producers. At a time when regulatory powers are being further devolved to a wider range of public and private interest institutions, the governance of food is likely to become more contested and further intensify the 'competitive battlefield of quality, regulation and consumption' (Marsden, 2004: 151). It is by continuously drawing attention to these wider considerations of quality that the singular pre-occupation with risk and safety of food might be challenged. Drawing support from a multi-level governance system would allow speciality producers to defend the local both nationally and globally (Morgan, Marsden and J. Murdoch, 2006). Finally, by demonstrating the significance of the relational properties of food networks, especially the technical competence and moral authority to exercise a co-responsible form of risk management, it might even be possible to explore prospects for a new architecture of food governance sensitive to the plurality of quality conventions of artisan producers.

Notes

1 A number of issues raised by farmhouse cheese producers are indicative of this tighter regulation, although perhaps the most critical is their categorisation as 'milk processing establishments', which puts them on the same basis as the industrial dairies. Elsewhere in the European Union such producers are listed as 'limited capacity establishments', where derogations can be sought from aspects of the Directive.
2 In the interests of clarity and due to constraints of space the position of the Department has been sharply drawn and it is recognised that this does not necessarily reflect the position of its entire staff, either then or now. Indeed, the election of a new government in 2007 brought a new perspective to this Ministry, one that is more sympathetic to the challenges faced by small producers. However, this chapter is exclusively concerned with events and discourse prior to 2006.
3 HACCP is a tool used by food businesses to monitor procedures at vital points in the manufacturing process where food is susceptible to contamination.
4 It was noted by the court that milk from the herd was marked by a low total bacterial count, demonstrating good hygiene, and by a low somatic cell count, reinforcing claims that there was an absence of mastitis among the animals. Thus it was highly unlikely, argued counsel for WCNC and supported by veterinary experts called by that side, that M. bovis was present in the mammary glands and therefore in the milk. The chief scientific witness called by DAF responded, 'You cannot prove absence'.
5 It should be noted that tissue samples from the supermammary glands were taken from the slaughtered animals and sent for analysis to the National Veterinary Laboratory. These more scientifically advanced tests were conducted during November and December 2002. In January 2003 the cheese

maker received notice from DAF that some samples had proven positive for
M. bovis, which would have indicated more extensive development of the
disease in those animals, with the strong possibility of infecting the milk.
Such findings would have deterred many from proceeding with a legal appeal
against the Detention Order, though not in this case. Just a few weeks before
the first court hearing (in December 2003) the solicitor representing the
cheese maker was informed that a labelling error had been made and that
the tests had actually all proven negative.

References

Allaire, G. (2004) 'Quality in Economics: A Cognitive Perspective', in M.
    Harvey, A. McMeeking and A. Warde (eds.), *Qualities of Food* (Manchester:
    Manchester University Press).
Ansell, C. and D. Vogel (2006) 'The Contested Governance of European Food
    Safety Regulation', in C. Ansell and D. Vogel (eds.), *What's the Beef? The
    Contested Governance of European Food Safety* (Cambridge, MA: MIT
    Press).
Apel, K.-O. (1996) 'A Planetary Macro Ethics for Humanity: The Need,
    the Apparent Difficulty and the Eventual Possibility', in E. Mendieta (ed.),
    *Karl-Otto Apel: Selected Essays, Volume Two, Ethics and the Theory of
    Rationality* (Atlantic Highlands, NJ: Humanities Press).
Barham, E. (2003) 'Translating Terroir: The Global Challenge of French AOC
    Labelling', *Journal of Rural Studies*, 19, 127–38.
Barling, D. (2004) 'Food Agencies as an Institutional Response to Policy Failure
    by the UK and the EU', in M. Harvey, A. McMeeking and A. Warde (eds.),
    Qualities of Food (Manchester: Manchester University Press).
Barling, D. and T. Lang (2003) 'A Reluctant Food Policy? The First Five Years
    of Food Policy under Labour', *The Political Quarterly*, 74, 8–18.
Beck, U. (1992) *The Risk Society: Towards a New Modernity* (London: Sage).
Beck, U. (1995) *Ecological Politics in an Age of Risk* (Cambridge: Polity).
Boltanski, L. and L. Thévenot (1991) *De la justification: Les économies de la
    grandeur* (Paris: Gallimard).
Bulkeley, H. and M. Betsill (2003) *Cities and Climate Change: Urban Sustain-
    ability and Global Environmental Governance* (London: Routledge).
Buonanno, L. (2006) 'The Creation of the European Food Safety Authority',
    in C. Ansell and D. Vogel (eds.), *What's the Beef? The Contested Governance
    of European Food Safety* (Cambridge, MA: MIT Press).
Busch, L. (2000) 'The Moral Economy of Grades and Standards', *Journal of
    Rural Studies*, 16(3), 273–83.
Busch, L. and C. Bain (2004) 'New! Improved? The Transformation of the
    Global Agrifood System', *Rural Sociology*, 69(3), 321–46.
Callon, M., C. Méadel and V. Rabeharisoa (2002) 'The Economy of Qualities',
    Economy and Society, 31(2), 194–217.

Cidell, J. and H. Alberts (2006) 'Constructing Quality: The Multinational Histories of Chocolate', *Geoforum*, 37(6), 999–1007.

Cunynghame, A. (2001) 'British Cheese-Makers under Threat', *The Ecologist*, June.

Dixon, P. (2000) 'European Systems for the Safe Production of Raw Milk Cheese', Report presented to the Vermont Cheese Council, Montpelier, Vermont, available at: www.vtcheese.com/vtcheese/rawmilk_files/rawmilk. htm (accessed 6 August 2008).

Donnelly, C. W. (2001) 'Factors Associated with Hygienic Control and Quality of Cheeses prepared from Raw Milk: A Review', *Bulletin of the International Dairy Federation*, 369, 16–27.

Eden, S. (1998) 'Environmental Issues: Knowledge, Uncertainty and the Environment', *Progress in Human Geography*, 22(3), 425–32.

Fold, N. (2004) 'Spilling the Beans on a Tough Nut: Liberalization and Local Supply System Changes in Ghana's Cocoa and Shea Chains', in A. Hughes and S. Reimer (eds.), *Geographies of Commodity Chains* (London: Routledge).

Food Safety Authority of Ireland (FSAI) (2005) 'On Farm Study of Consumption of Unpasteurised Milk', available at: www.fsai.ie/publications/other/ unpasteurised_milk.asp (accessed 6 August 2008).

Food Safety Authority of Ireland (FSAI) (2006) 'Legislation – Milk and Milk-Based Products', available at: www.fsai.ie/legislation/food/legislation_milk. asp (accessed 6 August 2008).

Fox, P. and P. McSweeney (2004) 'Cheese: An Overview', in P. Fox, P. McSweeney, T. Cogan and T. Guinee (eds.), *Cheese: Chemistry, Physics and Microbiology, Third edition, Volume 1: General Aspects* (London: Elsevier).

Friedberg, S. (2003) 'Culture, Conventions and Colonial Constructs of Rurality in South-North Horticultural Trades', *Journal of Rural Studies*, 19, 97–109.

Fulponi, L. (2006) 'Private Voluntary Standards in the Food System: The Perspective of Major Food Retailers in OECD Countries', *Food Policy*, 31, 1–13.

Grappin, R. and E. Beuvier (1997) 'Possible Implications of Milk Pasteurisation on the Manufacture and Sensory Quality of Ripened Cheese', *International Dairy Journal*, 7, 751–61.

Harvey, M., A. McMeekin and A. Warde (2004) 'Introduction', in M. Harvey, A. McMeeking and A. Warde (eds.), *Qualities of Food* (Manchester: Manchester University Press).

Holloway, L., M. Kneafsey, L. Venn, R. Cox, E. Dowler and H. Tuomainen (2005) 'Possible Food Economies: Food Production–Consumption Arrangements and the Meaning of "Alternative"', Cultures of Consumption Working Paper Series, No. 25.

Hooghe, L. and G. Marks (2001) 'Types of Multi-Level Governance', *European Integration, Online Papers 5, 11*, available at: http://eiop.or.at/eiop/ texte/2001-011.htm (accessed 6 August 2008).

Ilberry, B. and M. Kneafsey (1999) 'Niche Markets and Regional Speciality Food Products in Europe: Towards A Research Agenda', *Environment and Planning*, 31, 2207–22.

Ilberry, B. and M. Kneafsey (2000) 'Producer Constructions of Quality in Regional Speciality Food Production: A Case Study from South West England', *Journal of Rural Studies*, 16, 217–30.

Ilberry, B., D. Maye, M. Kneafsey, T. Jenkins and C. Walkley (2004) 'Forecasting Food Supply Chain Developments in Lagging Rural Regions: Evidence from the UK', *Journal of Rural Studies*, 20, 331–44.

Irish Farmers Journal (IFJ) (2005) 'David and Goliath', *Irish Farmers Journal*, 2, 2 April.

Khachatourians, G. G. (2001) 'How Well Understood is the "Science" of Food Safety?', in P. Phillips and R. Wolfe (eds.), *Governing Food: Science, Safety and Trade* (Montreal: McGill–Queen's University Press).

Kirwan, J. (2004) 'Alternative Strategies in the UK Agro-Food System: Interrogating the Alterity of Farmers' Markets', *Sociologia Ruralis*, 44(4), 395–415.

Lang, T. and G. Rayner (2003) 'Food and Health Strategy in the UK: A Policy Impact Analysis', *The Political Quarterly*, 74, 66–75.

Latour, B. (1998) 'To Modernize or Ecologize? That is the Question', in B. Braun and N. Castree (eds.), *Remaking Reality: Nature at the Millennium* (London: Routledge).

Marsden, T. (2003) *The Condition of Rural Sustainability* (Assen: Royal Van Gorcum).

Marsden, T. (2004) 'Theorising Food Quality: Some Key Issues in Understanding its Competitive Production and Regulation', in M. Harvey, A. McMeeking and A. Warde (eds.), *Qualities of Food* (Manchester: Manchester University Press).

Maye, D., M. Kneafsey and L. Holloway (2007) 'Introducing Alternative Food Geographies', in D. Maye, L. Holloway and M. Kneafsey (eds.), *Alternative Food Geographies: Representation and Practice* (Oxford: Elsevier).

Mol, A. and H. Bulkeley (2002) 'Food Risks and the Environment: Changing Perspectives in a Changing Social Order', *Journal of Environmental Policy and Planning*, 4, 185–95.

Morand, F. (2006) 'Integrating Concepts of Institutions: A Comparative Introduction to Thévenot's Conventions', Eco-Innovation Working Paper, available at: www.eco-innovation.net (accessed 6 August 2008).

Morgan, K., T. Marsden and J. Murdoch (2006) *Worlds of Food: Place, Power, and Provenance in the Food Chain* (Oxford: Oxford University Press).

Morris, C. and C. Young (2004) 'New Geographies of Agro-Food Chains: An Analysis of UK Quality Assurance Schemes', in A. Hughes and S. Reimer (eds.), *Geographies of Commodity Chains* (London: Routledge).

Murdoch, J., T. Marsden and J. Banks (2000) 'Quality, Nature and Embeddedness: Some Theoretical Considerations in the Context of the Food Sector', *Economic Geography*, 76(2), 107–25.

Murdoch, J. and M. Miele (2004a) 'A New Aesthetic of Food? Relational Reflexivity in the "Alternative" Food Movement', in M. Harvey, A. McMeeking and A. Warde (eds.), *Qualities of Food* (Manchester: Manchester University Press).

Murdoch, J. and M. Miele (2004b) 'Culinary Networks and Cultural Connections: A Conventions Perspective', in A. Hughes and S. Reimer (eds.), *Geographies of Commodity Chains* (London: Routledge).

Nestle, M. (2003) *Safe Food: Bacteria, Biotechnology, and Bioterrorism.* (Berkeley, CA: University of California Press).

Parrott, N., N. Wilson and J. Murdoch (2002) 'Spatialising Quality: Regional Protection and the Alternative Geography of Food', *European Urban and Regional Studies*, 9(3), 241–61.

Ponte, S. and P. Gibbon (2005) 'Quality Standards, Conventions and the Governance of Global Value Chains', *Economy and Society*, 34(1), 1–31.

Raikes, P., M. Jensen and S. Ponte (2000) 'Global Commodity Chain Analysis and the French filière Approach: Comparison and Critique', *Economy and Society*, 29(3), 390–417.

Renting, H., T. Marsden and J. Banks (2003) 'Understanding Alternative Food Networks: Exploring the Role of Short Food Supply Chains in Rural Development', *Environment and Planning A*, 35(3), 393–411.

Rowell, A. (2003) *Don't Worry: Its Safe to Eat* (London: Earthscan).

Sage, C. (2003) 'Social Embeddedness and Relations of Regard: Alternative "Good Food" Networks in South West Ireland', *Journal of Rural Studies*, 19(1), 47–60.

Sage, C. (2007) 'Trust in Markets: Economies of Regard and Spaces of Contestation in Alternative Food Networks', in J. Cross and A. Morales (eds.), *Street Trade: Commerce in a Globalising World* (London: Routledge).

Salais, R. and M. Storper (1992) 'The Four "Worlds" of Contemporary Industry', *Cambridge Journal of Economics*, 16, 160–93.

Salatin, J. (2004) ' "Sound Science" is Killing Us', *Acres*, 34(4), 5–8.

Sexton, R. (1998) *A Little History of Irish Food* (London: Kyle Cathie).

Skogstad, G. (2006) 'Regulating Food Safety Risks in the European Union: A Comparative Perspective', in C. Ansell and D. Vogel (eds.), *What's the Beef? The Contested Governance of European Food Safety* (Cambridge, MA: MIT Press).

Storper, M. and R. Salais (1997) *Worlds of Production. The Action Frameworks of the Economy* (Cambridge, MA.: Harvard University Press).

Strydom, P. (1999a) 'The Civilisation of the Gene: Biotechnological Risk Framed in the Responsibility Discourse', in P. O'Mahony (ed.), *Nature, Risk and Responsibility: Discourses of Biotechnology* (Basingstoke: Macmillan).

Strydom, P. (1999b) 'The Challenge of Responsibility for Sociology', *Current Sociology*, 47(3), 65–82.

Strydom, P. (2000) *Risk, Environment and Society: Ongoing Debates, Current Issues and Future Prospects* (Buckingham: Open University Press).

Taylor, G. (2003) ' "From the Slurry to the Curry": The Politics of Food Regulation and Reform in Ireland', *Irish Studies in International Affairs*, 14, 149–64.

Thévenot, L. (2001) 'Organised Complexity: Conventions of Coordination and the composition of Economic Arrangements', *European Journal of Social Theory*, 4(4), 405–25.

Thévenot, L. (2002) 'Which Road to Follow? The Moral Complexity of an "Equipped" Humanity', in J. Law and A. Mol (eds.), *Complexities: Social Studies of Knowledge Practices* (Durham, NC: Duke University Press).

Thévenot, L. (2005) 'Convention School', in J. Beckert and M. Zafirovski (eds.), *International Encyclopaedia of Economic Sociology* (London: Routledge).

Thévenot, L., M. Moody and C. Lafaye (2000) 'Forms of Valuing Nature: Arguments and Modes of Justification in French and American Environmental Disputes', in M. Lamont and L. Thevénot (eds.), *Rethinking Comparative Cultural Sociology: Repertoires of Evaluation in France and the United States* (Cambridge: Cambridge University Press).

Van Zwanenberg, P. and E. Millstone (2003) 'BSE: A Paradigm of Policy Failure', *The Political Quarterly*, 74, 27–37.

Watts, M. and D. Goodman (1997) 'Agrarian Questions: Global Appetite, Local Metabolism: Nature, Culture and Industry in *fin-de-siècle* Agro-Food Systems', in D. Goodman and M. Watts (eds.), *Globalising Food: Agrarian Questions and Global Restructuring* (London: Routledge).

Watts, D., B. Ilberry and D. Maye (2005) 'Making Reconnections in Agro-Food Geography: Alternative Systems of Food Provision', *Progress in Human Geography*, 29(1), 22–40.

Wilkinson, J. (1997) 'A New Paradigm for Economic Analysis?', *Economy and Society*, 26, 306–39.

Wynne, B. (1996) 'May the Sheep Safely Graze? A Reflexive View of the Expert–Lay Knowledge Divide', in S. Lash, B. Szerszynski and B. Wynne (eds.), *Risk, Environment and Modernity: Towards a New Ecology* (London: Sage).

7

Wasting Ireland and consuming sustainability: the 'Celtic Tiger' years and beyond

G. Honor Fagan

Introduction

This book addresses the culture of environmental politics through case study analysis of environmental discourse. This chapter critically addresses waste management, one of the most central environmental issues in the politics of the 'Celtic Tiger' years. It advances a multi-scalar analysis of the various actors involved in waste governance as they sought to deal with what has become known as the 'waste crisis', and identifies shifts and continuities within the counterposed sustainability and competitiveness paradigms in those years. The chapter examines the obstacles and opportunities afforded as the politics of governance shifted towards a communicative planning scenario. Of critical importance is the issue of sustainability, so to speak 'after the party' in the post-'Celtic Tiger' conjuncture. This chapter argues for prioritising, communicating and symbolising a 'green' component to Irish identity and developing a new reflective politics of consumption and a new approach to wasting.

From economic growth towards sustainability

Sustainable development as a concept contains two competing elements. The word 'development' can primarily refer to economic growth, increased production and increased profitability in production. On the other hand, 'sustainability' refers to a way of meeting our needs without compromising the capacity of the children of this generation to in turn meet its needs by depleting earth's resources or not taking into account its limitations. While sustainability is a nebulous concept, and has been critiqued for being so broad as to appear to be the conceptualisation of 'environmental politics gone astray' (Fisher and Hayer, 1999) there is evidence that to some extent indicators of sustainability will be quite concretely built into all future development.

The relevance of these distinctions becomes evident when one goes on to measure development. How does one evaluate a period of national economic growth in the twenty-first century? Economists typically measure it in terms of Gross Domestic Product (GDP). Sociologists typically measure it on the basis of increased household earnings, and other sociologists of a more radical persuasion measure it on the basis of increased equality in incomes, whether in terms of earnings between classes, spatially diverse locations, genders, or races. Increasingly at the micro-level citizens choose to understand, conceptualise and measure it on the basis of growth in their individual or family income, their increased spending and purchasing power and their greater access to social facilities such as education and health and their access and control over decision making in government policies that impact their lives and life chances. So there is variation – and, indeed, a politics – to measuring development.

Structures of economic development traditionally operate to increase production. Economic development is likewise dependent on growth in consumption, where the ability of consumers to buy the outputs from production is linked directly to the calculations on profit. While that equation works out quite well in the short term, it does not take into account the real material factor of the environment in which this structural activity is organised. In other words, it does not cost in the exploitation of the environment nor factor in the material reality of the earth as a limited resource, usually reduced by economists to mere 'externalities'. From a structural perspective it can be argued, then, that the prioritisation of economic growth has led to a total array of structural conditions that support production for profit regardless of the lack of sustainability of such patterns of production and consumption. However, more recently, an interesting shift is occurring at the macro-level of economic governance in the global era where measuring the success of growth through GDP indicators is being subtly but irreversibly altered. Now the argument is being developed, due to environmental pressures, for a shift from GDP indicators to 'smart' GDP measurements where good things count positively and bad things count negatively (McGlade, 2007).

Measurements of GDP are inaccurate and misleading given that it can soar after a natural disaster, for example, because of the inevitable increase in production to rebuild after the loss of human life and infrastructure. Given the current pressures on the environment, global sustainability necessitates the re-design of production and consumption patterns. So called 'smart' GDP (McGlade, 2007) indicators will drive this, regulating production in ways that provide opportunities for systemic changes in diets and lifestyles. The re-design is currently under development in the context of the action plans of the European Commission, such as the dual and interlinked development of the Action Plan on Sustainable Consumption and Production and the Action Plan on Sustainable Industrial Policy.

To feature sustainable development – or, from a more culturist perspective, to reinvent the 'Green Ireland' of song and Tourist Board nostalgia – a genuine conceptual paradigm shift is called for. While benefiting greatly from globalisation, there have been environmental downsides to Ireland's economic success that need to be reviewed. Waste has been, and is, generated at a series of spatial levels or scales, both long-term and attendant on the recent accelerated growth created by the 'Celtic Tiger'. A multiplex response in terms of the structures of production, governance, consumption patterns, scientific advances, national mindset and personal attitudes is required. The challenge is to plan and implement a waste future where Ireland takes up a leading position in the wider evolving green revolution. It would be a shame if the globally renowned cultural and social capital that has marked Ireland's success story was not now turned towards innovation for environmental sustainability in the approaching post-consumerist phase of globalisation.

One way of engaging the degree to which Ireland is approaching sustainability in its policies is to focus on the period of the 'Celtic Tiger' economic growth and observe its growth in the context of sustainability. The policy making context has shown evidence of a shift from government to governance, a shift that involves decentralisation and delegation of deliberation and decision making from the parliamentary complex to a wider range of intermediate institutions embracing greater levels of societal participation. A move towards communicative planning has accompanied this shift. In this chapter, the manner in which the various social actors in the Republic of Ireland have approached the issue of waste within this communicative framework will be explored. In particular, it will examine how sustainability principles have been addressed in relation to production, consumption and waste policy in the 'Celtic Tiger' years, roughly in the decade from 1996 to 2006, considering the various forces that have shaped waste policy and the degree to which rival considerations of sustainability or competitiveness entered calculations.

Economic growth and waste in the 'Celtic Tiger' years

Internationally, the pattern of waste flows in the 1980s and 1990s was marked by wholesale increases in the production of waste, with particularly fast increases in the richer nations. US waste generation grew from 2.7 pounds per person in 1960 to 3.3 pounds per person in 1980 and up to 4.4 pounds per person in 1993.[1] Over 1.8 billion tonnes of waste was generated each year in Europe, equivalent to 3.5 tonnes per person. This was mainly made up of waste coming from households, commercial activities (e.g. shops, restaurants, hospitals, etc.), industry (e.g. pharmaceutical companies, clothes manufacturers, etc.), agriculture (e.g. slurry), construction and demolition projects, mining and quarrying activities and from the generation of energy.

In all EU countries, the quantity of waste is continuously increasing; however, in the Republic of Ireland there was an above-average growth rate in its production due to the economic boom of the 'Celtic Tiger'. Between 1995 and 1998, waste flows in Ireland increased by a phenomenal 89 per cent. Clearly one principal child of the economic boom was unsightly and unsustainable waste production, and equally clearly the debris of globalised Ireland's production and consumption boom left a visible malign geographic footprint. The position on waste management in 2000 was, according to an EPA staff member interviewed then, that:

> We have done very little in the waste area through the 1970s and 1980s, and it wasn't until the 1990s that any kind of focus started on waste. And because we didn't start when we should have, we are twenty-five years behind others. (Fagan, O'Hearn, McCann and Murray, 2000: 13)

In other words, before the Republic of Ireland was networked into a European system of waste management it was simply not governing waste, it was 'disposing' of it in landfill sites. Figure 7.1 shows which sectors produce waste in the Republic of Ireland.

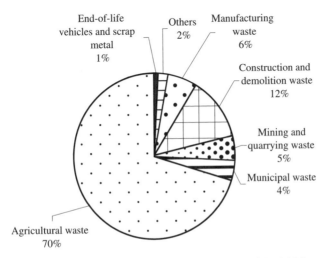

Fig. 7.1 National profile of waste generated in 2004

Agricultural waste, at 70 per cent of the total, constitutes the largest proportion, although it has decreased from previous years. Construction and demolition waste constitutes the next biggest proportion, at 12 per cent of the total. The bulk of the 15 per cent increase in total generation of waste between 2001 and 2004 is attributed to the trebling of the waste produced in this category. Municipal waste, which got a disproportionate amount of attention in the 'waste crisis' debate, constitutes only 4 per cent of the waste produced. However, it too is fast increasing.

Municipal waste increased by 1 per cent from 2001 to 2002, but from 2002 to 2003 it increased by 10 per cent, where for the first time it exceeded 3 million tonnes (EPA, 2003: 6).[2] While municipal waste did increase in 2004 by 4 per cent (Table 7.1), a new statistical calculation on the part of the EPA leaves the overall figure still just over 3 million tonnes (EPA, 2004: vii).

At the level of individual consumption, each person in the Republic of Ireland in the year 2000 'produced' practically double the European average of 1 kg of municipal waste per day. The Irish EPA (EPA, 2002) estimated that in 2000 every citizen of the Republic produced an average of 600 kg of waste a year. The average generation of household waste per person was calculated at 398 kg *per capita* in 2003, still increasing from 2002, but with just a 2 per cent rate of increase (EPA, 2003: 8).

Table 7.1 Irish total waste generated (2004)

Waste category	2004	
	Tonnes	**%**
Construction and demolition waste	11,167,599	13.1
Manufacturing waste	5,044,243	5.9
Mining and quarrying waste	4,044,511	4.7
Municipal waste	3,034,566	3.6
End-of-life vehicles and scrap metal	491,960	0.6
Hazardous waste	366,291	0.4
Contaminated soil	307,340	0.4
Energy, gas and water supply waste	284,647	0.3
Dredge spoils	238,565	0.3
Drinking water sludges	59,741	0.1
Urban wastewater sludges	42,298	0.0
Sub-total: non-agricultural waste	25,081,660	29.4
Agricultural waste	60,175,025	70.6
Total	85,256,685	–

(Source: EPA, 2004)

The methodologies for calculation have been changed and there have been improvements in the collection of data from local authorities since 2003 (EPA, 2004: 8). However, while there is variation between countries' calculation methods, and data to some extent may not be comparable, still Ireland ranks as the largest *per capita* generator of municipal waste in the European Union (EEA, 2005).

Applying the concept of environmental sustainability to recent economic development trends in Ireland highlights the boom's disastrous eco-social consequences. Are there any real achievements in terms of waste reduction given increased pressure from the European Union to regulate waste? Table 7.2 shows the major waste indicators for 2001, 2002 and 2003. It provides figures for the waste produced, recovered and disposed of in landfill for these years, during which there has in fact been an implementation of waste management policy.

While the figures highlight the huge efforts to manage waste, particularly at the three lower levels of the waste hierarchy, as in the rest of Europe these efforts are not effectively counteracting the increases. National and EU regulations are not enough in themselves to stem flows in waste.

In addition to this policy failure, there has been in Ireland considerable illegal waste activity recorded since the introduction of the Waste Management Act 1996. Large-scale dumping occurred in Wicklow from

Table 7.2 Irish waste indicators (2001–3)

Indicator	2001	2002	2003
Municipal waste			
Municipal waste collected/ person (tonnes)	0.59	0.61	0.65
Municipal waste arising/ person (tonnes)	0.69	0.69	0.77
Disposal rate for household and commercial waste collected (%)	86.7	79.3	71.6
Recovery rate for household and commercial waste collected (%)	13.3	20.7	28.4
Number of landfills accepting municipal waste (%)	48	39	35
Number of bring banks (%)	1,436	1,636	1,692

Table 7.2 *Continued*

Indicator	2001	2002	2003
	Household waste		
Household waste collected/ person (tonnes)	0.34	0.36	0.36
Household waste arising/ person (tonnes)	0.37	0.39	0.41
Disposal rate for household waste (%)	94.4	90.7	86.9
Recovery rate for household waste (%)	5.6	9.3	13.1
	Commercial waste		
Commercial waste collected/person (tonnes)	0.25	0.25	0.29
Disposal rate for commercial waste collected (%)	76.2	62.5	52.7
Recovery rate for commercial waste collected (%)	23.8	37.5	47.4
	Packaging waste		
Best estimate of total quantity arising (tonnes)	872,917	899,125	1,006,287
Packaging waste arising/ person (tonnes)	0.223	0.229	0.257
Best estimate of packaging waste recovered (tonnes)	221,266	296,389	419,600
Packaging waste recovered/ person (tonnes)	0.056	0.076	0.107
National recovery rate (%)	25.3	33	41.7
	Hazardous waste		
Quantity of hazardous waste exported (tonnes)	275,309	249,439	389,199
	226,904 recovery	203,156 recovery	224,749 recovery
	47,979 disposal	42,419 disposal	162,821 disposal
	475 unspecified	3,364 unspecified	1,629 unspecified

(Source: EPA, 2004: 28)

1997 to 2002, and in 2005 there were still twenty-five unauthorised landfills and fifteen unauthorised waste handling facilities (EPA, 2005: 1). There has also been considerable cross-border illegal movement of waste. Statistics for 2003 show that one in five households were either not served, or were not availing themselves of, a waste collection service, which in itself could involve almost 300,000 tonnes of waste unaccounted for annually (EPA, 2005: 2). The EPA report on *The Nature and Extent of Unauthorised Waste Activity in Ireland* (EPA, 2005) indicates that first the nature of illegal activity is changing, in that large-scale illegal dumping no longer takes place, that illegal cross-border movement of waste has been reduced significantly, but that there has been increased unauthorised waste collection, fly-tipping (sporadic, small-scale dumping) and uncontrolled burning of waste. It is estimated that seventeen of the twenty-five unauthorised landfills contained commercial and industrial waste, with construction and demolition waste accounting for the greatest level of illegal activity. Over 80 per cent of the waste found in unauthorised landfills was construction and demolition waste and local authorities had received more complaints about this type of waste than about all the other streams put together. Given these figures on illegal activity, the EPA strongly advocates enforcement as key to progress on waste management (EPA, 2002: 2). However, while enforcement in these cases is indeed a priority, it is clearly the mark of the failure of Irish policy in general. Focusing on enforcement is indeed a distraction given the seismic shifts necessary to address the problem of waste and to engineer a sustainable future for Ireland. Having looked at the material reality of waste production and disposal in the 'Celtic Tiger' years, the chapter now turns to the emerging opportunities and obstacles in the policy arena.

Technocratic problem solving or communicative planning?

Ireland at the height of its economic boom moved into the grip of what has been commonly referred to as a 'waste management crisis' (Fagan, O'Hearn, McCann and Murray, 2001) in the late 1990s and the early 2000s. There were two aspects to this crisis. First, there was the material and environmental problem of the increase in the quantity and types of waste and, second, the interlocked problem of its management. With the European Union able to enforce sanctions on the nation-state and the national Government needing to radically change the direction and composition of waste flows, the drawing up and implementation of strategy quickly became an issue of governance at a national level.

Stoker argues that 'governance recognises the blurring of boundaries and responsibilities for tackling social and economic issues' (1998: 21). Government by central decree on the waste management issue was not an option since the Irish Government had moved to a governance model patterned on consensual politics and multi-agency partnerships. From this perspective, self-governing networks for the fulfilment of waste management functions were very much favoured by the Irish state. The capacity to 'get things done' did not simply rest on the power of Government to command, and commands would only be invoked in a last-instance scenario.

This reflects the European context where the communicative turn had begun to take effect in policy development. Consultation on policy was a legal requirement of the European Union, although the extent or parameters of that consultation were not legislated for. In the European governance scenario, planning, the main tool to change society, was to shift towards a collaborative or communicative form. Good governance was about bringing citizens and stakeholders together to *participate* and take responsibility in a well-functioning planning *process*. Communicative planning, according to Sager (1994), is characterised by a view of planning as a long-term process in which the focus lies on the process and on communications within that process, as much as on calculations and the planning object.

In terms of the levels of power of different actors in the waste governance scenario, the European Union is a key player in that it regulates waste and sets the scene for its regulation at national level. The cornerstones of European policy on waste were established as hierarchically organised objectives:

• Prevent waste in the first place
• Recycle waste
• Turn waste into a 'greenhouse neutral' energy source
• Optimise the final disposal of waste, including its transport.

While the European agenda informed by sustainable environment concerns can be clearly seen with its hierarchisation of objectives, equally the market-driven notions of development are being played out when it comes to its implementation, with its fourth objective at that point often being prioritised. Waste legislation clearly takes cognisance of networked green politics, but at the implementation stage the contradiction between the concepts of development (market-driven in its capitalist form) and sustainability (the earth as limited resource) are in constant contention with each other. European policy in the 1990s pointed towards degrees of sustainability in its waste hierarchy, but the

European Union also put legislation in place that set targets for its constituent countries to reduce all waste streams, and set very specific timeframes for national governments to meet these reductions. For example, for the Republic of Ireland's municipal waste stream there is a national target to be achieved of 35 per cent (currently at 34 per cent) recycling by 2013 and a household waste diversion from landfill target of 50 per cent (currently at 19 per cent) by the same year.

In the Republic of Ireland in 2001 there was a need for an estimated investment of 1 billion euros, over a three- to five-year period to implement the waste development plan (Forfás, 2001: vi) and the National Development Plan envisaged this coming mainly from the private sector. Clearly, given its history of reliance on landfill, Ireland faced a gruelling task to organise a strategy to divert waste away from landfill, to reach targets set at a five-fold increase in recycling and to find the finance for the infrastructure, especially if the objective was for the private sector to answer this call as envisaged in the National Development Plan. Private capital was thus seen as a key stakeholder, as a necessary 'node' in the governance of waste management (Fagan, 2004). In particular the government's gaze focused on the private sector and on the waste industry's multinational giants, and sustainability concerns became secondary to costs and to citizens' and communities' concerns. In order to reach the targets it was considered necessary by the government of the day to bring key players such as 'private enterprise' into some form of partnership – in other words, a prioritisation of the 'stakeholder' over the citizen was clearly part of the solution to the waste problem. Waste governance, from this perspective, could not be resolved at its most radical level – that of sustainability. As it emerged the plans relied heavily on the treatment of waste through regional 'thermal treatment plants' and on recycling to be funded primarily through private enterprise.

The plans were brought to a standstill as opposition focused around the local planning authorities at regional level where the incineration plants were to be sited. Those environmentalists and environmental scientists who contested waste management plans were worried about the growing influence of commercial interests, specifically waste companies coming into the Irish globalised waste market. The key concern from the environmentalist's point of view was the role of 'big business', i.e. incineration companies, in the implementation of the plan. They argued that there had been aggressive attempts by incinerator companies to lobby the government (Fagan, O'Hearn, McCann and Murray, 2001: 17) and to lead strategy. This concurs with O'Brien's interpretation at a global level where he comments on waste industrialists:

This is a market whose rational economic actors are begging, cajoling, threatening and coercing the states of Europe to intervene politically into the circulation of wastes precisely because the 'spontaneous' emergence of markets does not generate the values they want out of the rubbish heap. (O'Brien, 1999: 292)

Environmentalists argued that the new government response of building incinerators simply mirrored the previous landfilling strategy – 'Okay so we can't dump everything anymore, so let's just burn it' seemed to be the strategy. They believed that in both cases the government was 'being wooed by, or was wooing', large international companies and taking little responsibility for negative impacts on localised communities (Fagan, O'Hearn, McCann and Murray, 2001: 16–17). Those in opposition to the plans felt that they failed to contextualise waste in anything other than a framework for industrial 'competitiveness' and profitability as opposed to sustainability.

While governance necessitated a consultation process and the introduction of key players into the process, the unequal balance of power in the consultations and the fact that some partners were 'more equal than others' resulted in outright contestation of the plans, and thus the situation spiralled into a political crisis. On what discursive basis did communities and activists contest the Irish government's preferred waste management strategy? The environmentalists and local communities, feeling threatened by incineration plans, were deeply critical of what they perceived as the 'façade' of consultation that had been put in place (Fagan, O'Hearn, McCann and Murray, 2001: 18). There was a widespread perception at community level that government 'consultations' (often dictated by EU regulations) on the development of incinerators were simply empty rhetorical exercises for communities to 'let off steam' but were not designed to change decisions already taken on technical grounds (Fagan, O'Hearn, McCann and Murray, 2001: 19).

The opposition to the location of incineration plants began, fuelled by anger about the nature of the consultation process that had produced the plans, and drove the waste management strategy into political crisis in 2000–1 as local communities blocked the sub-regional plans. The state, however, reacted and the Minister at the time, Noel Dempsey, removed local councillors from the decision making process who had been subject to public will and replaced them with the county manager, a government employee. So here, in response to challenge from 'below', a central decree, government as opposed to governance, was used to achieve the localising or embedding of waste management. This is not to say that the state moved entirely back to traditional government or rejected the principal of consensus politics and failed to involve itself in multi-agency partnership but, rather, that they removed the locality from involvement in the decision making process. The Environment Minister, Martin Cullen, stated quite openly that the planning process on waste management was 'overdemocratised' and that he did not believe it was 'adding anything to it by having so many layers involved' (*Irish Times*, 12 August 2002). The so-called 'fast-tracking' for waste management plans had to be implemented, and An Board Pleánala (The Planning Board) became a 'one-stop shop' for assessing all plans for new waste management facilities. The Minister, rather contradictorily, insisted that he was not removing any groups or individual rights to express their views – 'That is sacrosanct, but I don't see a need for these views to be expressed at so many different levels' (*Irish Times*, 12 August 2002). In other words, a repeat of oppositional views at multiple levels in a multi-layered process of governance was a source of irritation for government.[3]

Power, communication and conflict

The issue of power of the various actors became central in the multi-faceted and shifting dynamic of the governance process and to the communicative planning scenario. Some actors had more power than others. Some gained more power than others because of their alignment with technocratic, short-term, profit-oriented solutions given the urgency of the waste crisis. Others lost considerable power in the complex political process that unfolded, local authorities and communities being big 'losers'. That local communities were important players in the dynamic is without question, but there were ebbs and flows in their political power.

Theoretically, expanding governance through such mechanisms as consultation processes, increased participation and communicative planning should deliver better democracy, quicker consensus and greater legitimacy. Theories of communicative planning have been derived from Habermas' theory of communicative action which argues for a new universal model for discursive rationality (de Sousa Santos, 1995). Communicative planning relies on the potential of communicative rationality as a system of critical assessment of alternative means of reaching consensus. However, conflict, unequal power bases, short-term solutions and decreased legitimacy mark the implementation of environmental planning in the 'Celtic Tiger' years, even within that expanded governance scenario.

Consultation processes, and more specifically communicative planning, are designed to give different actors access to decision making processes. Indeed it often holds out the promise of equalising their influence on the planning process. However, it failed to deliver in the development of Irish waste management policy, where the 'façade' of the consultation processes described by citizens and communities was central to triggering their anger with the process, and central to their articulation of grievance. Secondly, the political crisis erupted in reaction to what was seen as the false assumption – from the point of view of the government – or false promise – from the point of view of the communities and environmentalists – of a communicative process equalising different actors' influence on the planning process. The environmentalists saw the 'wooing' of the government by big incineration businesses as central to the outcome, and they saw that the technocrats dictated it, given that the government employed one engineering company to 'manage' the consultation process with communities and citizens.

In terms of analysing obstacles and opportunities for implementing sustainable planning locally through communicative planning, Mannenberg and Wilbourg (2008) argue that communicative planning is a planning ideal that, in applied contexts, carries certain risks for delivering sustainable development and indeed for democracy more generally. First, there is the risk of the communicative process becoming the focus rather than the plan itself; secondly, the traditional model of representative democracy is challenged; thirdly, legitimacy is challenged and, fourthly, it relies on achieving consensus and this entails the risk of suppressing political conflict (Mannenberg and Wilbourg, 2008: 36). In terms of the variety of outcomes possible for different actors, they argue that where communicative processes are strong the citizens and stakeholders can gain influence and correlatively the autonomy of the professional planner and the publicly accountable local politician is weakened. Nonetheless, they argue that in actuality 'communicative planning has proven to be a friend of all strong actors and a foe to those in less favourable positions' (Mannenberg and Wilbourg, 2008: 42).

In the case of the planning process in Ireland, the citizens and communities definitely found communicative planning, or what they would consider the illusion of communicative planning, a foe. The communicative planning process advantaged stakeholders with economic capital and oriented to profitability. In the short term the government's advantage was that it could change the rules of the communicative game at will, removing weaker players from the planning process. This is not to infer that the governance processes described above adhered to the ideal of communicative planning, but rather that in practice the discourse of communicative planning and the illusion of communicative planning marked the development of Ireland's waste management policies.

Policies in the Republic of Ireland were legitimated on the basis of a weak communicative process, and the government responded to contestation of these policies with a further weakening of the process.

Given the symbiotic relationship between the social and the environmental, a major challenge for governance is to identify the means by which to implement sustainable development practically and concretely. A major challenge for governance at this particular moment, when powerful corporate actors who produce and 'dispose' of waste are strengthening their role, is to ensure that the discourses of all the players are heard, that all the nodes in the networks are uncovered and that all are contextualised within a broader framework than economic profitability. The repercussions of the above débâcle in the exercise of governance are as yet unknown. However, what is interesting is that with a communicative process, or the illusion of a communicative process in place, conflict and contestation was still the fate of the waste management plans. This outcome makes clear the limitations of communicative rationality as a universal model insofar as it downplays power struggles and political contradictions.

Productivity and sustainability: binary opposites?

To focus on waste alone, rather than on regulating production and consumption when engineering sustainability is simply not logical, and the fact is that the early waste management plans did just this. It would be the equivalent of legislating for how to bin the shavings that came off the platform of a nuclear reactor's base, rather than legislating around the production and use of the nuclear reactor itself. Without production being governed by criteria of sustainability, there is no point in managing its waste.

In essence the waste situation is deteriorating and waste disposal policies are not improving the situation as quickly as the problem warrants internationally. This is certainly the case for Europe and for Ireland. Waste policies were officially seen to be clearly failing as early as the end of 1999 in Europe. The EU environmental action programmes were unable to stem the generation of waste and were thus failing to meet their foremost objective – the prevention of waste in the first place. Despite the hierarchisation of objectives and targets set by the European Union, the EEA by the year 1999 presented a chaotic scenario unfolding: 'The expected waste trends during the outlook period [up to 2005] suggest that existing policies, although providing some degree of success, will not be sufficient to stabilise waste arising, meet policy objectives, or progress towards sustainability' (EEA, 1999: 215).

The sheer material quantity of waste in circulation during this period was extraordinary. The EEA statistics on the European Union for 1999 showed that 2,000 million tonnes of waste were being generated per year and that the amount had increased by 10 per cent per annum over the previous six years. It was estimated that *all* waste streams would continue to increase steadily (EEA, 1999: 215). Essentially waste generation was spiralling out of control. To begin with, a wide range of different waste streams was increasing in volume, from consumers generating too much household waste to more wastewater treatment plants producing larger amounts of sewage sludge. Waste disposal methods were not coping with the increased loads, with several countries increasing the amount of biodegradable waste sent to landfill. Gradually, and most importantly, what was known in lay terms began to be officially recognised – that *waste generation was strongly linked to economic activity*, meaning that, as Europe's economy grew so, too, would the waste problem. The data generated under the EU Directives revealed a particularly close link between economic growth and waste from the construction industry (EEA, 2000). The Republic of Ireland statistics directly reflected this trend of increased economic growth, and the out-of-control spiral of waste emerging from the construction industry.

In the light of the failure of previous policies a further phase of policy making began in the early 2000s. While the waste hierarchy was not removed as a solution further emphasis was placed on the first point, the prevention of waste, and the link between economic activity and waste production became the focus of further policy. The sixth EU Environment Action Programme (EAP) called for 'absolute decoupling' – that is, an overall reduction in the volumes of waste generated. Decoupling occurs if the growth rate of waste amounts is less than the growth rate of a given economic driving force over a certain period of time. Relative decoupling occurs when waste amounts continue to grow, although at a slower rate than the underlying economic driver. Absolute decoupling is when environmental pressure is decreasing during a period of economic growth (EEA, 2005: 27). Projections drawn up for the years 2000–20, on the basis of current policy in place, indicates that in the European Union most waste streams are expected to decouple relatively, but not significantly, from GDP by 2020 (EEA, 2005). None are expected to decouple absolutely. So the further waste target of absolute decoupling will not be met in the foreseeable future. The construction, demolition and industrial waste streams are expected to produce about 650 million tonnes per year by 2020 and municipal waste is expected to produce 250 million per year by that year (EEA, 2005: 32). Policy, therefore, at the European level, is destined to fail to achieve its principle objectives (EEA, 2005).

So it can be argued that current trends in waste management are unsustainable and that increases are not being counteracted effectively. Options to treat and dispose of waste are seen to be diminishing as quantities increase and concerns about their potential impacts grow (EEA, 2005: 6). Decisions on the location of incinerators was and is very controversial in many countries, but particularly so in Ireland. There is growing evidence of the harm caused by their toxic emissions and they are increasingly being perceived as at core 'dirty technologies' (Murray, 2004: 7). Landfill options are often limited by space as well as by fears of soil and groundwater contamination and their impacts on human health. 'The European Environmental Agency state that: The current policy tools for dealing with waste are inadequate and need to be complemented by approaches that promote smarter resource use by changing production and consumption patters and through innovation' (Murray, 2004: 6).

Arguably, Ireland is at a turning point in relation to waste management. Efforts to manage waste, with or without enforcement, are no longer seen as sufficient unless integrated with processes of production and consumption. Discussing waste amounts and striving for the waste management hierarchy of more recycling and less disposal is still a necessity. However, there is also need for a more integrated approach that would examine where and from what mechanisms the waste comes, what types of waste should not be produced, what resources go into the waste stream and what resources can successfully be lifted out of the waste stream altogether. Understanding waste flows and paving the way for better waste regulation would thus become integrated into the debate on production and consumption patterns and resource management. This redefinition of waste, according to Murray, 'promises to be, along with the information and knowledge revolution, one of the defining features of the post-industrial era' (2004: 17).

The structures and consumption patterns of contemporary society encourage wasteful consumption and unsustainable patterns of production that lead to waste. Sustainable production and consumption are the only viable long-term options for society. Factoring in the production of waste to economic growth and providing a waste costing system where the allocation of waste costs to producers and consumers would be conducted fairly would provide part of a structural solution only. Scientific innovation is also a necessary component of the switch to sustainability. Building on resource productivity is one of the key ways the scientific community can transform structural conditions. Very

156 Irish environmental politics

interesting in this regard is the new 'materials revolution' being proposed by environmental engineers and scientists, and some are making the argument that materials productivity as opposed to labour productivity will form the basis of the post-industrial era (Weizsaker, Lovins and Lovins, 1998). It is only in the shift towards this 'materials revolution' and social patterns of sustainable consumption that production and sustainability can be complementary as opposed to oppositional.

Towards a green Ireland?

While natural scientists and politicians already have a clear role to play in regard to environmental sustainability, the role of the social sciences and humanities are also vital to developing a holistic and sustainable approach. Changing the social practices around consumerism should be part of developing sustainable consumption. A social practice approach looks at how patterns of social behaviour create, support and recreate structures, suggesting that there are no structures without supporting behaviours. If this approach to wasting is followed, a waste future where lifestyles in relation to wasting are addressed could emerge. The environmental pressures of consumption are generally lower than those of production, but are expected to grow significantly. Consumption in the areas of eating, housing, travel and tourism is growing significantly and this marks a shift in the environmental burden away from production to consumption. Given this shift, it can be argued that it is necessary to develop innovative governance strategies for dealing with sharply rising patterns of consumption. The development of these governance strategies would be designed by citizens and governments together inspired by the critical need to organise sustainable patterns of consumption. Shifts in lifestyles and societal preferences can make a huge difference in a world organised around consumerism (Spaargaren, Moll and Buttel, 2000). Restructuring various consumption patterns can be crucial in the future, and this is possible if the focus is on the intersection of the structure of production with the lifestyle of the citizen/consumer, and not on the individual or the structures alone. Artists and literary scholars, likewise, have their role to play in creating the imagery that will inspire the innovative generation of green environments and repulsion for the environmental destruction currently advancing.

Without a lead being given in the matter of innovation in production and consumption, the reality is that the imagined 'Green' Ireland is fast disappearing in the sense that its air and water quality is being progressively compromised. It's continued 'greenness' is possible only through an ecological transformation whereby production and consumption patterns and their resultant waste streams are re-organised to protect the health of the environment and its dependants. Ireland's future depends on the ability of its politicians, citizens, scientists and business leaders to plan a more progressive Irish role in the wider evolving green revolution that it is hoped will mark the post-consumerist phase of globalisation.

It is necessary to reconstruct our theoretical conceptions of productivity, profit and consumerism in ways that 'build in' the waste component in a world beginning to take the principles of global economic sustainability seriously. Waste policy in the 'Celtic Tiger' years – and all understandings of wasting that disassociate it from the production and consumption processes – waste 'Ireland',[4] and consume its future potential as a healthy and sustained imagined community. A critical analysis is needed that engages the politics of contingency[5] where the socio-economic politics of limiting wasting and greening production come into vogue as something more structured than a cosmopolitan lifestyle choice, where 'good waste' (Murray, 2004) (i.e. recyclable) is instantly recognisable and promoted, and where unsustainable production, unrecyclable waste and wasting consumption patterns are immediately recognisable as bad things in a 'new' Irish model of sustainability. Such a model should re-configure the image of Ireland as a green networked nation. In this sense, 'green' directly symbolises a positive ecological future sustained through an 'ecological' democracy in which global environmental citizenship and deliberative engagement are key referents.

Notes

1 Figures available at: www.epagov/grtlakes/seahome/housewaste/src/intro. htm (accessed 20 August 2008).
2 The EPA could not account for this 10 per cent increase other than to say that local authorities believed that the dramatic increase from 2002–3 was likely to be because of increased quality of data as well as increased resource use and waste generation on the part of consumers and business (EPA, 2003: 7). In 2004 they calculated that the municipal waste was at just over 3 million tonnes although there had been a 4 per cent increase, because they had produced the figures based on a new methodology.
3 For discussion on how the multi-level governance approach of waste management has impacted at the local level, see Murray (2003).
4 Authors such as Declan Kiberd (1995) explore the cultural and discursive constructions of Ireland as an 'imagined community' that have been so critical to its political and social leadership roles in the globalised era.

5 Laclau and Mouffe (1985) assert that nothing is predetermined and that
   points of contingency hold potential for transformative change.

References

Becker, E. and T. Jahn (eds.) (1999) *Sustainability and the Social Sciences*
    (London: Zed Books).
Boyle, M. (2002) 'Cleaning up after the Celtic Tiger: Scalar "Fixes" in the
    Political Ecology of Tiger Economies', *Transactions of the Institute of British
    Geographers*, NS, 27, 172–94.
de Sousa Santos, B. (1995) *Toward a New Common Sense* (New York:
    Routledge).
Dirlik, A. (1999) 'Place-Based Imagination: Globalism and the Politics of Place',
    *Review, A Journal of the Fernand Braudel Center for the Study of Econom-
    ics, Historical Systems and Civilizations*, 22(2), 151–87.
Environmental Protection Agency (EPA) (2002) *Environment in Focus, 2002:
    Key Environmental Indicators for Ireland* (Dublin: Environmental Protection
    Agency).
Environmental Protection Agency (EPA) (2003) *National Waste Database
    2003, Interim Report* (Wexford: Environmental Protection Agency).
Environmental Protection Agency (EPA) (2004) *National Waste Report 2004*
    (Dublin: Environmental Protection Agency).
Environmental Protection Agency (EPA) (2005) *The Nature and Extent
    of Unauthorised Waste Activity in Ireland*, Press Release, Thursday 15
    September 2005, available at: www.epa.ie/NewsCentre/Press Release/
    MainBody,7789,en.html (accessed 20 August 2008).
European Environment Agency (EEA) (1999) *Environment in the European
    Union at the Turn of the Century* (Luxemburg: EC Publications).
European Environment Agency (EEA) (2000) *Environmental Signals* (Luxem-
    burg: EC Publications).
European Environment Agency (EEA) (2005) *European Environment Outlook
    Report No.4* (Luxemburg: EC Publications).
Fagan, G. H. (2003) 'Sociological Reflections on Governing Waste', *Irish
    Journal of Sociology*, 12(1), 67–85.
Fagan, G. H. (2004) 'Waste Management and its Contestation in the Republic
    of Ireland', *Capitalism, Nature, Socialism*, 15(1), 83–102.
Fagan, G. H., D. O' Hearn, G. McCann and M. Murray (2001) *Waste Man-
    agement Strategy: A Cross Border Perspective* (Maynooth: National Institute
    for Regional and Spatial Analysis).
Fisher, F. and M. A. Hayer (1999) 'Beyond Global Discourse: The Rediscovery
    of Culture', in F. Fisher and M. A. Hayer (eds.), *Environmental Politics:
    Living with Nature* (Oxford: Oxford University Press).
Forfás (2001) *Key Waste Management Issues in Ireland* (Dublin: The National
    Policy and Advisory Board for Enterprise, Trade, Science, Technology and
    Innovation).

Kiberd, D. (1995) *Inventing Ireland: The Literature of the Modern Nation* (London: Jonathan Cape).

Laclau, E. and C. Mouffe (1985) *Hegemony and Socialist Strategy: Towards a Radical Democratic Politics* (London: Verso).

Luke, T. (1977) 'Green Consumerism: Ecology and the Use of Recycling', in T. Luke, *Ecocritique* (Minnesota, MN: University of Minnesota Press).

Mannenberg, M. and E. Wilbourg (2008) 'Communicative Planning – Friend or Foe? Obstacles and Opportunities for Implementing Sustainable Development Locally', *Sustainable Development*, 16, 35–43.

McDonald, F. (2002) 'Minister Wants To Fast-Track Planning On Waste', *Irish Times*, 12 August.

McGlade, J. (2007) 'Finding Pathways Towards Sustainable Consumption and Production in Europe', at the EEA Conference, Time for Action: Towards Sustainable Consumption and Production in Europe, Ljubljana, 27–29 September 2007, available at: www.eea.europa.eu/pressroom/peeches/finding-the-pathways- (accessed 20 August 2008).

Murray, M. (2003) *Waste Management in Ireland: A Case Study on the Impact of Transnationalisation on Governance* (NUI Maynooth, PhD thesis).

Murray, R. (1999) *Creating Wealth from Waste* (London: Demos).

Murray, R. (2004) *Zero Waste* (London: Greenpeace Environmental Trust).

O'Brien, M. (1999) 'Rubbish Values: Reflections on the Political Economy of Waste', *Science as Culture*, 8(3), 269–95.

Sager, T. (1994) *Communicative Planning Theory* (Aldershot: Avebury).

Spaargaren, G., G. Moll and F. Buttel (eds.) (2000) *Consuming Cultures: Power and Resistance* (Basingstoke: Macmillan).

Stoker, G. (1998) 'Governance as Theory: Five Propositions', *Journal of International Social Science*, 155, 119–31.

Urry, J. (1999) *Global Citizenship and the Environment: An ESRC Funded Research Project* (Department of Sociology, Lancaster University), available at: www.comp.lancs.ac.uk/sociology/jures.html (accessed 20 August 2008).

Urry, J. (2000) *Time, Complexity and the Global* (Department of Sociology, Lancaster University), available at: www.comp.lancs.ac.uk/sociology/soc057ju.html (accessed 20 August 2008).

Weizsaker, E., A. Lovins and L. Lovins (1998) *Factor Four, Doubling Resources, Halving Resource Use* (London: Earthscan).

8

Promoting participatory planning: a West of Ireland case study

Catherine Corcoran and Ciaran Lynch

This chapter outlines the development of a collaborative planning process through a partnership between a local authority and a community in the West of Ireland. The process, which was subsequently called Integrated Area Planning (IAP), offers an opportunity to the parties concerned to develop a shared vision and agreed set of objectives and actions around local development priorities within a collaborative planning framework. The process offers possibilities for the building of capacity in local structures and institutions to enable them to act as effective development agents. A collaborative approach to local planning may open up channels for a more collective community voice about a range of issues and thus offer increased opportunities for wider participation in local governance. However, unless the institutions of the state offer adequate time and resources to community groups – and, crucially, if they fail to address power imbalances between themselves and the communities involved – then such processes are unlikely to be successful in bringing about real change.

The model of participation that is discussed in this chapter finds its theoretical foundations in a variety of commentators on societies and their processes. Among these are Jurgen Habermas, Anthony Giddens and James S. Fishkin. While these commentators have provided insights that inform and explain the model, they are exemplars of perspectives rather than providers of process details. The work of Patsy Healey in the United Kingdom and Judith Innes and David Booher in the United States has proposed models and analysis within the field of collaborative planning that have used the work of Habermas and Giddens in particular. It should also be noted that the perspectives that have been learned from the work of these three authors has provided a basis for explanation of practice rather than being used in its development. However, these explanatory insights have assisted in the refinement and development of the processes.

Introduction

The Habermasian view that through authentic dialogue citizens could come to agree on 'universal truths', not through some reflective ontological process that can be conducted in isolation but through the exchange of thoughts and ideas in a rational context and from which consensus can be drawn, is fundamental to the IAP approach. This anti-relativist and anti-post-modernist stance of Habermas has given foundation to the perspective that at the level of a small rural community, those that may appear to come from very different conceptions of reality and of what is right can agree on many matters and can, in particular, come to agree on actions and activities from which all will benefit and to which all can assent. In other words, the relativism of the post-modernist perspective that Habermas confronts at a philosophical level can also be addressed at the practical level of the local community in which the seemingly irreconcilable can be brought to consensus through the communicative process.

The concepts of 'ideal speech' and 'authentic dialogue' are central to this approach as is the belief that a capacity to reason and to accept the dictates of reason are universally shared characteristics. Habermas specifies the following requirements for an 'ideal speech' situation to exist:

1 The speakers cannot contradict themselves
2 The speakers are required to assert only what they believe
3 Every person who has the competence to speak and act must be allowed to participate
4 Everyone is permitted to question every assertion
5 Everyone is allowed to enter any assertion into the discourse
6 Everyone is allowed to express his/her attitudes, desires and needs
7 There should be no internal or external coercion that prevents the speakers from exercising their rights under 3 and 4 above. (Quoted in Samovar, 2006).

It can readily be seen from this description that in a real and locally bounded situation, the process will require time, protection and assistance from others outside it so that the conditions of ideal speech can be met.

Speaking of authentic dialogue in the context of multicultural environments, Habermas prescribes the following:

• The parties must renounce the violent imposition of their convictions
• They must acknowledge each other as partners of equal rights regardless of their reciprocal conditions and forms of life

- They must acknowledge that they are participants in a discussion in which each party can learn from the other
- There must be openness and willingness by participants to view things from the perspective of the other. (Samovar, Porter and McDaniel, 2006)

Again in a small community environment the need for external assistance with the process is clear. What is also clear and what has been learned from experience, however, is that it can be relatively easy for the powerful to subvert the process either by not participating at all or by participating in a way that merely pretends to authentic dialogue.

While Habermas brought the concepts of communicative action and ideal speech to the process, Giddens provided the concept of structuration:

> The basic domain of study of the social sciences, according to the theory of structuration, is neither the experience of the individual actor, nor the existence of any form of social totality, but social practices ordered across space and time. Human social activities, like some self-reproducing items in nature, are recursive. That is to say, they are not brought into being by social actors but continually recreated by them via the very means whereby they express themselves as actors. In and through their activities agents reproduce the conditions that make these activities possible. (Giddens, 1984: 2).

The concept of structuration is important for three reasons. First, it contains implicit in it a focus on the structuralist aspects of society. Such a view underpins the collaborative planning approach which is based on a belief that, in the right circumstances and at least in smaller communities, individuals and groups can work together with a positive purpose and seek common outcomes rather than, necessarily, being subjected to the conflict and domination envisaged by other perspectives. The second important element of structuration is its key perspective of the interaction of agency and structure. This perspective posits that human beings acting as agents both respond to and work within certain structures that provide them with some degree of security of meaning while, at the same time, their acts of agency can work to moderate and change the structures themselves.

The third element of Giddens' approach that is relevant is that of tacit knowledge – or 'practical consciousness', as Giddens calls it. This reflects the understanding that we know our own context well from a practical, executive perspective, even if we do not have the time, space or opportunity to reflect on that knowledge. That knowledge is, however, a key community resource and when reflected on in the context of a

Habermasian space can provide insight and opportunity to effect consensual change that might not otherwise arise and impact on the social structures and processes of a community in a particular place and time.

When this thinking is applied within a small-scale, bounded geographic space and in a structured but safe context of dialogue, individuals are provided with a conscious and purposeful opportunity to reflect on the structures within which they work; to understand those structures and their operation more clearly; and, by their agency, to start the process of modifying those structures. In other words, the structuration processes identified by Giddens are put in motion in a more conscious and organised way than might occur in the more fluid, contradictory and multifaceted activities of day-to-day living. As a result, the outcomes in terms of amendments to structure are also more purposeful and conscious.

The third element that provides a backdrop to the IAP model is the 'deliberative democracy' concept promoted by Fishkin (1997). When considering the 'deliberation' element of the concept, Fishkin has identified the importance of information, dialogic completeness, diversity and conscientiousness to the quality of the process. He suggests that the quality and accuracy of the information provided; the extent to which opposing views are presented and discussed; the extent to which the views of different stakeholders are brought to the consideration of the issue; and the extent to which people are willing to be swayed by rational argument all contribute to the overall quality of the process. In some of these perspectives he reflects the 'authentic dialogue' and 'ideal speech' concepts of Habermas.

In the context of the IAP model, Fishkin's perspective creates the awareness of the need for expertise to be provided to the process at an appropriate time while also recognising the tacit knowledge that is available to us all. Fishkin's use of methods to develop groups that are truly representative of a society and to provide those groups with accurate information and a broad range of perspectives is reflected in the IAP's use of the community steering group, and the effort that goes into making it as representative as possible of all significant sectors; in the linking of the expertise of public bodies with the process so that those participating in deliberation in an 'ideal speech' environment are expressing judgements and beliefs that are well grounded in fact and with the expectation that good information assists those who are coming to the process honestly, ready to change perspective if their original view is based on factual error.

The model of communal decision making that has been implemented by the IAP is based unashamedly on the belief that the best outcomes for most people in a community emerge from honest dialogue in a well-informed context. However, the spaces for such dialogue are limited. By helping to create such spaces in a way that is informed by the insights of the three authors referred to here, among others, it is hoped that the argument that often passes for debate, and the oppression that often markets itself as consultation, can be reduced.

Partnership and the planning process

Since the late 1980s the concept of 'social partnership' has become a cornerstone of public policy in Ireland. 'Social partnership (or corporatism) is at the core of public policy in Ireland and underpins recent economic performance. Social partnership can be defined as the search for consensus on economic and social objectives between sectoral interests – trade unions, business, farming organisations – and government' (Walsh, Craig and McCafferty, 1998: 15). In the mid-1990s, with the realisation that economic growth had produced inequitable outcomes for certain people and for certain areas, the community and voluntary sector was invited to participate in social partnership. For Crickley (1998) partnership became one of the main influences on the development of the voluntary and community sector during the 1990s.

Partnership structures established to deal with issues emerging from uneven economic development such as rural decline and unemployment have also been challenged to deal with another issue, which is the increasing and in some cases overwhelming demand for housing in rural areas since the mid-1990s. Issues relating to planning are causing major problems for many local authorities in the country and are impacting on local authorities at professional, political and managerial levels (Lynch, 2003); there is a clear breakdown in trust at many levels and in many areas. The objectives considered appropriate by technical planners, by policy managers, by politicians and by communities and individuals are often at odds and incompatible, and this has led to a great deal of difficulty for all those involved.

While planners and central government might insist on concentration of housing within towns and villages, rural and farming organisations argue that social sustainability demands that rural housing be located in the countryside, that the current practice of concentrating dwellings in the urban areas is restrictive and that rural housing can contribute positively to the future well-being of rural villages (Lynch, 2003). It may be argued that one of the underlying causes of the disagreement in this area is the lack of a shared vision about what and how the rural areas of the country *should be*. While the planning process as set out in the law has many excellent characteristics, it lacks a good process and opportunity for the creation of the shared visions that must underlie any attempt to create a set of goals and policies that will have widespread consent.

This difficulty is symptomatic of a more endemic problem inherent in the way in which many of the policy decisions regarding local development are made. Often, communities and other groups are asked to participate in discussions regarding the mechanisms for implementing visions that are decided elsewhere rather than being asked to participate in the setting of those visions. The involvement of local people as part of partnership structures is only likely to be meaningful if those local structures have real power to make decisions (Fraser, 1996). If the visions and the goals can be agreed locally by the various interest groups, and if this process is accepted by the policy makers, reaching consensus on the mechanisms is often far less difficult.

The idea of participation in planning

The concept of a participatory approach that involves citizens in the planning process is not new. The seminal work by Sherry Arnstein in the United States in the late 1960s, developed while she was involved in developing processes for citizen participation in planning and urban renewal projects, has been highly influential in shaping both participatory theory and collaborative planning approaches (Arnstein, 1969). Arnstein developed an eight-rung 'Ladder of citizen Participation', with each rung corresponding to the extent of citizens' power in determining the end product. At the bottom of the ladder are Rung 1/Manipulation and Rung 2/Therapy. Using these two rungs she describes levels of non-participation that have been contrived by some to substitute for real participation, while really designed to 'educate' or 'cure' the participants. She uses rungs 3, 4 and 5 to illustrate progress to levels of tokenism that allow the 'have-nots' to hear and to have a voice. But under these conditions they lack the power to ensure that their views will actually be heeded by the powerful. Further up the ladder, Arnstein describes levels of citizen power with increasing degrees of citizen involvement in decision making. At Rung 6, citizens can enter into a partnership that enables them to negotiate and engage in trade-offs with traditional power holders. At the topmost rungs, 7/Delegated Power and 8/Citizen Control, 'have-not' citizens obtain the majority of decision making seats or full managerial power. Thus Arnstein maintains that participation has significant gradations. The distinguishing factor in the typology is the degree of power that the 'have-nots' gain in order to compel key institutions to become responsive to their views, aspirations and needs.

At about the same time that Arnstein was publishing her work, the issue of public participation in the planning process was being considered in the United Kingdom. This was exemplified by the Report of the Committee on Public Participation in Planning known as the Skeffington Report (1969), produced on behalf of the Ministry of Housing and Local Government. As noted by the Royal Town Planning Institute:

> That report accepted the need to involve the public in planning and made far-reaching recommendations which influenced subsequent legislation in the early 1970s. Publicity and consultation became required components of the statutory planning system providing local people with opportunities to comment on and object to development plans and planning applications. Planners in the 1970s embraced this new responsibility with some enthusiasm, and time and effort was spent preparing exhibitions and organising public meetings. Despite the enthusiasm, the response from the public was typically disappointing. Gradually this led many councils to reassess their commitment to public consultation and to carry out only the minimum necessary to meet the requirements of the planning acts. (Illsley, 2002: Introduction)

It might be argued, of course, that while this process referred to 'participation', it was, in fact, more akin to a process of consultation. There are a number of models that reflect this more participatory approach to decision making, including models of deliberative democracy and collaborative planning.

The planner Patsy Healey has been to the forefront in developing the collaborative model in a planning context and has incorporated some of the thinking of Habermas and Giddens in her approach. In summary, the collaborative planning model is based on getting diverse groups of people together to decide on a common area of planning. It maintains that parties must begin with their interests rather than their positions and that they must neither give in nor insist on their way. They must learn about each other. They must seek mutual gain solutions that as far as possible satisfy all interests and in the process, when possible improve matters for all. As a result, rather than making enemies, they make allies. They must persist in both competing and cooperating and accept this norm. The tension between cooperation and competition, and between advocacy and inquiry, is the essence of collaboration.

Healey (1997) argues that collaborative planning has the following characteristics:

- It is grounded in relation-building processes and is focused on relational webs or networks.
- It recognises that people operate across a multiplicity of networks and that the dynamic of social change arises through the mobilisation of such networks.
- It recognises that governance is far wider than government by formal institutions and is dependent upon a wide range of informal processes (see Fagan, Chapter 7).
- It can help to build up 'institutional capacity', i.e. the quality of the relational networks within a locality.
- It recognises the importance of creating links at the level of neighbourhood, town and city, thus working to build up links across networks improving relational capacity in these places.
- It builds upon a process of inclusionary argumentation which 'generates conviction'. This focuses upon how participants come together and establish a basis of trust and understanding.
- It leads to a dialogue where there is a process of mutual learning, allowing for consensus-building, which in itself is specific to the time and place. This allows for conditions of cultural difference to be accommodated, and recognises that there is a diversity of ways of knowing.
- It recognises that building a strategic process by identifying key stakeholders and relying on pre-existent groups leaves out those who have no voice in public arenas, and that an inclusionary ethic means that techniques need to be employed to overcome this problem.

Healey also points out that there should be a right to challenge decisions. There should also be a right to call to account. This would help ensure that full collaboration took place. Collaborative planning needs a variety of resources to function properly and these should be made available. The system of governmental competencies also needs to be reviewed.

Critiques of collaborative and partnership approaches

While participation and collaboration have been part of the language of governance for many years, and even more so in recent times, the concepts are not without their critics. These range from those such as Fainstein (2000), who is critical of collaborative models for both theoretical and practical reasons, to writers such as Shapiro (2003), who has been in debate with Fishkin over the latter's promotion of models of deliberative democracy. Critics of collaborative models suggest, among other things, that such approaches are not possible even in theory; that they expect a level of self-sacrificing behaviour and an other-focus that is not likely in practice; that they lead to outcomes that reflect the lowest common denominator; that the level of 'authentic dialogue' that they require is impossible to achieve in practice; that better results are often achieved by 'expert' rather than collaborative dialogue; and that power relationships are ultimately little impacted on by the processes involved.

While it can be acknowledged that some of these criticisms are not without merit, the response that is proposed here is that the criticisms point to the need for a more careful design of the process; to the creation of a more knowledgeable and capable lay community; to a focus on the elements of decision making that a collaborative process can most easily affect; to considering the nature of social and geographic units to which such models can be most successfully applied; and to changes in the structures of governance that would support such processes.

The Tipperary Institute and collaborative planning

There are many ways that the requirement to involve local communities in the planning process in Ireland can be fulfilled. At its most basic, local authorities can involve the community in a process of consultation around plans that are drawn up at a central level. Local people may be invited to participate in a planning process by being consulted about what will happen in their area, and problems and solutions may be modified in the light of people's responses. Using Arnstein's typology, this would involve a very low level of participation and be labelled 'tokenistic'. At another, more significant level, local people can be invited to participate in a joint analysis of needs in tandem with the local authority, leading to the development of action plans and the formation of new local institutions or the strengthening of existing ones. The degree to which local actors could exercise power to make the target agencies responsive to their views, aspirations and needs is an important feature here. In effect, this model is based on the concept of developing a partnership approach to planning. In Arnstein's view, a partnership arrangement means that power to make or influence policy and decision making is redistributed through negotiation between citizens and traditional power holders (Arnstein, 1969: 221). The parties agree to share planning and decision making responsibilities through such structures as joint policy boards, planning committees and mechanisms for resolving conflict.

The Tipperary Institute works with community groups, government agencies and local and national associations involved in rural development in its many aspects. One of the areas of focus for the Institute is developing partnerships between the various stakeholders involved in land-use and development planning. The Institute has been involved with a number of communities and local authorities in developing local area plans. From this work, it began developing a framework which it subsequently called Integrated Area Planning (IAP) and sees the development of the framework as work in progress. The present working definition used for IAP is:

> IAP is an empowering, practical and participatory process to collect, analyse and compile information while developing the skills and structures needed to prepare and implement an inclusive and multifaceted plan for a defined geographical area.

The next part of this chapter goes on to describe the various phases within the emerging IAP framework. It outlines the conceptual aspects of the framework to date and examines its practical application in a West of Ireland town.

Stages in developing an IAP framework

The contracting phase

In November 2000, the Kinvara Community Council approached Galway County Council about the need to prepare a development plan for the village area. A coastal community, located seventeen miles from Galway City, Kinvara has become an increasingly attractive area for residential development. Kinvara has always been a market town and its location on Galway Bay has defined its role as a port, a harbour and more recently as a tourist centre. It is Galway's gateway to the Burren which is one of the most important botanical sites in Europe and is of major importance to the cultural and economic life of the town. Despite outmigration and the decline in sea transport and agriculture in the last century, Kinvara has developed as a thriving community. Now like many towns and villages situated in relatively close proximity to a major city, it has experienced substantial development pressure over the past few years. This pressure led to growing concerns over pollution in the bay and the unplanned nature of the housing development in the vicinity. The Kinvara Community Council identified the need to prepare a development plan to manage the increasing pressure for development and to set parameters regarding the level, scale and nature of the development that would take place for the future.

In July 2001, having successfully secured funding, Galway County Council agreed to proceed with the preparation of an Integrated Area Plan as part of a pilot Community Planning Project. Conscious of the need to adopt a new and innovative approach, Galway County Council engaged the Tipperary Institute as facilitators for the planning process. Prior to the initiation of the process, the Department of Food, Business and Development at University College Cork (UCC) were invited by the Institute to act as mentors and evaluators of the project and to assist in further developing the IAP Framework. Much of the analytical material included in this article is derived from their work.

Data collection

The first activity in the project that directly involved the local population was a baseline study of the existing attitudes and opinions of the people of Kinvara about the priority needs in the community and about their views on the existing decision making processes and planning procedures of the local authority. It was intended to gather this information prior to the public announcement and formal initiation of the planning project. For the purposes of representation, and in order to allow people to contribute, it was proposed that this data were to be gathered using focus group discussions. This involves inviting small groups of people (usually six–twelve) who share one particular social or economic feature to discuss a specific topic in detail. Nine meetings were held in late March and early April 2002 with various interest groups in the area, based on open invitations. One of the surprising aspects of this part of the process was that there was such a convergence of opinion in relation to the principal issues affecting the town and the performance of the local authority. This allowed the facilitators to identify the main issues that needed to be tackled in the plan. At a later stage in the process, task groups were appointed to investigate these issues further, but it was at this stage essential that the broad issues that underpinned the plan were identified.

Establishment of the Steering Group

A major step in the project was the appointment of a Steering Group for the IAP. The main responsibilities of this group were guiding the IAP process by developing an overall set of visions for the plan, participating on task groups and ensuring that local people were consulted at all stages in the plan's development. Perhaps the most essential principle in establishing a Steering Group was that the group be as representative as possible and that all of the different groups within the community would have an opportunity to be represented. This reflects collaborative planning models which call for both diversity and interdependence among stakeholders in any planning process if the benefits of collaborative dialogue are to be achieved. All stakeholders should be at the table, or engaged in some way, if agreements are to be durable and fully informed (Innes and Booher, 2000: 7). Healey talks about a dialogical process of mutual learning (1997: 225) and allowing for consensus-building in that particular context. These writers maintain that stakeholders need to be diverse if the process is to take full advantage of the creativity that can arise from a wide set of competing interests.

Capacity-building of the Steering Group

Fundamental to the IAP approach is a belief that the process of developing the plan is as important as the plan itself. The actual paper plan is just one side of the coin; the other is developing the capacity of local people to become agents of change in their own local area through their involvement in developing that plan. In Healey's view (1997: 57), spatial planning can help to build up institutional capacity or the quality of relational networks within a locality. Various UK studies on community regeneration projects found a clear need for long-term investment in social and community infrastructure and other forms of support if they are to be successful (Burton, 2003). The methodology adopted therefore needs to maximise the opportunity for the group and individuals involved to develop skills that they could use in the future on various groups or committees active in the area. This view is shared by the Planning Officers' Society: 'Capacity building and other support will assist communities in need to influence regeneration initiatives and secure beneficial and sustainable outcomes that address real needs' (Addison and Associates, 2004: 6).

In order to address this, the Institute developed and implemented a detailed programme of group capacity-building. Skills development in areas such as communication and networking to develop the capacity of members to run effective meetings, reach decisions by consensus and operate as an effective unit were an initial focus for group training. This is an essential aspect of collaborative planning as outlined by the theorists. The group needs to define its own mission, ground rules and tasks (Innes and Booher, 2000). It must create its own tasks and working committees which have both the interest and the ability to work effectively and make progress. This is what is described as 'collaborative dialogue'.

Establishment of visions and objectives

Following the initial group training exercises, the Steering Group began the process of developing the plan. The model in development suggested that a strategic approach to planning would start by establishing a broad vision with the group as to the type of place in which they would like to live. This 'vision development', while informed by the issues identified by the focus groups, was not constrained by the present reality of living in the town but rather demanded of the group that they project into the future and come up with a series of statements that described a shared ideal about the kind of place they wished Kinvara to become. It therefore demanded of the group that they put aside current realities and project an ideal future. The aims of this aspect of the IAP are, first, to create a shared understanding among the group around a common set of priorities; secondly, to create a focus on the broad issues that affect the area; and, thirdly, provide a context within which the development decisions can be examined.

An advantage of taking a vision-led approach is that it serves to move people away from disagreement on small issues and focuses them on the wider picture. They state that current best practice in planning would indicate that planners have a key role in articulating, promoting and leading an agreed vision, making use of integration and collaboration skills to ensure the involvement of communities and partners in the planning process: 'The vision would identify regeneration priorities, objectives, opportunities and drivers, along with an overall approach (e.g. conservation led)' (Addison and Associates, 2004: 5). This approach was adopted in Kinvara.

If the vision statements within IAP are the core of the plan then the objectives can be seen as the detail. Objectives are the more specific targets that need to be achieved if the visions are to be realised. The Steering Group drew up these vision statements over two meetings. Objectives were also developed by the group and further refined and actions allocated to each objective by the task groups established to deal with researching the issues in greater detail.

Establishment of task groups

One of the most detailed and time-consuming elements of the process, but perhaps the most satisfying for members, was that of working on one of the task groups. These task groups were established to develop the detail that was to form the core of the plan. Their task was to take the visions and objectives established by the overall Steering Group and to propose how these visions and objectives could be realised. In all, fifteen task groups were established at different stages of the process, reflecting the broad range of issues identified at the first public meetings as well as the information required to complete the statutory aspects of the planning process.

A significant aspect of the workings of these groups was that membership was widened to include members of the community who were not members of the Steering Group and who had a specific knowledge about or interest in a particular issue. Thus the members of the education group, for example, included local education providers, parents and a local man who is a senior academic. The environment and heritage group took on board members of existing local organisations concerned with these issues. This step in the plan may be used as a further opportunity to broaden community 'ownership' of the IAP process. It may also serve to increase local knowledge and awareness of issues and stimulate local debate.

Another vital aspect of the task group membership is that significant players from relevant local authority departments were included as working members of the groups. When the task groups made recommendations around particular topics such as sewerage, traffic, etc. they were therefore informed both by local people's knowledge on local conditions and the staff's expertise and experience about the issue concerned.

While there is some disagreement among the Steering Group members as to the success of the task groups, there is widespread agreement as to the usefulness of the task group approach in gathering information regarding the different elements/issues which need to be covered in the development plan. There is also agreement among the Steering Group that task groups are a convenient means of dividing some of the work of the Steering Group into more manageable parts.

Drafting stage

The reports from the various task groups were collated into a working draft document. The document contained a condensed statement of visions and objectives along with a series of actions, nominated stakeholders and a timeframe. The task groups themselves did all of this work. At this point, it was believed that the document would benefit from including a policy context within which strategic issues emerging from the process could be structured. Broad policy statements reflecting government policy and recognising good practice in areas such as education and housing were drafted. Guidance on these areas was sought from documents such as the National Development Plan and the draft County Development Plan to help establish general benchmarks against which various proposals made by the task groups could be measured. The staff of the Institute and Galway County Council drafted this part of the document.

At the end of this process some members of the group complained of 'participation fatigue' and expressed frustration at the length of the process. It would seem that the best way to negate this would be to ensure a shorter process. However, participatory processes tend, by their nature, to be lengthy. Any attempt to make the process shorter could compromise the effort to promote greater participation. However, despite this faltering in the operation of the Steering Group, there was, at the end of this stage of the process, general agreement as to its success overall as a working body. For the most part, the Steering Group acknowledged that while problems may have arisen towards the end, the body was quite successful in that it fulfilled its remit of guiding the community to creating a development plan for Kinvara.

Validation

The purpose of this stage of the plan is to gain public support for, and agreement with, the broad thrust of the IAP. As with the earlier stages of consultation, efforts were made to communicate with all members of the community. A series of meetings was held over three days in April 2003 in Kinvara in order to present the draft plan to the public and to get verbal feedback. Hundreds of draft plans were copied and made available to buy or rent from various outlets in the town. The public was also invited to send in written feedback. The response to this was mixed. Attendance at meetings was not very high but those that did attend gave detailed feedback. A number of very well-thought-out and comprehensive pieces of written feedback were received and all were published as appendixes to the final document.

The use of focus groups, task groups and public meetings were, in this particular project, successful in getting some members of the community to participate. In addition, the creation of a Steering Group, which represented as wide a spectrum of the community as possible, also helped in the pursuit of an inclusive process. However, these initiatives did not, on their own, encourage the participation of those members of the community who were more difficult to reach. The UCC evaluation revealed that there were people in the area who did not get involved in the process and recommended that it would seem necessary to employ methods which were more tailored to those in the community for whom the thought of participating presented significant challenges. These challenges may range from physical disabilities to transport difficulties, from fear of public engagement to lack of personal social skills.

Approval stage

In order to complete the circle the plan needed to have the official approval of two primary stakeholders – Kinvara Community Council and Galway County Council. This was achieved by the Steering Group at meetings with these bodies where the group formally presented the plan in detail and held a question-and-answer session with both the elected and executive members of Galway County Council and the officers of the Community Council.

Implementation

The Kinvara IAP was completed in 2003. Within one year of its completion, the statutory Local Area Plan (LAP) was produced by Galway County Council. While the process of developing the LAP followed normal practice, it differed greatly from the norm in terms of content, in that the strategic thrust of the LAP and most of its key elements mirrored the IAP produced and approved by the Kinvara community. This was a very important success and a validation of both the IAP process and of the partnership arrangement between the community and Galway County Council. Despite this, however, there were a number of issues that many in the community were concerned about. One interpretation of the LAP that many locals objected to was the fact that the consolidation of the town centre agreed in the IAP was not given precedence over the development of other parts of the town. Another concern was the inclusion in the statutory plan of a proposal to develop a new street in the town, seen by many as unnecessary and not part of any discussions during the IAP process. A major issue for the community was the fact that the amount of land zoned for residential development far exceeded the recommendations implicit in the IAP. This was further compounded when the Council's elected members voted to further increase this zoned area. Many residents therefore felt that key issues prioritised in the IAP were not adequately reflected in the LAP, and that certain proposals in the statutory plan militated against proposals contained in the IAP. Also, because the LAP does not contain an action plan nor a list of priorities, it remains a set of uncoordinated aspirations and statements of best practice. Unlike the IAP, it does not clearly define what it is seeking to achieve and consequently lacks coherence and prioritisation.

On the other hand, a wide range of actions in specific areas has been identified in the IAP. The defined actions and associated objectives have been categorised into short-, medium- and ongoing/long-term activities. Associated with each activity is a range of stakeholders and agencies, with various responsibilities in relation to the actions outlined. Since the publication of the IAP, the local community has been active on a number of fronts. Major projects such as plans for a playground and community crèche, the refurbishment of the community centre, the protection of an ancient church and burial ground and a successful campaign to retain and develop secondary education facilities in the town, as well as the achievement of runner-up status in the all-Ireland Pride of Place competition, are among the initiatives undertaken. The entire implementation process, however, requires an underpinning commitment by the community supported by the statutory agencies to ensure that the spirit and the essential material elements of the plan are realised. This calls for ongoing community mobilisation and continuous inputs from officials in lead agencies.

Galway County Council has had a direct and significant input into the preparation of the plan. This input needs to continue through the implementation of many of the elements and to support other aspects. Ongoing support from councillors is required to ensure that estimates are prepared and approved which reflect the various objectives in the plan and that resources are subsequently allocated. It is also critical that members of the Council continue to provide support with the implementation stages of the plan and in particular the key priority, the sewerage in the bay, as expressed by all groups in the town through the IAP process. Until this system is funded and built the people of Kinvara say that, for them, little will have changed. A plan remains a plan until it is implemented.

Conclusions

The Kinvara IAP is an example of a partnership approach to local planning. It was completed by a series of groups made up of members of the local community and from statutory agencies, principally the Local Authority. The overall process succeeded in producing the plan and in developing relationships between the parties involved. The initial objectives of the project were more or less realised. The process demanded a significant commitment in terms of time and resources from all parties concerned and this commitment was a vital component in ensuring project completion. In their evaluation of the process, UCC concluded that there was a combination of factors necessary for the creation of a more open and involved planning process. In order to maximise public participation in a process, such as that undertaken in the development of the Kinvara IAP, a number of themes require consideration.

Resources

The above case study would suggest that, in order to maximise community participation in a process such as this, significant investment is needed. Merely offering the community the opportunity to participate is not always enough to increase participation rates. In his examination of the constraints facing community groups Fraser (1996: 49) maintains that involving local communities in partnerships in a way that is meaningful takes time. Some partners in these processes have been very reluctant to devote the necessary time and resources to empowerment. Promoting participation among the most marginalised in the community requires extra effort. There are numerous causes behind people's unwillingness to participate, ranging from straightforward reasons such as time constraints to more complex ones such as lack of belief in the process or in their ability to participate. In order to overcome these problems, it is necessary to go out into the community and actively encourage participation through a range of targeted measures. These measures may range from offering alternative times and venues for meetings to capacity-building and training. However, all of these exercises require a significant investment of both time and financial resources. The time commitment made by Steering Group members in Kinvara was very significant, and the comparative nature of the IAP produced reflects this commitment.

The process highlighted the resource limitations within which the different sections of the County Council operate. Involvement in a process such as this requires a large amount of time and personnel, which is not always available within normal resources. For instance, it was noted by participating officials that administration took approximately two-thirds of the time spent on this process. In addition, a lot of time was spent working in the community attending meetings, etc., which also put a significant strain on resources. Resource constraints must be recognised when planning how best to become involved in a process such as this.

Facilitation

The presence of an external facilitator is pivotal to the success of the participatory process. This is particularly so in the initial stages when the various actors require a mediator through which to come together.

This role can evolve as the process develops, ensuring that any communication problems are recognised and dealt with to ensure a fair and balanced process. In addition to fulfilling the role of mediation, an outside body is required to act as a support, especially for the members of the community who are involved in guiding the process. The complexity of the planning process can often be a considerable barrier to those in a community who may have little or no knowledge of these complexities. The fact that there are unequal power relations between statutory agencies and local communities has to be acknowledged and recognised. The role of facilitator as 'power-broker' may not be inconsiderable in these situations. A key issue in the process, however, is who 'owns' the process and to whom the facilitator is ultimately answerable. If the Local Authority is the employer, can the facilitator have the freedom to negotiate processes that may not be in line with what the Council wants? It is perhaps more desirable that the community has a role in selecting the facilitator, who may then be accepted by the contracting agency as having sufficient experience to facilitate the process.

Communication

The element of communication is fundamental to a successful participatory process. Clear communication is necessary at a number of levels. One of the intentions of the opening up of the planning process is to create improved relationships between the public and Local Authorities. In order to achieve this, the building of a communication network between both parties is critical if the community is to begin to build a trusting relationship with the Local Authority. In Fraser's view the statutory agencies need to build up confidence and trust in the community sector and to learn to respect the different skills, cultures and ways of working and constraints that affect the community sector. Equally, the community sector needs to trust the agencies and move from a confrontational and 'blaming' mode to work towards developing a shared vision and common objectives (Fraser, 1996: 51). Communication between the wider community and bodies such as the Steering Group, which is responsible for guiding the process, is also key in harnessing the interest of the community. There are any number of existing communication networks which can be utilised for this purpose – e.g. noticeboards, local radio and print media, parish newsletters, existing community clubs and organisations, etc. – in addition to holding public meetings. Internal communication within the Local Authority and within the Steering Group is also crucial if the participatory process is to be successful.

Length of process

If a process is to attempt to be as participatory as possible, it is inevitable that it will be a lengthy one. However, the length of a process such as this can often be one of the reasons that prevents people from participating. There is little that can be done about the length of the process, but the frustration with this aspect can be limited somewhat. It is vital that those who are involved in the process – especially those members of the community who may be unfamiliar with this type of situation – are aware from the beginning of the timescale involved. If participants have prior knowledge of the time factor they may be less likely to become discouraged by the seemingly slow progress of such a process. In addition, the above case study has shown that it is important to get participants actively working on the plan as early as possible in the process.

Power

In Arnstein's typology, if partnership is to be achieved it means that power needs to be redistributed through negotiation between citizens and power holders. These two groups must agree to share planning and decision making responsibilities through such structures as joint policy boards, planning committees and mechanisms for resolving impasses. In Arnstein's opinion, however, in most cases where power has come to be shared it was taken by the citizens, not given by the city. Power had to be wrested by the powerless rather that proffered by the powerful. She maintains that partnership can work most effectively when there is an organised power-base in the community to which the citizen-leaders are accountable and where the group have resources to pay for independent technical advice and support. With these ingredients citizens have some genuine bargaining power over the outcome of the plan and can approach the agencies with 'hat on head instead of in hand' (Arnstein, 1969: 222).

For Fraser (1996: 51), the empowerment of local communities as part of partnership structures is only likely to be meaningful if partnerships themselves have real powers. Where partnerships are ad hoc arrangements which statutory agencies can opt into or out of at will, then they will remain unlikely to share any of their power or control over their resources. Thus those at the centre who hold power must delegate that power to local partnership groups to draw up integrated plans for their areas. This will mean those who currently have power and resources being required to share control over them with others. Echoing Arnstein's writing of thirty years before, Fraser points to the fact that there are still very unequal relationships between the statutory and community sectors. A change to a more collaborative approach would challenge power structures at the levels of the community and Local Government; it would ask experts to adopt a far less prescriptive approach; it would ask politicians to share some of their decision making power with lay members of the communities they represent; it would ask existing community leaders to act in ways that reflected the views of the community more than their own personal views. In addition to such structural changes, a new approach would require changes in the education of planners and other professionals; in the resourcing of community organisations and their volunteer leaders; and in the relationship between those elected to political office and their constituents. These are substantial changes to the structures that presently prevail and would require commitment and leadership at the highest levels if they are to be effectively implemented.

Structures

Sadhbh O'Neill (1998) maintains that, traditionally, local authorities in Ireland have had a poor relationship with community groups. Even where a local authority has a progressive approach in relation to the consideration of the views of the community on a particular issue or development, in general there are often no structures in place at local level to formally engage communities in policy making. The Community Workers Co-Operative (CWC, 2000) concludes that in fact there are now new or enhanced structures for participation emerging, but that they are largely small-scale, explorative and at the lower end of the decision making spectrum. There is a failure on the part of local authorities to move beyond rhetoric to action, and to move from ad hoc consultation with communities to establishing local policy making and implementation bodies with decision making powers and the resources to implement action. In examining community planning in Scotland, Atherton, Hashagen et al., (2002) find that there is a need for and an onus upon local authorities to build up the infrastructure of the community sector – the local support and umbrella bodies, networks and forums which facilitate groups, organise cooperation among them, build up long-term assets and endowments and conduct dialogue between the community sector and the state bodies (Atherton, Hashagen et al., 2002: 11).

   In initiating the IAP process in Kinvara, Galway County Council have moved significantly in both facilitating and funding a local group to come up with a development plan for their area. In developing the plan together with the community, the seeds of a partnership approach have been sown. With ongoing commitment by all parties concerned to implementing the agreed plan and the required investment in local community infrastructure and services, an improved quality of life for local residents in Kinvara should result. Linkages to the County Council structure may result in ongoing improved relationships between the community and the local authority. An openness to a move from what O'Neill calls 'abstract physical planning approaches to a more intuitive, flexible and people-centred vocabulary enabling and encouraging participatory decision-making' (1998: 41) on planning issues may result. The local government reform process, coupled with a more empowered and confident community sector, may offer improved prospects for shared governance and more democratic decision making on the key issues that affect people in rural Ireland.

References

Addison and Associates (2004) *Moving Towards Excellence in Planning: Regeneration* (London: Planning Officers' Society).

Arnstein, S. R. (1969) 'A Ladder of Citizen Participation', *Journal of the American Planning Association*, 35(4), 216–24.

Atherton, G., S. Hashagen, with G. Charan, C. Garratt and A. West (2002) *Involving Local People in Community Planning in Scotland* (London: Community Development Foundation Publications).

Booher, D. and J. E. Innes (2008) *Planning with Complexity: An Introduction to Collaborative Rationality for Public Policy* (London: Rontledge).

Burton, P. (2003) *Community Involvement in Neighbourhood Regeneration: Stairway to Heaven or Road to Nowhere?*, available at: www.neighbourhoodcentre.org.uk (accessed 14 April 2008).

Community Workers Co-operative (CWC) (2000) *Partnership, Participation and Power* (Galway: CWC).

Crickley, S. (1998) 'Local Development and Local Governance: Challenges for the Future', in CWC, *Local Development in Ireland: Policy Implications for the Future* (Galway: CWC).

Department of Food, Business and Development, University College Cork (UCC) (2003) 'Unpublished Evaluation of the Kinvara Integrated Area Planning Project' (Cork: UCC).

Fainstein, S. S. (2000) 'New Directions in Planning Theory', *Urban Affairs Review*, 35(4), 451–78.

Fishkin, J. S. (1997) *Public Opinion – The Voice of the People and Democracy* (New Haven, CT: Yale University Press).

Fraser, H. (1996) 'The Role of Community Development in Local Development', in *Partnership in Action: The Role of Community Development and Partnership in Ireland* (Galway: CWC).

Giddens, A. (1984) *The Constitution of Society: Outline of the Theory of Structuration* (Cambridge: Polity).

Habermas, J. (1987) *Theory of Communicative Action*, Vol. II (Boston, MA: Beacon Press).

Healey, P. (1997) *Collaborative Planning: Shaping Places in Fragmented Societies* (Basingstoke: Macmillan).

Illsley, B. (2002) *Planning with Communities: A Good Practice Guide* (London: Royal Town Planning Institute).

Innes, J. E. and D. E. Booher (2000) 'Collaborative Dialogue as a Policy Making Strategy', Working Paper 2000–5, Institute of Urban and Regional Development, University of California at Berkeley.

Lynch, C. (2003) 'Capacity and Community: The Balance between the Social and the Environmental in a Specific Cultural Context', in L. O. Persson, A. Satre Ahlander and H. Westlund (eds.), *Local Responses to Global Changes: Economic and Social Development in Northern Europe's Countryside* (Stockholm: National Institute for Working Life).

O'Neill, S. (1998) 'Local Partnerships, Sustainable Development and Agenda 21', in *Local Development in Ireland: Policy Implications for the Future* (Galway: CWC).

Samovar, L. A., R. E. Porter and E. R. McDaniel (eds.) (2006) *Intercultural Communication – A Reader, 11th edn.* (Belmont, CA: Thomson Wadsworth).

Shapiro, I. (2003) *The State of Democratic Theory* (Princeton, NJ: Princeton University Press).

Skeffington Report (1969) *People and Planning: Report of the Committee on Public Participation in Planning, Ministry of Housing and Local Government* (London: HMSO).

Walsh, J., S. Craig and D. McCafferty (1998) *Local Partnerships for Social Inclusion?* (Dublin: Combat Poverty Agency).

Irish environmental discourse: towards an ecological ethic?

Patrick O'Mahony

Introduction

One of the most pressing problems in contemporary theory ranging across the social sciences, political theory and philosophy is the problem of the normative. The social sciences struggle to find a place for the normative at all, either ignoring it as a dogma that precludes the proper value-free foundations of the search for truth or merely 'ethicising' it as the expression of the standpoint of an excluded group. The problem is not that either objectivity is a bad epistemic value or that ethically laden struggles fail to produce moral learning but that neither position addresses the question of the normative in a dynamic and yet systematic way, as both an innovation and a foundation stone of social integration, as a complex whose dynamics can be reconstructed through research and whose instituted form can be justified or criticised beyond particular positions. These concepts of 'reconstructive' and 'justification' recur when the position of political theory and political philosophy is considered. Here, there has never been a problem of shunning the normative; indeed, normative justification or critique is at the heart of the endeavour.

Yet, in contemporary theory, the enterprise faces new challenges. The reconstructed spatio-temporal narratives – the realisation of individual autonomy, the ethos of democracy – that ground the necessity of particular versions of the normative – for example, liberal or republican theories in their many instantiations – have lost resonance given the facts of pluralism, complexity, worsening injustice and the weakening of the territorial container of the nation-state. Beyond this, the justification of the normative today brings in train the constant questions of justification for, by, or with whom, in which spatio-temporal societal configurations and with what effects. In this sense, one might speak of a 'relevance crisis' of normative theory.

The problems of normative theory outlined above evince a recurring dilemma; normative theory is never more needed than when it is never

more difficult. In the following paragraphs one contemporary version
of normativity will be briefly explored, the discourse ethics of Jurgen
Habermas and Karl-Otto Apel. Therefore, in a first step, key ideas of
Apel's proposals for a communicative transformation of philosophy will
be outlined. These derive, on the scholarly plane, from a reconstruction-
oriented critique of 'traditional' philosophical argument and, on the
application plane, from what he calls the 'macro-ethical' crises of a
human civilisation that has become irrevocably planetary in scale. These
reflections on Apel's work will help develop a number of key requirements for contemporary normative theory, its procedural quality, its
projective horizons, its spatio-temporal re-scaling, its participative
openness, its substantive orientation and its collective epistemic
foundations.

Such horizons, however, remain abstract unless put in the framework
of a composite theory embracing both normative innovation and institutionalisation. In a second step, therefore, an account of moral learning
theory that is suggestive for understanding the societal dynamics of
normative innovation will be developed that utilises Habermas' account
of rational political will formation. In a third step, the contemporary
moral learning that has resulted in the formulation of an ecological ethic
will be outlined. On this basis, in a fourth step, the chapter moves on
to consider how the conditions of normative innovation within the
framework of ecological discourse is being played out in a particular
theatre, Irish environmental discourse, showing how a kind of repressive symbolic hegemony blocks the possibility of eco-ethical learning
processes, which nonetheless retain an insistent force given their greater
embedding in the wider institutional and discursive contexts.

Discourse ethics and moral learning processes

Apel's proposals for the transformation of philosophy (Apel, 1980) take
leave from the communication-independent, monological orientation
of 'traditional' philosophy whether empiricist, rationalist, or transcen-
dentally oriented. Such a philosophy saw itself as independent of the
communication context in its focus on the formal truth conditions of
statements in an axiomatised syntactical and semantic sentence system
and monological in that perception was reduced to individual acts of
understanding and knowing the world, without relating such perception
to the intersubjective context of communication with others. According
to Apel, this radical freedom of the individual was taken in various
philosophical lineages – Descartes via Kant to Husserl, on the one side,

from Hume to Locke and the empiricist tradition on the other – to ground the capacity for autonomous judgement free from prejudice and external authority (Böhler, 2003; 15–16). Apel (1978: 89–90) claims that this philosophical inheritance goes in two directions that notwithstanding their apparent mutual competition actually ideologically complement one another; the rationalist and empiricist tradition moves in the direction of an objective and value-free foundation for science as the privileged rationality of Western civilisation and the transcendental tradition ends up in a self-consciously ir-rationalist existentialism concerned with subjective decisions of conscience. The value-free scientific rationality emphasised by the one grounds the ethically neutral ideal of 'publicly valid rationality'. The subjectivisation of conscience emphasised by the other consigns morality to the sphere of private decision. Apel describes this as the Western 'complementarity system', specifying value-free public rationality and subjective moral freedom.

In Apel's view, this complementarity system as an orientation complex is both epistemologically and ethically problematic in an intertwined manner. Epistemologically, the single, knowing subject is unable to perceive the further consequences of any given action in the complex action systems of modern society and hence she is incapable of ethically responsible action. However, Apel's claim has a re-constructive intent; the Western complementarity system has a non-obsolete core in that the freedom and responsibility of individuals as behavioural agents must be rescued from the domain of irrational decision, if its potential for *collective responsibility* arising from of the post-conventional outcomes of socialisation is to be mobilised.

Apel proposes a communication-theoretic reformulation of epistemology and ethics in order to rescue the possibility of responsible action in modern social conditions. For this purpose, he develops the idea of a communication community following Peirce's reformulation of Kant. Instead of monological presuppositions of something inherent in individuals that works outwards to the world, the individual *a priori*, Apel instead proposes an intersubjective *a priori* of communication that has two related components. First of all, in the real communication community, in a manner similar to G. H. Mead, meaning is conceived as a fundamentally social accomplishment. One can only judge what is meaningful and communicatively significant by learning the cultural codes and the linguistic and interactive rules of a real communication community. Such a communication community in this sense temporally precedes the actions of the individual and her action horizons can only be formed in the light of its existence.

Secondly, claims to the meaningfulness and validity of statements raised in the real communication community point beyond it to the *argumentation a priori* of the unlimited communication community. Beyond prejudice, power and individual judgement, the claim to *validity* of statements in the real communication community presupposes the will to argue this validity within an unlimited argumentation community that can raise objections and ask questions. Practical argumentation processes within the presupposed context of the unlimited communication community can only ever generate provisional agreement – and often don't get this far. Nonetheless, the integrative foundations of a common social life cannot be sustained if certain basic epistemic and moral norms cannot be tested and agreed upon and built into the moral, legal and ethical frameworks of real communication communities that are adequate for the challenges of their times.

The idea of a potentially unlimited community of argumentation is at the heart of the discourse ethics programme of Apel and Habermas. In modern conditions, where ethical ideals are irreversibly pluralist and often opposing, moral norms can no longer follow particular ethical standpoints. Instead, moral–practical disputes can only be resolved according to the basic Kantian insight by designing procedures for conflict resolution that respect the substantive conviction that all individuals are free and equal. Discourse ethics, in line with the above, however, breaks with Kant's idea of moral individualism in which morally acting individuals are separated from one another by what Honneth, following Habermas' critique of Kant, describes as an 'abyss of speechlessness' (Honneth, 2007: 105). Instead, following discourse ethics, the individual subject must check through procedures of linguistic intersubjectivity that include all affected parties whether moral validity may be ascribed to the norms of her action. Moreover, such procedures must take place in appropriate conditions of publicity, participative opportunity and information adequacy. Discourse ethics describes itself as a transcendental–pragmatic position; transcendental in the sense of the *a priori* necessity of a discourse free from domination and pragmatic in the sense of the necessity of intersubjective assent to norm formation by all those affected.

The transcendental idea of the possibility of a discourse free from domination marks out discourse ethics as a moral theory. It may be regarded as containing an indirect and direct application to the conditions of social integration: indirectly, the transcendental–pragmatic conditions of the possibility of argumentative discourse in an unlimited communication community endlessly make possible the grounding of valid, intersubjectively binding moral norms; directly, any form of social integration that can be said to conform to moral standards of justice and responsibility must contain instituted moral norms that satisfy the justification condition of the assent of all in the real communication community.

However, not all norms are moral norms; ethical discourses produce ethical norms; epistemic discourses produce epistemic norms of valid knowledge ('truth'); and legal discourses produce enabling and constraining legal norms. Apel and Habermas ground the ethical-ladenness of all communicative acts in four formal–pragmatic validity claims; comprehensibility, truth, appropriateness and sincerity, all of which pertain to distinct ethical world relations. However, when Apel speaks of the macro-ethical challenges facing humanity today – global justice, ecological re-orientation, capacity for species destruction – he conceives of these challenges as necessitating a new kind of collective responsibility – or, more accurately, co-responsibility – between interacting agents, that could only arise from the interweaving of epistemic, ethical, moral and legal discourses, which individually and integrally must be guided by the above formal validity claims that underpin all argumentative discourse.

Of the various discourses, central to discourse ethics are those relating to moral norm formation, since these are fundamental to the communicative achievement of social integration. As Habermas emphasises, the combined legal–political framework of public and private rights is intrinsic to the institutional realisation and social distribution of moral norms. Seen from the vantage point of a communicative ethics, moral norms historically tend to a wider participatory quality and faced with the continuously expanding ethical pluralism of modern societies their justification and application come to depend on ongoing deliberative procedures, rather than substantive grounding in a shared set of values.

Classically, social integration is communicatively achieved via the combined force of moral and ethical discourses within a concretely situated socio-political community. However, in the conditions of modern societies that depend for their material reproduction on complex formally organised spheres, which to a high degree follow non-normative functional logics, social integration increasingly depends on indirect legal steering. The universality that accompanies the formation and application of moral norms has therefore to be set in a wider range of discourses and normative complexes. In *Between Facts and Norms* (1996), Habermas proposes the following tableau that he entitles 'A Process Model of Rational Political Will Formation' (see Figure 9.1).

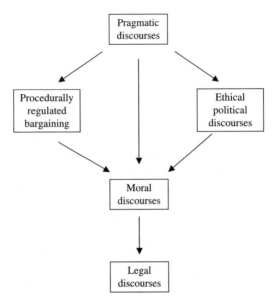

Fig 9.1 A process model of rational political will formation (Habermas, 1996)

This process model is intended to clarify how discursively structured opinion and will formation in a legislature is interwoven with communicative power. The process model starts with pragmatic issues, advances along what Habermas calls the branches of compromise formation (bargaining) and ethical discourse to the clarification of moral questions and ends with a 'judicial review of norms', understood also in the wider sense of legislative norm specification (see Arjomand, 2003 on the intertwining of legislature and judiciary).

In pragmatic discourse, an 'ought' is directed towards the free choice of actors who can make intelligent decisions on the basis of hypothetically presupposed interests and value preferences. In ethical–political discourse, an 'ought' is relative to the maintenance or alteration of a community or group specific conception of the authentic, good life. Habermas claims that entry into moral discourse requires a step back from all 'contingently existing normative contexts' and that 'the categorical "ought" of moral norms is directed towards the autonomous will of actors who are prepared to be rationally bound by insight into what all could will' (Habermas, 1996: 164).

Habermas conceives of the three alternatives of bargaining, ethical and moral discourses as three ways to continue to explore issues that are first broached pragmatically. Figure 9.1 shows various paths through the process model. Political will formation culminates in legal institu-tionalisation, 'in resolutions about policies and legal programmes that must be formulated in the language of law' (1996: 167). The latter takes the form of a judicial review of norms that have been re-contextualised in the medium of a multifaceted political discourse.

Habermas' intention in developing this process model is to clarify the component discourses of political will formation and the multiple ways in which they can combine. The efficacy of this model to clarify political will formation depends both on the formal specification of the compo-nents – i.e. types of discourses and associated norm complexes – and the processual specification of the ways in which they can combine, including their relative strength over time.

Normative orders and political will formation

Habermas' process model of political will formation as described above can be extended into a differentiated tableau of political norms and associated standards and processes (Table 9.1).

The emphasis on norms rather than discourses in Table 9.1 is designed to address the institutional structure of modern societies that discourses reproduce or challenge. The normative dimension allows for the speci-fication of enduring institutional patterns in different societies that can vary significantly. 'Norms', in this sense, may be understood as distinct complexes that can be formally differentiated – as in Table 9.1. This formal specification, as developed below, takes on a substantive form when applied to particular cases – e.g. the Irish normative order. Such an order may be regarded as temporally enduring though subject to constant potentials for transformation. The clarification of such trans-formation processes – or successful resistance to them – leads into the sociological task of the specification of normative dynamics.

As a formal typology, Table 9.1 cannot be directly applied to concrete cases because the constitution of a specific normative order does not

Table 9.1 A legal-political typology of norms

	Pragmatic	Bargaining	Ethical	Moral	Legal
Norm type	Instrumental	Compromise	Evaluative	Universal	Positive
Process	Decision	Fair Bargaining	Reciprocal	Procedural Justification	Rule Application
Standard	Control	Equilibrium	Appropriateness	Rightness	Coherence

obey strict formal classifications but depends on how the component elements are discursively interwoven in the given interaction order (Goffman, 1983; Eder, 2007) or relational setting (Somers, 1995). Such a task requires a further concretisation of Habermas' process model as outlined above. The idea of 'normative dynamics' does not presuppose a 'progressive' normative teleology. As will be argued below, it can just as well mean the stabilisation of a repressive normative hegemony.

In relation to the above formal specification, then, *pragmatic* norms specify what consequences predictably follow from certain actions, leaving aside ethical and moral considerations or endogenously building them in. Such norms result from the interplay of the aggregated logic of consequences and – putatively – rational collective or individual action, and typically take the form of action-guiding maxims such as 'do this to achieve that'. They are decision-oriented in the sense of the confidence engendered by the anticipated predictability of the relation between action and aggregated consequences. The technologically conceived standard is that of control, where aggregated systemic logics compensate for the opacity of disaggregated contexts of action.

Bargaining norms fall between ethical and moral norms, on the one side, and pragmatic norms, on the other. On the former plane, Habermas (1996) draws attention to the legal institutionalisation of fairness codes in the design of bargaining procedures so that all affected interests can come into play and have an equal chance of prevailing. Nine (2008) further draws attention on the ethical plane to the importance to jurisdictional legitimacy of perceived outcome equality over time between interest groups engaged in ongoing societal bargaining processes. The normative standard in bargaining shifts from that of control in pragmatic norms to that of equilibrium in which societally representative, legitimate parties seek to advance their interests but within a framework that respects other interests and the collective viability of an underlying common project such as productivity/wage trade-offs or environmental sustainability (Elster, 1989).

Ethical norms or values constitute collective and individual identities. They represent commitments that underpin shared forms of life, specifying membership criteria and terms of esteem and solidarity within a particular small- or large-scale community. Ethical norms thereby specify certain kinds of recognition relation between members of a common lifeworld, who are prepared to make sacrifices for the common good or the good of disadvantaged members of the community (Habermas, 2001; Honneth, 2007). The modern nation-state has been regarded as the proto-typical ethical community in modern social organisation. However, ethical allegiances exist below and above the nation-state in groups of all kinds and individuals bring to bear ethical differences in various kinds of procedures – such as, for example, hospital ethics committees. The standard for ethical norms is appropriateness implying, on the one hand, the social validity of what is right by 'us' in this time and place and, on the other, the recognition in the post-metaphysical pluralism of modern life that 'our' commitments must take proper account of the differing commitments of others.

In the tradition of discourse ethics *moral norms* take on an unconditional quality; they are agreed by all and, correspondingly, are binding on all. They are not therefore situation- or group-relative. Moral ideas and the moral imagination are open to argument (see Fesmire, 2003); moral norms acquire institutional force in the here and now as the outcome of norm-building procedures. This viewpoint of discourse ethics is not dissimilar to the norms of public reason as understood by John Rawls and the device of the original position in Rawls has something like the same architecture as Habermas' deliberative and universalist account of norm formation (Habermas, 1995; Rawls, 2005 [1993]). The most fundamental norm is the norm of universal inclusion in the communicative process leading to the formation of – other moral – norms. Moral–political norms in Habermas' sense can be understood as those corresponding to the framework of individual private rights, on the one side, and public rights of communication and participation, on the other. In modern conditions of ethical pluralism and contingent contexts of experience, moral norms depend on an increasingly procedural form of justification. Hence, intersubjective agreement on what is unconditionally right – the standard of moral norms – depends on procedures – public, legal, parliamentary – that specify the relationship between universalistic criteria and specific situations – e.g. fair treatment for women depends on women's situations and experiences and does not simply consist of the extension of existing individual rights to women in the name of formal equality.

Legal norms take on a double character. On the one hand, they have an enacted quality in the sense of legal statutes that are factually observed because they emanate from a recognised legal procedure and are backed by coercive power. On the other hand, the legitimacy of legal norms depends on normative justification processes that reach beyond the legal system in the narrow sense to include the moral, ethical and pragmatic discourses that shape statute formation in the legislative process (Habermas, 1996: 30). This double character emphasises, then, on the one side, the necessary social applicability of law as a system of coercive rules that make possible the liberty of individuals to pursue their interests and, on the other, the shaping of legal rules by pragmatic, ethical and moral discourses of legitimacy. In the latter case, it is not simply the *de facto* acceptability of law that is at issue but the overall legitimacy and symbolic standing of the legal system itself.

Today, there is an increasing interpenetration of legal and political norm-setting, described by Arjomand (2003: 24) as the judicialisation of politics and the politicisation of the judiciary, comprising judicialised legislation by parliaments and administrative organs and legislative jurisprudence by the constitutional courts and supranational judiciary organs (Arjomand, 2003: 9). These multifarious processes demonstrate the strains on the legal system in its normative roles of social regulation and political steering. At bottom, though, legal norms have to translate the heterogeneity of ethical and pragmatic positions into applied rules that do not contravene basic moral norms.

Normative innovation and collective learning

The consideration of the normative complexes as laid out above within the framework of political dynamics returns us to Apel's Peirce-inspired ideas of communication communities. Whereas Apel rather starkly – though with regard to his intention, correctly – distinguishes between the real and the unlimited communication community, it is possible to think of the real communication community in terms of its exploration of epistemic, moral and ethical horizons that lie beyond itself and that pertain to the construction of an already virtually imagined new normative order reaching beyond the level of practical rationality established in that society.

Real communication communities are constantly engaged in argumentative conflicts, then, that exceed their existing practical rationality and the stake of this conflict is societal learning processes that are either adaptations or challenges to this established practical rationality. The relationship between learning frameworks and rationality will be left aside for now, and returned to in the substantive treatment of an ecological ethic in Ireland below. Instead, three gradations of the real communication community that respectively depart progressively further from the level of practical social rationality will be specified.

The first of these will be called the 'normal' communication community, in which communicative and argumentative positions are embedded in a close relationship to an existing practical rationality. Such a practical rationality is sustained by a specific, temporally enduring organisation of the normative order of society, variously involving translation arrangements between the normative complexes, power relations between social groups lying within and between these complexes, the availability of epistemic and social resources and so on. Such a communication community achieves a practical equilibrium between its historical sense of its identity and instituted practices and its 'horizontal spatial' distinctiveness from other communication communities.

The relation to other communication communities separated on the spatial plane brings in a second gradation of the real communication community, the degree to which a given community engages with the cultural frameworks of other real communication communities bringing into play new learning potentials that elsewhere – i.e. in these other communities – have been transposed into a practical social rationality. What appears in *this* communication community as an innovation that merits consideration has been already implemented in *that* communication community. The prospects for the innovation to be adopted in this communication community will crucially depend on whether learning needs to be fundamental, which essentially entails far-reaching ethical or moral learning, though changes in the structure of bargaining processes can also have radical implications.

The third gradation of communication community is the furthest from practical social rationality and the nearest to the counter-factual horizons of the unlimited communication community. At this third level, fundamental ideas are at issue that have major implications for existing practical rationality but run counter to its existing logic. It can be conceptualised as a moral, ethical and epistemic 'diagnostic' critique of the normative content of existing social arrangements, a diagnostics that can in the right circumstances transpose into a prognostic demand for innovation in moral norms. History is replete with many examples of this kind of constitutive, actor-borne learning processes – the ethic of capitalism, minority rights in majoritarian democracies, the status and rights frameworks affecting women and, today, the call for an ecological ethic in the form of a transformed foundation for human relations with external nature.

However, as Klaus Eder points out, it is also replete with examples of learning processes that cannot find an evolutionary pathway at a given point in time (Eder, 1996). The example Eder gives is of the new nature relation that emerges in European societies with the advent of the Romantic Movement, including its vegetarian eating culture, a culture that could not in the early nineteenth century find a social evolutionary path into societal rationality. Hence, this culture is forced to give way in the nineteenth century to the more powerful force of an anthropomorphic and nature-dominating scientific rationality and its mechanistic relation to nature (Eder, 1996). According to Eder, it goes underground to emerge again in changed circumstances with new social carriers.

The traditions associated with critical theory, both the discourse ethics of Apel and Habermas and the learning theory of Eder (1985), Strydom (1987), Miller (Forthcoming) and others, are unusual in the contemporary landscape for the emphasis they put on moral learning processes and instituted moral–legal norms. Elster, for example, by contrast excludes moral and legal norms from the domain of social norms (Elster, 1989). In both political theory, outlined in Apel's account of the Western complementarity system as described above, and other variants of normative sociology, moral learning processes appear as the ineluctable outcome of other forces such as the dynamics of interests, technological change, the rise of certain social classes and so on. While these and other factors can by no means be excluded as critical contextual conditions of moral learning, they do not explain how such moral learning can be regarded as an indispensable condition of radical social change or how such change must be in substantial part conceptualised in the medium of moral learning itself.

Moral learning and moral norm formation are pivotal to social change because they specify unconditional normative principles that regulate incontrovertible – in the here and now – rules of social interaction. Moral learning processes can therefore either involve the substantive specification of moral norms – e.g. rights or practical justice commitments – or they can, additionally or alternatively, involve changes in the procedural forms of legal–political organisation. In one of his other major works, for example, Eder (1985) characterises the pathological history of moral–legal learning processes in Germany, manifested in the failure to build a consensual, democratic institutional framework out of the interplay of ethical–political associations. In further work (see Eder, 1996, 2007; see also Miller, Forthcoming), in the emphatic cognitive sociology of Strydom and in Honneth's recognition theory, the medium of collective moral learning is located in the classificatory struggles between social groups over the specification of the kind of rational–critical, intersubjective meaning out of which moral norms can be forged. The classificatory practices of social groups in such discursive struggles do not take place in a rarefied 'moral' space; moral norms are forged from collective learning that is conditioned by pragmatic, bargaining, ethical and legal discourses.

In the concrete cases of real communication communities, moral innovation may not actually emerge from successful outcomes of classificatory struggles, or the moral normative framework may be partial or contradictory. Furthermore, within the moral and constitutional frameworks of actual societies, moral norms do not usually emerge from deliberative and discursive practices that are practically equivalent to Habermas' counter-factual universality condition; they mostly emerge from dislocated discursive and deliberative processes that nonetheless succeed in gaining universal assent, frequently after the relevant moral norm has actually been instituted.

Moreover, discursive and deliberative processes in many cases can by-pass moral learning altogether and address social problem in need of a solution via pragmatic, bargaining, ethical and legal innovations. In such cases, the influence of power differentials is likely to be far higher than if moral learning processes come into play. The cost of non-moral learning can be experienced differentially across advantaged and disadvantaged groups or, in the case of regressive and/or authoritarian learning, it can be felt by the society as a whole.

As analysed above, moral learning processes sometimes lead to moral norm formation in the institutionalised frameworks of rights, justice and responsibility. However, such moral norms are interpreted and become effective in concrete forms of life – i.e. real communication communities – that are structured by ethical, bargaining, legal and pragmatic norms and practices. Hence, moral norms always co-exist with non-moral norms and practices; they offer a set of unconditional standards and rules, in the sense that all could assent to them, but they are in most cases conditionally applied. For example, the process of jury selection or judicial prejudice may compromise the right to a fair trial or the right to freedom of speech may in certain restricted circumstances be justifiably curtailed – as, for example, curbs on race hate speech.

From a macro-sociological standpoint, it is important to grasp the structures that determine the capacity to innovate in or successfully resist moral norm formation. Such innovation or resistance will take place in real communication communities that position themselves in relation to their context in the three ways described above – historically, comparatively and imaginatively. All modern societies in one way or another sustain ongoing communicatively achieved reflection on their own historicity and comparative situations. However, whether across groups or the whole society collective learning takes place, and whether this kind of learning becomes transposed into practical social rationality will crucially depend on the alignment of social forces on the normative plane of social integration. Hence, taking the lead from various sociological frameworks and the account of types of norms above, four kinds of normative (dis-)integration that can be assumed to be present in all democratic societies are outlined below:

- *Schizmogenesis:* This is essentially a state of societal *disintegration* or integration that is only sustained by non-normative means, i.e. by domination potentially backed by violence. Examples are extreme ethnic conflict in cases where irreconcilable ethnic groups are encased within territorial jurisdictions or cases in which there is no functioning state and anarchy is let loose. In relation to ethical and moral innovation in the environmental sphere in democratic countries, this kind of societal 'integration' tends to occur only on some issues as – for example, issues to do with GM crops, abortion or animal rights (see O'Mahony, Chapter 4).

- *Repressive hegemony:* Repressive hegemony involves circumstances in which the ethos of a particular social group comes to dominate over the other – actual or potential – identities of other social groups in a given society. This can occur across the society as a whole – the domination of a particular class, for example – or can be differentially present in different social spheres. In the latter case, for example, economic relations could be conducted on a basis of – relatively – fair bargaining where the gendered domestic sphere or the environmental sphere may be based on strongly asymmetrical and symbolically latent power. Repressive hegemony may involve either or both ideological distortion and subterfuge or the unchallenged belief, even by the dominated, in the desirability of the domination of the values of a particular group for the good of all.

  Situations of repressive hegemony characteristically bring to the fore certain kinds of ethical norm that are not tested in public discourse. Ethical norms of this kind have an extensive influence on the selection of available moral norms – on rules of distributive justice or conceptions of autonomy, for example. They also influence agendas for bargaining. Perhaps most decisively from the standpoint of innovation, they structure what can be pragmatically thematised, i.e. what is allowed to come on the agenda and the initial form it takes. The emphasis on ethical norms often involves foreclosing on innovation in bargaining – standards for negotiation on environmental issues that recognise ecological values – and moral norms, building unconditional normative standards such as animal and information rights.

- *Compromise:* If structures of repressive hegemony operate largely on the *latent* plane, in terms of the symbolic concealment of the play of social power, normative integration achieved through compromise and rational dissensus (see Miller, Forthcoming) operates *manifestly* as the outcome of bargaining or more diffusely societal argumentation processes. This kind of normative integration presumes a high degree of symmetry in the distribution of social power, including the epistemic and communicative capacity to effectively represent social positions. It therefore represents a filtration process in which issues characterised by such symmetry move beyond the conditions of hegemonic domination to become explicitly thematised and practically addressed within bargaining or argumentation processes. The ideal of compromise is relatively well understood as a process of the aggregation and reconciliation of interests while that of rational dissensus refers to the inability to agree how to pragmatically advance, though the difference of views is both understood and respected. Following Apel above, this kind of compromise-based or dissensual integration may be regarded as conditioned by moral norms; the play of interests occurs within a morally regulated constitutional framework (Apel, 1978). However, the underlying constitutional framework cannot itself be constructed from the play of rational interests, since such interests can only issue in contract-type arrangements between consenting parties and do not include all those potentially affected by the norm who are not parties to the contract. Nor does it include those who put the interests of others before their own in given social conditions and issues.

• *Consensus:* Consensual kinds of normative integration are already anticipated in the latter remarks on compromise. Consensual normative integration is characteristic of moral norm formation. While such norms are not exclusively constructed in deliberative processes oriented to the production of consensus – their impulse arises from societal struggles over moral concepts and their application – such deliberative processes, especially constitutional legal ones, have a big and sometimes decisive roles to play in the *actual specification* of these norms.

Consensus is, however, not only of a moral kind. It is also characterised by shared epistemic and wider symbolic assumptions on the nature of factual, social and emotional worlds. Such shared background assumptions do not precisely correspond with moral norm formation – this always has an additional reasoned and post-conventional dimension – but they create the kind of social stability out of which moral norms can be framed in given societies. However, this kind of stability does not usually pre-exist *new kinds* of moral norm formation; innovation in moral norms rather emerges from the end of a phase of collective learning by conflict involving category struggle over the very idea of what is 'moral' in a given case or situation.

Democratic moral norms, ideal-typically, are conditioned by consideration of the good of all, whether understood in the framework of liberal private rights emphasising autonomy and freedom or the framework of public autonomy emphasising justice and solidarity. Moral norms offer foundational rules of the game that should not be transgressed. However, there is considerable historical contingency and variability in collective, public conceptions of morality as these are typically weakly institutionalised in rights frameworks. Apel's idea of a macroethic of responsibility also corresponds with the consensus mode of societal integration; since it has the status of a macro-ethic, it exhibits a consensual quality that is not simply ethical in nature but also, depending on processes of social selection, potentially gives rise to moral–legal institutionalisation.

In concrete societies, all the above types of societal integration tend to find a place in various combinations. Certain social issues, for example, may be subject to bargaining; others to rational dissensus; some issues are prone to indivisible-type conflict and exhibit a schizmogenetic quality; moral norm processes are put into play by consensus formation; repressive hegemony excludes or minimises the impact of certain innovative ideals. These processes, both individually and relationally, are complex and multifaceted. Understood sociologically, Habermas' concept of political will formation as sketched above takes place in societies with historically formed cultures, structural situations and preferences orders that shape both the conditions of public discourse and will formation, on the one side, and normative outcomes, on the other.

Further to the initiation or repression of learning processes, Max Miller (Forthcoming) develops an account of types of conflict and learning processes blocked by different kinds of social pathology. The three kinds of social pathology identified by Miller are infinite conflicts, finite conflicts and conflicts that result in consensus. These correspond to the various modes of societal coordination sketched above. The first corresponds to the schizmogenetic type of irreconcilable disagreement; the second to finite conflicts that are characterised by rational dissensus; and the third to consensual processes of the kind just outlined.

In its essentials, then, Miller's framework of conflict corresponds to three of the integration types already identified. The exception is his exclusion of the type of repressive hegemony, which will be explored further below. Miller outlines four kinds of blocked learning process that he claims prevents infinite conflicts from becoming finite conflicts – or, more unusually, finite conflicts that produce a consensual outcome. The first of these is *authoritarian learning* that involves the assumed right and capacity to be dogmatic and hence to enforce a predefined consensus; the second is *defensive learning* that is based on a defensive avoidance of dissensus and thus represents a more subtle kind of pre-defined consensus; the third is *ideological learning* that actually entrenches dissensus by promoting the belief that whatever can be learned must respect the permanence of certain kinds of antagonisms and falsely presumes that particular interests have the status of general ones; finally, *regressive learning* involves the use of *ad hominem* argu-ments and hence the *a priori* commitment to the dissensual exclusion of certain groups and individuals.

Miller classes the first two of these kinds of blocked learning as 'con-sensus pathologies', in that dogmatism and exclusion grounds a false kind of consensus which should not be equated with the above consen-sual model of social integration. The second two he classes as dissensus conflicts, with the committed belief in the insuperability of antagonism and the willingness to engage in *ad hominem* arguments.

Returning to the account of modes of normative integration, it is useful to apply these four learning types and associated consensus and dissensus pathologies both to infinite or schizmogenetic types of conflict and coordination *and* to what is described above as repressive hegem-ony. Repressive hegemony is different from Miller's account of infinite conflict in that it involves a form of conflict resolution – either by the exercise of power or by symbolic artifice – that ends conflicts or prevents them from forming. Miller's typology of learning blockages and forms of pathology can be extended to repressive hegemony as the very idea of consensus pathology intrinsically includes the avoidance of conflict in the sense that both those in hegemonic positions and those subject to hegemony may not see that conflict is necessary. In particular, the latter may see the given state of affairs as normal. As Honneth has continuously emphasised, conflicts only become manifest when percep-tual categories related to the denial of recognition are activated (Honneth, 2007).

The construction of an ecological ethic

This chapter, drawing on ideas of Peirce, Apel, Habermas and Miller, has assembled a conceptual framework that is designed to explore the nature of an ecological ethic and more particularly those factors that contribute to its poor development in the Republic of Ireland. Before turning to this latter task of application, the elements of this framework will be drawn together. On the basis of Apel's Peirce-inspired account of real and unlimited communication communities, an account of real communication communities as they cognise potential kinds of practical rationality that lie beyond their direct, immediate experience was developed – e.g. found in an ecological ethic.

The first case is when such real communication communities seek to learn from reflecting on their own practices; the second is when they learn from other real communication communities; and the third is when they are capable of independent learning. This capacity for learning in communication communities was related, following Habermas, to mechanisms of political will formation and transposed his account of the discourse of political will formation into its normative implications, identifying pragmatic, ethical, bargaining, moral and legal norms.

However, these two moves were still not sufficient for a normative critique in real societies. To complete the picture, the normative framework had to be related to types of social integration that organise normative structures into different patterns that reflect historically formed cultures, structural situations and power balances.

Finally, this model drew from the work of Miller to specifically articulate the nature of the learning blockages and learning pathology that impede innovation. Throughout the chapter, the pivotal significance of ethical and moral learning processes was emphasised, as these are intrinsic to decisive innovation in normative integration.

In terms of the structure designated above, an ecological ethic built upon a post-conventional ethic of responsibility would take the form of a collective identity that could generate a framework of moral norms, embracing rights, obligations and shared commitments that would specify a new relationship to external nature. The emergence of moral norms of this kind would acquire a constitutional standing through their fusion with legal norms that in turn shape ethical values and bargaining processes. All of this creates a relevance structure that conditions what kind of issues pragmatically come onto the political agenda in the first place, and the ways in which they do so.

Temporally, macro-societal ethics with moral significance on this scale take a long time to form, as can be instanced by examples such as the rights of women, ideas of social justice and political cultures that sustain democracy. The time duration for the formation of an ethic is, however, conditioned by the degree of exigency of the issues that call it into being. Given that some significant transformation of ecological values is generally today regarded as indispensable given the scale of ecological challenges on a planetary scale, the formation of an ethic of this kind acquires great urgency. Epistemic judgement on how far such value transformation needs to go nonetheless arises in the light of varying estimations of the requirement for fundamental cultural change, as opposed to those material changes that can be delivered without cultural transformation. Of course, such comments reference only one motive for the formation of such an ethic, the extent of the material crisis that demands it as a solution. It leaves out the wider context of *preference* for the normative implications of adopting an ethic that is not simply introduced as a solution to a societal crisis, whether social, material or ecological in form. In other words, such a preference would reflect an *intrinsically* moral learning process of the kind specified earlier in this chapter.

As Döbert (1994) correctly, if rather pessimistically, suggests, the path to an intrinsic ecological ethic is a difficult one and given present societal priorities hard to confidently anticipate, even given the contemporary perception of ecological crisis on a world scale. Amongst the issues that one can loosely identify as barriers to the realisation chance of such an ethic is the materialism and individualism of the socialisation system, the continuing need for other values that compete with ecocentric ones, the anthropomorphism of legal norms and dominant political philosophies and the spatial and temporal regulation of embedded systemic processes that are antagonistic to such an ethic. In these circumstances, even though they do not speak decisively against the long-term chances of an ecological ethic, it is perhaps best to settle on normative learning processes that indicate the potential to move towards an ecological ethic, rather than establishing an unbridgeable chasm between normative potentials and actual empirically observable normative tendencies.

In the following, attention will be given to some features of the culture of Irish environmental politics that generally point against the establishment and maturation of an ecological ethic, before tentatively suggesting some indications that this may be changing. This goal will be pursued by outlining some general preliminary requirements for the emergence of an ecological ethic, then turning to explain its relatively poor realisation by following Miller's account of learning blockages before finally turning to some more positive concluding reflections.

An ecological ethic of responsibility, as understood by Apel, should include all those actually and potentially affected both now and in the future. This is consistent with two key criteria of the doctrine of sustainable development that already itself goes some way to specifying an ecological ethic – respect for future generations and adequate levels of participation to realise combined ecological and material justice goals. However, an ecological ethic assumes, beyond the idea of sustainable development, a commitment to far-reaching post-conventional value change oriented towards *intrinsic respect* for nature. In this sense, the precautionary principle is intrinsic to an ecological ethic in that it marks recognition of limitations in the human capability to assess risk and to fundamentally know in advance how natural processes will react to human interventions.

Hans Jonas developed this idea in terms of the need to recognise that humans cannot perceive all the nature-regarding secondary consequences of their actions, as these are mediated through complex human and biotic systems with unforeseeable consequences. Hence, they cannot predict the ethical implications of their actions *a priori* and must therefore proceed with caution and the potential for reversibility (Apel, 1987: Jonas, 1979). An emergent ecological ethic, then, in the general systemic, institutional and cultural climate of modern societies is related to (a) commitment to participatory innovation on complex environmental issues, necessarily extending to inclusion of multiple perspectives; (b) commitment to practices of precaution, at least as a principled willingness to build such principles into risk assessment; (c) commitment to nature and all living being as containing a good deserving intrinsic respect, though such respect may be differentially specified.

In general, even in more pragmatic terms, an ecological ethic is not well established in Ireland. First, if some of the contributions to this volume are taken into account, it is evident that what Nancy Fraser calls 'participatory parity' is not in place (Fraser and Honneth, 2003). In Sage's Chapter 6, for example, there appears to be an intent to invoke the law to impose the most stringent of risk standards on raw milk cheese producers while it was frequently averred by pro-GM actors, including representatives of the public authorities, in the case conducted by O'Mahony that it is impossible to prove the absence of risk – i.e. in essence meaning that some degree of reasonable risk is intrinsic to human activities (see Sage, Chapter 6 and, O'Mahony, Chapter 4). The apparent contradiction is perhaps not there if one allows for the new authority of science in Irish risk culture; scientific standards of risk assessment will find against raw milk cheese producers while legitimating the existence of some measure of risk in scientific innovation. The contradiction, in other words, is sublated by the perception of scientific authority.

However, this elevation of scientific authority is a symptom of the degree to which science is entrenched as *the* standard for risk assessment, hence trumping an inclusive vision of participation and the autonomy and efficacy of practical reason and running the risk of scientific overconfidence and the neglect of the precautionary principle as diagnosed by Jonas (1979). In an extensive case study, O'Mahony,

Skillington, Murphy and Burke found a systematic elevation of science over practical reason in which, contrary to recent epistemological and political learning processes, hard facts were taken to reign over soft values (O'Mahony, Skillington, Murphy, Burke and O'Sullivan, 2006). In her contribution to this report, Skillington described this as a form of neo-positivism and O'Mahony outlined a 'cognitive model of participation' that because it privileged the values of science and economy so much inevitably reduced the potential importance of practical discourse and learning that involved the public.

In a whole range of areas ranging from waste management performance, the implementation of Local Agenda 21, preference for the epistemic and evaluative standard of 'sound science' over the precautionary principle, spiralling carbon outputs and failure to meet Kyoto targets, to instance only some, Ireland falls behind in its international commitments and lags in comparative terms with countries at a similar level of development. The commitment to economic development is paramount and environmental considerations are a distant second, far from the commitment in sustainable development doctrine to give environmental considerations primacy where there is a conflict.

Moreover, the generally restricted nature of policy coalitions on environmental matters and the evaluative weight given to economic and political–bureaucratic positions over environmental ones lock in a strong commitment to scientific enlightenment and consumer capitalist values and practices. It would be possible to continue and to document a state of affairs that has until very recently manifested relatively low and belated commitment to environmental values. However, the path of scholarly assessment is relatively clear; the moral and ethical significance of ecological questions have only weakly and, by comparison with other similarly developed countries, relatively poorly influenced either public values or policy culture in Ireland. Both from the standpoint of collective learning through reflection on a collectively shared past or learning from other societies, the Irish public is relatively poorly equipped to move towards an ecological ethic.

Miller's typology of blocked learning processes as outlined above offers insight into this state of affairs. Taking each element of the typology in turn, ideological blockages to learning processes are associated with dogmatism, and Miller relates this to an understanding of power as the ability not to learn. In Ireland, this is manifested in a mode of societal coordination based on the repressive hegemony of, first, Catholic traditionalism, and then economic rationalism. These complexes have enjoyed such dominance that competing or additional societal value systems have been unable to assert themselves. Dogmatism runs hand in hand in Ireland with a well-documented anti-intellectualism and the latter dramatically reduces the capacity for learning through critical reflection. The consensual pathology is expressed in the idea that anything outside of the established customary – and, latterly, rationalistic – canon is irrelevant. Between the twin poles of systemic rationalism and quasi-aesthetic compensation in consumerism – Apel's complementarity system – a normatively reflective critique has a hard time gaining a voice.

Defensive learning as a modality for the consensual avoidance of dissensus is remarkably well developed in Ireland. It frequently takes the form of assertion of achievement even where the record is poor. Official environmental documents variously claim that Ireland is an advanced case of sustainable development or even a high-participation society, though both are manifestly not the case. In these circumstances, instead of overtly disagreeing with environmental values and goals, which is effectively the case, and taking up an argumentative position, consonance with these goals and values is asserted. The predefined consensus that Miller speaks of is manifested in the merely rhetorical assertion of environmental values; the presumed consensus lies in the belief that such rhetorical assertion is adequate and generally acceptable to the public.

The first kind of dissensual pathology outlined by Miller arises from ideological learning in which there is a presumption of irreconcilable antagonism. This is clearly manifested in O'Mahony's Chapter 4 on GM, and there are dimensions of it also in Sage's and Skillington's Chapters 6 and 5. Notwithstanding the manifest commitment to environmental goals and values, policy makers nonetheless assume that the values held by environmentalists cannot be accommodated within the existing policy culture. This policy culture sees itself as committed above all to furthering economic development goals, subject to minimal environmental safeguards. Furthermore, on the GM issue, for example, there is an easy presumption that the pro-GM coalition of scientists and economic actors, both epistemically and ethically, is in the right. Clearly, as the analysis of the environmental actor's discourse in Chapter 4 shows, ideological learning expressed in the belief in antagonism also extends to the other side.

However, this appears more a response to the fact that the institutional system is closed and apparently exclusive. Ideological learning is not a promising recourse on this side of the divide as it entrenches separation from institutional influence. However, it is also common in certain movement cultures that make a virtue of their exclusion from institutional influence and develop an anti-institutional critique. Finally, regressive learning is present in the prevalence of *ad hominem* arguments on both sides, with assumptions respectively of either arrogance or indifference, on the one side, and irrationality and irrelevance, on the other.

In general, these learning pathologies entrench a particular ideological reading of the world that subordinates environmental goals to economic ones. They block potentials of forming public will in a direction consistent with an ecological ethic. This may be articulated in terms of the conceptual framework developed above in three ways. First, the real communication community is conceived narrowly. Historically circumscribed outcomes of achieved learning that privilege values largely indifferent to ecological ones reduce the general public willingness to voluntarily learn from other communication communities. They still further reduce the will to consider a more radical relation to the further horizons of an unlimited communication community engaged with forming both an ecological reason and, beyond it, an ecological morality.

Secondly, learning blockages generally exclude the potential for ethical and moral learning in the environmental field, while legitimating primarily pragmatic learning. As long as the principles of an ecological ethic do not gain leverage through either or both public and external transnational institutional support, consensual learning blockages can be accepted, even encouraged. However, when sustained challenges arise from public and institutional contexts, dissensual learning modalities come into play. The GM plants issue in Chapter 4 illustrates how this happens and how it can rapidly escalate, tending towards schizmogenesis.

Thirdly, Ireland has on many issues exhibited, and continues to exhibit, a mode of governance based on repressive hegemony. While consensual coordination historically provided a moral and legal framework of norms and rights, and ethical and bargaining norms underpin consensual outcomes on certain issues, the prevalence of embedded cultures, learning blockages and power imbalances diminish the potential for the exercise of these consensual modes of coordination (see Corcoran and Lynch, Chapter 8). Environmental issues have tended towards strictly pragmatic norm-setting and problem solving and this increases the likelihood that path dependency in a manner inimical to an ecological ethic, rather than path innovation towards it, will result.

A major emerging question arising in relation to an ecological ethic is just how much it is possible to address both nature crisis and nature-related value systems without the moral learning processes underpinned by such an ethic. On the surface, at least from a non-specialist reading, it does appear that environmental problems have mounted in Ireland and elsewhere, more or less in line with the predictions of the less dystopian wing of radical ecology going back thirty years or more. This has coincided only partly in terms of cause and effect with a rising interest in participatory innovation, though it is not certain how such innovation can be made consistent with the existing representative governance system.

Furthermore, according to the work of Inglehart there has been a shift to so-called 'post-material values', which incorporate a new orientation to nature, over the last thirty years or so (Inglehart, 1977). These international tendencies indicate the necessity for moral–legal innovation in the sense of an ecologically oriented framework of rights and responsibilities that all countries must meet. It is now generally accepted that countries at an advanced level of development, moreover, should accept greater responsibility because of their greater capacity and greater historical guilt for environmental degradation. For the construction of such moral learning capacity, ethical learning in an ecological register is essential.

On the whole, there has been relatively little progress in Ireland with respect to the formation of such an ethic. Crucial thresholds such as radical shifts in public consciousness and governance innovation in the field have not been attained to the degree they have in other countries, even counting those within the same transnational governance regime such as Germany and the Scandinavian countries. However, looking across the essays collected in this volume, there are some indications of progress in these directions. For example, Skillington in Chapter 5 explores how cosmopolitan themes of ecological responsibility entered into public discourse and normative orientations through an adversarial court case, helping to dissolve the 'anti-historical' inability to learn from history.

Barry in Chapter 2 also draws attention to a significant recent development, the advent of the Green Party into government, particularly the holding of the critical Ministry of the Environment, Planning and Local Government. He ties this to the possible advent of a republican political philosophy that would increase reflective capacity, green leadership and deliberative problem solving.

Such developments indicate a shifting of the cognitive order and institutional models through which environmental politics have historically been addressed in Ireland. Above all, they indicate a changing moral–normative foundation of environmental communication. The communicative form of environmental politics in Ireland shows tentative signs of recognising the interconnected intra-societal and transsocietal ecological challenges that confront modernity. The country is late in responding to these challenges, and significant blockages to learning and practical innovation endure. Nonetheless, it remains an open issue whether a cosmopolitan ecological ethic may now make headway given cultural–political change, the dissolution of older repressive macro-social religious ethics and the relativisation of economic development goals with achieved prosperity, even if this prosperity is not as secure as it once looked.

References

Apel, K.-O. (1978) 'The Conflicts of our Times and the Problem of Political Ethics', in F. R. Dallmayr (ed.), *From Contract to Community: Political Theory at the Crossroads* (New York: Marcel Dekker).

Apel, K.-O. (1980) *Towards a Transformation of Philosophy* (London: Routledge & Kegan Paul).

Apel, K.-O. (1987) 'The Problem of a Macroethic of Responsibility to the Future in the Crisis of Technological Civilization: An Attempt to Come to Terms with Hans Jonas's "Principle of Responsibility"', *Man and World*, 20, 3–40.

Arjomand, S. (2003) 'Law, Political Reconstruction and Constitutional Politics', *International Sociology*, 18(1), 9–34.

Böhler, D. (2003) 'Dialogreflexive Sinnkritik als Kernstück der Transzendentalpragmatik: Karl-Otto Apel's Athene in Rücken', in D. Böhler, M. Kettner and G. Skirbekk (eds.), *Reflexion und Verantwortung: Auseinandersetzungen mit Karl-Otto Apel* (Frankfurt: Suhrkamp).

Döbert, R. (1994) 'Die Überlebenchancen unterschiedlicher Umweltethiken', *Zeitschrift für Soziologie*, 23(4), 306–22.

Eder, K. (1985) *Geschichte als Lernprozess? Zur Pathogenese politischer Modernität in Deutschland* (Frankfurt: Suhrkamp).

Eder, K. (1996) *The Social Construction of Nature: A Sociology of Ecological Enlightenment* (London and Thousand Oaks, CA: Sage).

Eder, K. (2007) 'Cognitive Sociology and the Theory of Communicative Action: The Role of Communication and Language in the Making of the Social Bond', *European Journal of Social Theory*, 10(3), 389–408.

Elster, J. (1989) *The Cement of Society: A Study of Social Order* (Cambridge: Cambridge University Press).

Fesmire, S. (2003) *John Dewey and Moral Imagination: Pragmatism in Ethics* (Bloomington, IN: Indiana University Press).

Fraser, N. and A. Honneth (2003) *Redistribution or Recognition: A Political – Philosophical Exchange* (London: Verso).

Goffman, E. (1983) 'The Interaction Order', *American Sociology Review*, 48, 1–17.

Habermas, J. (1995) 'Reconciliation through the Public Use of Reason: Remarks on John Rawls's Political Liberalism', *Journal of Philosophy*, 92(3), 109–31.

Habermas, J. (1996) *Between Facts and Norms* (Cambridge: Polity).

Habermas, J. (2001) *The Postnational Constellation: Political Essays* (Cambridge, MA: MIT Press).

Honneth, A. (2007) *Disrespect: The Normative Foundations of Critical Theory* (Cambridge: Polity).

Inglehart, R. (1977) *The Silent Revolution: Changing Values and Political Styles among Western Publics* (Princeton, NJ: Princeton University Press).

Jonas, H. (1979) *Das Prinzip Verantwortung: Versuch einer Ethik für die technologische Zivilization* (Frankfurt: Suhrkamp).

Miller, M. (Forthcoming) *Discourse Learning and Social Evolution: The Emergence of Novelty* (London: Routledge).

Nine, C. (2008) 'Democracy, Self-Determination and Territory', unpublished ms, Philosophy Department, University College, Cork.

O'Mahony, P., T. Skillington, M. Murphy, G. Burke and S. O'Sullivan (2006) *Public Participation in the Environmental Field: Models and Prospects*, Report to Environmental Protection Agency, Ireland (Cork).

Rawls, J. (2005) [1993]. *Political Liberalism* (New York: Columbia University Press).

Somers, M. R. (1995) 'Citizenship and the Place of the Public Sphere: Law, Community and Political Culture in the Transition to Democracy', *American Sociological Review*, 58, 587–620.

Strydom, P. (1987) 'Collective Learning: Habermas's Concessions and their Theoretical Implications', *Philosophy and Social Criticism*, 3(13), 265–81.

Index

animal rights 40–1, 196
Apel, K.-O. 5, 16, 17, 27, 126,
    184–7, 192–4, 197–9, 201–2,
    204

Beck, U. 16, 19, 55, 56–7, 61, 64,
    65–6, 100, 124, 126
Boltanski, L. 105, 118, 119–20
Brundtland Commission 17, 20, 70
Brunkhorst, H. 20–1, 102

Celtic Tiger 31–2, 36, 48, 98,
    140–3, 151
citizenship 10 n. 1, 20–3, 33–8,
    87–90, 91, 93–4, 102–4, 106,
    110, 114, 165, 179
    see also democracy
civil society 7–8, 10, 18–26 *passim*,
    88
    see also globalisation
climate change 17, 20, 31–2, 36,
    43–6, 48, 50 n. 3, 50 n. 5, 57,
    70
cognitive order 2–8 *passim*, 12,
    14–16, 23–7 *passim*, 28 n. 1,
    58, 75–6, 79–95, 97, 102, 112,
    119, 121, 194, 203, 206
    see also cultural models
cosmopolitanism 12–15, 20–8,
    99–102, 103, 105, 206–7
cultural models 1–2, 4, 7, 22–3,
    75–6, 79–80, 90–1, 92–5, 95 n.
    2

Delanty, G. 7, 23, 24, 99
democracy 7–9, 19–21, 23, 32–4,
    37, 38–42, 55, 100–4, 109–12,
    151–2, 193–6, 198
    accountability 10, 98, 99–101, 132
    deliberative 20, 163, 166, 167
    participation 7–9, 62–3, 78–9,
        90–2, 111–12, 160–9, 174–5,
        177–81, 202–4
    public sphere 7–8, 22, 24, 67, 71,
        76, 79, 90
discourse 6, 7, 10, 12, 15–18, 21–8,
    33, 40–7, 50 n. 3, 57, 64–8, 70,
    76, 91, 93, 102–4, 107, 112,
    122, 143, 161, 183–8, 191, 194
    ecological 16, 75, 80–92, 128,
        140, 183–8, 204
    political 2, 40, 46, 75, 79–80,
        152, 188–9, 200
    public 5, 7, 13–14, 16, 196, 206
    scientific 59–60, 64–5, 66, 118,
        122, 124

ecological modernisation 20, 45
economic growth 31, 44–5, 68, 76–7,
    108, 110, 140–3, 154–5, 164
Eder, K. 22, 76, 190, 193–4
equality 35–6, 69, 141, 151–2, 186
European Union (EU) 9–10, 19, 31,
    42, 43, 77, 78, 81–2, 95, 101,
    103, 107, 111, 118, 122, 124,
    134 n. 1, 141–2, 143, 145,
    147–50, 153–5

food safety 84, 107, 118, 119, 121–5, 128, 129–34
Fraser, N. 8, 105, 202

genetically modified organisms (GMOs) 3, 10, 75–95, 103–12, 124, 196, 202, 204–5
Giddens, A. 38, 55, 57, 64, 160, 162–3, 166
globalisation 12, 14, 17–22, 24–31 *passim*, 45, 68, 72, 100, 142–3, 149, 157
  global civil society 16, 22, 23, 26, 28, 62, 85, 111
  neo-liberalism 17, 19, 23, 33, 108–9
Goffman, E. 76, 190
Green Party 31–2, 36, 46, 47–9, 206

Habermas, J. 2, 5, 16–24 *passim*, 56, 57–8, 76, 94, 100, 103, 108, 151, 160, 161–3, 166, 184, 186–91, 194, 195, 198, 199–200
Honneth, A. 99, 105–6, 186, 190, 194, 199, 202
human rights 10 n. 1, 20–1, 60, 81, 99–114, 167, 187, 191, 193–5, 198, 200, 205–6

Jonas, H. 16, 202
justice 44, 105–8, 113–14, 183, 187, 194–6
  ecological 23, 33, 40–1, 100–1, 102–4, 111, 114
  social 27, 69, 93, 99–102, 104

Kant, I. 14, 26–7, 184–6

Laclau, E. 55, 158 n. 5
learning 18, 21–8, 34, 80, 94–5, 97–8, 102, 104, 112, 167, 171, 183–4, 192–207
Luhmann, N. 2, 20, 26

Miller, M. 22, 194, 196, 198–204
Mol, A. 20, 124

Mouffe, C. 55–6, 158 n. 5
multinational corporations (MNCs) 22, 23, 54, 59, 60–1, 63, 66, 72 n. 2, 78, 82–4, 85, 88, 90, 100, 103–14, 110, 113, 117, 123, 133, 153

non-governmental organisations (NGOs) 7, 18, 22, 23, 45–6, 77–8, 82, 83, 85, 86–7, 90
nuclear technology 14, 15–16, 47, 57, 70, 91, 153

peak oil 32, 36, 45–8, 54, 70
Peirce, C. 27, 185, 192, 199
planning 8–9, 47, 54–7, 66–71, 147–52, 160–81
pollution 3, 16, 54, 57, 63, 69, 72 n. 2, 93, 169
power 7–10, 20, 36–7, 55–6, 57, 59, 66–7, 70–2, 79–80, 91–2, 107–12, 133, 148, 150, 151–3, 160–8 *passim*, 178, 179–80, 186–95 *passim*, 196–7, 199–205 *passim*
precautionary principle 77, 89, 202–3

quality of life 3, 50 n. 4, 54, 60, 68–9, 181

Rawls, J. 2, 81, 191
reflexive modernisation 55–6, 57, 62
responsibility 5–8, 27, 37, 61, 106, 185, 198, 200–2, 206
  co-responsibility 16, 126–30, 132, 187
risk 14–17, 19–20, 25–7, 47, 57, 60–8 *passim*, 72 n. 3, 76–8, 85–6, 87, 90–1, 93–4, 100, 103–9, 112, 113, 124–9, 133, 134, 202

social learning *see* learning
Spaargaren, G. 20, 156
Strydom, P. 15, 16, 22, 25, 28 n. 1, 76, 107, 126, 194

sustainable development 31, 33,
37–8, 41–2, 45–6, 49 n. 1, 57,
70–2, 140–2, 152–3, 155–7,
201, 203, 204
see also Brundtland Commission

Teubner, G. 20, 23, 113
Thévenot, L. 5, 118, 119–121, 133

United Nations (UN) 14, 17, 19–20,
21, 23, 50 n. 5, 70, 73 n. 5